CITIES AND PRIVATIZATION

REAL POLITICS IN AMERICA

Series Editor: Paul S. Herrnson, *University of Maryland*

The books in this series bridge the gap between academic scholarship and the popular demand for knowledge about politics. They illustrate empirically supported generalizations from original research and the academic literature using examples taken from the legislative process, executive branch decision making, court rulings, lobbying efforts, election campaigns, political movements, and other areas of American politics. The goal of the series is to convey the best contemporary political science research has to offer in ways that will engage individuals who want to know about real politics in America.

CITIES AND PRIVATIZATION:
PROSPECTS FOR THE NEW CENTURY

Jeffrey D. Greene
University of Montana

UPPER SADDLE RIVER, NEW JERSEY 07458

Library of Congress Cataloging-in-Publication Data

Greene, Jeffrey D.
   Cities and privatization: prospects for the new century/Jeffrey D. Greene.
     p. cm.—(Real politics in America)
   Includes bibliographical references and index.
   ISBN 0-13-029442-X
     1. Municipal services—Contracting out—United States.   2. Social service—Contracting out—United States.
   3. Privatization—United States. I. Title. II. Real politics in America series.

HD4605.G74 2002
363.6'0973—dc21
                                                          2001036359

VP, Editorial director: Laura Pearson
Senior acquisitions editor: Heather Shelstad
Assistant editor: Brian Prybella
Editorial assistant: Jessica Drew
Editorial/production supervision: Kari Callaghan Mazzola
Prepress and manufacturing buyer: Ben Smith
Electronic page makeup: Kari Callaghan Mazzola and John P. Mazzola
Interior design: John P. Mazzola
Cover director: Jayne Conte
Cover design: Bruce Kenselaar
Cover photo: PhotoDisc, Inc.

This book was set in 10/12 Palatino by Big Sky Composition
and was printed and bound by Courier Companies, Inc.
The cover was printed by Phoenix Color Corp.

Real Politics in America
Series Editor: Paul S. Herrnson

 © 2002 by Pearson Education, Inc.
Upper Saddle River, New Jersey 07458

Printed in the United States of America
10 9 8 7 6 5 4 3 2 1

ISBN 0-13-029442-X

Pearson Education LTD., London
Pearson Education Australia PTY, Limited, Sydney
Pearson Education Singapore, Pte. Ltd
Pearson Education North Asia Ltd, Hong Kong
Pearson Education Canada, Ltd., Toronto
Pearson Educación de Mexico, S.A. de C.V.
Pearson Education—Japan, Tokyo
Pearson Education Malaysia, Pte. Ltd
Pearson Education, Upper Saddle River, New Jersey

To my mother and father:

Without their support, encouragement, and insistence,
this book might not have been written.

CONTENTS

CHAPTER 3

CHAPTER 4

PREFACE

The writing of *Cities and Privatization: Prospects for the New Century* stems from a long-standing personal interest in politics, economics, public policy, and urban studies. Specifically, the book focuses on cities and privatization. Privatization was one of the most significant public-policy issues of the past century, and the policy debate has carried over into the new century. Privatization involves increasing the use of the private sector for producing and delivering a broad range of public services. The services range from collecting garbage in our cities to providing human services, such as social welfare or public health care. Privatization comes in many forms, ranging from completely getting government out of the business of producing and delivering certain services to simple contractual arrangements with private firms. Although using private firms to provide services for government has a long history in America, during the 1980s privatization quickly evolved into an intense, ideological policy debate because it threatened to alter a fifty-year pattern of government expansion. Privatization also became controversial because it involved politics and money. The critical choice involved in the debate is between market or government provision of services that were once considered to be the exclusive domain of the public sector. There are consequences for using either method to deliver services, as we shall see in this book.

This book deals with the policy debate over and the use of privatization in the real world. For cities, stressed to find ways to pay for expensive public services, privatization provides the possibility of maintaining or even expanding service levels without raising taxes or having to search for alternative revenue sources. The promise of privatization rests on the fact that private firms can produce services more efficiently (for less money) than government can. Why would this create a debate that spans more than a quarter of a century? There are many reasons that will be discussed in this book, but foremost among them is that politics is interwoven into the debate and in the implementation of privatization in the real world. Politics is about power, and those in power usually do not voluntarily give away their advantages. Privatization also involves money, and in many instances it is about taking money from city coffers that was once used to fund in-house city departments and paying private contractors to perform the same tasks for less money. Turning over functions to the private sector might cause some public employees to lose their jobs, and no one usually volunteers to give up his or her job. In the real world of cities numerous services must be provided, many of which most of us take for granted. Cities must provide these services within an environment that is affected by many factors that influence their finances. And when cities run low on funds to pay for services (a condition referred to as *fiscal stress*) they often look toward alternative ways to provide services: Privatization, in one form or another, is one of the alternatives.

Cities and Privatization: Prospects for the New Century is intended to be a supplemental reader for undergraduate and graduate-level urban politics, public policy, and state and local government classes, or a freestanding book for anyone who is interested in privatization at the municipal level. Although many excellent books have been published on privatization, the inspiration for writing this book came from the lack of a concise book that focused on privatization at the municipal level, blended theory with practical matters, and included real-life examples of privatization. This book blends many dimensions of privatization into a short, readable text. It contains the practical arguments and theoretical frameworks for and against using privatization, summarizes the evidence on efficiency between public and private organizations performing similar tasks, and includes numerous examples of privatization taken from the real world of city management. In short, the purpose of this book is to take the reader on a brief journey through the world of cities and their experiences with privatization. The book closes by looking at the prospects for privatization in the twenty-first century. I hope that you enjoy reading *Cities and Privatization: Prospects for the New Century*.

ACKNOWLEDGMENTS

This book represents an interest in privatization and cities that spans many years. Writing a book is a unique endeavor, and along the way one becomes indebted to those who have helped turn an idea into a product that can be shared with others. Special thanks must be given to Paul Herrnson, a professor at the University of Maryland and the editor of Prentice Hall's *Real Politics in America* series, and to Beth Gillett Mejia, former political science editor at Prentice Hall (now director of marketing). It was a pleasure to work with such competent, high-quality professionals. Both were instrumental in developing *Cities and Privatization: Prospects for the New Century* into its final form. I would especially like to thank Paul Herrnson for his assistance in editing the original manuscript and his helpful suggestions. I would also like to thank Nicholas L. Henry of Georgia Southern University and Michael E. Milakovitch of University of Miami for reviewing the manuscript and making helpful comments. Finally, I would like to thank the students at the University of Montana who read the early drafts of chapters. It was important for this book to be written in a style that was readable for both undergraduate and graduate students; the University of Montana students provided valuable feedback toward that end.

Jeffrey D. Greene

INTRODUCTION:
CITIES AND THE PRIVATIZATION DEBATE

Does it really matter whether a private company or a city's own sanitation department picks up residential garbage? Could the savings be significant enough between public and private garbage collection to justify a city shutting down its public department and contracting with a private vendor, or even turning over the service to the open market? Newark, New Jersey, privatized part of its garbage collection and saved around $1 million.[1] Is it worth using privatization if a city could save a million dollars? But if a municipal service is turned over to a private company, what is the impact on concerns other than saving money, such as efficiency, equity, and public accountability?[2] Will garbage be collected at the same quality level in both poor and wealthy neighborhoods? Who do citizens call if their garbage is not collected?

Questions about routine municipal services, such as garbage collection, may appear mundane but local officials and members of the academic community have debated the merits of public versus private provision of services for nearly three decades.[3] In fact, few public-policy topics have drawn more attention or been more controversial than privatizing public services.[4] Providing public services through the private sector is not a new idea, but since the mid-1970s, local governments have increasingly turned to privatization to reduce operating costs. This shift is not surprising to many observers, considering the fiscal dilemmas faced by many local jurisdictions in an era characterized by reinventing government[5] and federal devolution of responsibilities to state and local governments.[6] Fiscal dilemmas are evidenced by cases like Orange County, California, and Ecorse, Michigan. Orange County, one of the nation's largest and wealthiest local jurisdictions, filed for bankruptcy in 1994 after losing $1.5 billion in risky investments.[7] In 1986, Ecorse, a small town located in fiscally depressed Wayne County, Michigan, was placed in receivership by a state court after the city failed to resolve its financial problems. The city privatized virtually every municipal function and erased its $6 million of red ink in four years.[8] Although bankruptcies are rare in local governments, fiscal stress is not. Many believe that all cities can reduce their operating costs by using privatization.[9]

Privatization is associated with increasing the private sector's role in providing public services and transferring many traditional government functions to the private sector.[10] Government has frequently been lambasted for its waste and inefficiency, but the pace of criticism seems to have quickened in recent years as privatization emerged as an alternative for delivering public services. Although criticizing government and making comparisons between the public and private sectors is not a new phenomenon, the attention privatization has received is unprecedented. It exceeds that of the Progressive Era when reformers sought to make government more businesslike in its operations. The reform era tension, often referred to as the competence–democracy dichotomy, has carried over into the privatization debate. The quest for competence in local government stems from the widely held belief that government is inherently inefficient.[11]

Increasing the role of private firms in the delivery of municipal services has generated criticism. Skeptics have questioned whether it is possible for private firms strongly motivated by self-interest to serve the public good, much less be made responsible for provision of many of the critical functions typically performed by cities.[12] Local governments have been propelled to center stage of the Great Privatization Debate because of their widespread use of privatization. Surveys indicate that more than 80 percent of American cities use some form of privatization.[13] Proponents consider local governments to be the leading innovators of privatization.[14]

This book focuses on privatization and cities, or what some call the "local privatization revolution."[15] Many controversial and often conflicting issues emerge in discussions about privatization. Like most policy areas, privatization contains many dimensions. There are aspects regarding whether cities "should" use privatization and practical questions relating to its impact once implemented. Part of this book is devoted to whether or not cities "should" use privatization but more attention is given to issues such as efficiency—the cost-effectiveness of private vendors versus the publicly managed organizations for producing and delivering services. This chapter provides an introduction to the concept of privatization and examines the arguments for and against its application. Although many forms of privatization will be reviewed in this book, greater attention is given to contracting out with private for-profit or non-profit firms.[16] Chapter 2 focuses more specifically on the actual use of privatization at the municipal level and reviews the evidence concerning efficiency in a variety of services. The chapter also examines the amount of privatization used by cities. Chapter 3 explores questions about privatization and cities, such as the following: What types of cities actually use privatization? Where are they located? Do certain types of cities use more privatization than others do? Why do some cities use more privatization than others? What is the effect of political ideology and political culture on privatization? What effect do certain fiscal and socioeconomic factors have on cities' propensity to use privatization? Chapter 4 focuses on real world examples that illustrate privatization's successes and some of its failures. And finally, Chapter 5 examines the prospects for municipal privatization in the era of reinventing government (an idea that believes government should be managed in a businesslike manner and have an action- and results-based orientation). Chapter 5 also addresses a series of questions that develop in the book, including the politics of privatization and whether privatization serves the public's interest. This book examines many aspects and dimensions of municipal privatization. However, there remains an intense ideological controversy associated with the concept. Before beginning our journey through the world of cities and their experiences with privatization, the concept of privatization and its ideological underpinnings should be reviewed.[17]

THE CONCEPT OF PRIVATIZATION

Despite the attention that privatization has attracted over the years, the concept is often misunderstood.[18] This is partly because the privatization debate is frequently discussed on a philosophical level rather than in practical terms.[19] It is easy to fall into philosophical platitudes when discussing privatization because of the ideological controversy that surrounds the concept and the breadth of the concept itself. The ideological controversy pits the merits of positive government action and responsibility against the virtues of capitalism and free markets as the best means for achieving public goals. The breadth of privatization is illustrated in its description, which has been described as lamentably imprecise.[20] It can signify something as broad as shrinking the welfare state to something as narrow as substituting a team of private workers for an all-but-equal team of civil servants to carry out a particular task.[21] Privatization is difficult to define because it encompasses a variety of ideas and practices that are loosely housed under a single umbrella. However, these ideas and practices share a common ideal that involves increasing private-sector participation in areas typically considered public-sector responsibilities. Broadly speaking, *privatization is the attainment of any public-policy goal through the participation of the private sector.*[22]

Privatization comes in many forms, which include simple contractual arrangements with private businesses and nonprofit organizations. The purest version involves getting government completely out of both the production and delivery of a wide range of services. Privatization also encompasses a much broader range of activities such as deregulation, tax reduction, voucher systems, and public divestiture of government properties. The activities associated with privatization are intended to enhance efficiency and reduce government involvement in economic activities.[23]

The ideological underpinnings of privatization rest in the virtues of a freely functioning market economy.[24] Proponents of free markets believe that a market economy produces many desirable things, such as economic and technological progress, efficient utilization of society's resources, a rising standard of living, a reasonable, equitable distribution of wealth, and a society characterized by social mobility and political freedom.[25] In this view, government intervention beyond its minimal functions (those dealing with purely public goods, such as national defense) impairs efficient resource use, impedes economic progress, and inhibits social mobility and political freedom. This perspective is grounded in a theory based on an idealized model of a perfectly competitive market tending toward full employment for the economy as a whole and efficient use of resources by firms and individuals.[26] Proponents of privatization believe that government should confine itself to those activities related to governing and let the private sector produce society's goods and services.[27]

Privatization is not a new idea. Government contracting, the most common form of privatization in the United States, predates the Constitution. Historically, the private sector performed many functions, including many urban services, which eventually were taken over by the public sector.[28] As society became more complex because of industrialization, urbanization, and changing social values, government assumed more economic and social responsibilities. The idea of a large and expanding government became the norm as the expectations and demands placed on government mushroomed. For many, government action was viewed as the solution to society's problems. Consequently, government began providing an increasing array of services. Some have suggested this caused government to become overloaded and resulted in excessive public spending and proliferation of the bureaucracy.[29] In a philosophical sense, privatization represents the ideals of a countermovement that opposes the expansion of government and seeks to redefine the proper balance between the public and private sectors.[30] It is noteworthy to point out that the process appears to be running in a circular pattern. That is, in the nineteenth century the private sector handled many services that would eventually be taken over by the public sector to strengthen public accountability and later, to address concerns over equity. Because of escalating costs and the inefficiency of the public sector, many services were being returned to the private sector by the 1970s via contracting and public-private partnerships.[31]

Political debates over economic issues tend to possess ideological components and the privatization debate is not an exception. It is generally believed that government has three basic economic responsibilities.[32] They are *stabilization of the economy, distribution of wealth, and allocation of resources to their best use.* All of these issues are part of the privatization debate and all are highly ideological in nature. Considerable disagreement exists over whether expanding the role of the private sector is desirable. Critics argue reducing the size and leverage of government during the periods of "boom and bust" associated with the business cycle could destabilize the economy.[33] For example, we have grown dependent on the government increasing welfare spending during economic recessions. No one knows what would happen if the government stopped using its fiscal powers during recessions. Or, what the impact on the economy would be if the government failed to rescue large companies, like the federal government's loan guarantees for Chrysler Corporation in the early 1980s, or to help with major public-sector crises, like New York City's severe financial problems in the 1970s.[34] Moreover, reducing the role of government as a provider of services that benefit the poor might exacerbate inequalities in the distribution of wealth.[35] Many believe that services for the poor would be inadequate if the government stopped providing these services or turned them over to the private sector. Welfare programs are involved with redistributing wealth. Efforts to contract out welfare programs have become increasingly popular. For example, in the mid-1990s, Montana experimented with several locally based pilot programs that contributed to its current statewide, privatized program.[36] Evaluations of Montana's contracted program have been positive thus far. Privatizing welfare has become a big business and examples similar to Montana's experience can be found nationwide.[37] However, the most prominent issue has been *the allocation of resources to their best use*. It is this function that is judged by the *efficiency criterion*. It is also within this sphere that most of the privatization debate has occurred. Efficiency has been one of the driving forces behind the reinventing government movement and the push toward performance measures for government agencies and services. Although ideology has been deeply involved in discussions about efficiency, mainly in terms of balancing efficiency with other concerns like equity and public accountability, most of the debate has been concerned with whether privatization can actually deliver public services more economically than traditional government auspices. It is this area that has attracted the interest of local governments.

THE LOCAL GOVERNMENT FOCUS

The decision to privatize has been especially intense at the local government level. That is, local governments have turned to privatization due to expediency rather than ideology.[38] Local governments have taken the pragmatic approach largely due to the necessity created by a variety of fiscal conditions.[39] Fiscal stress became a major concern for many cities during the 1970s. Prior to that time, most cities based their fiscal projections on the expectation of growth. A developing tax base provided incremental revenue increases with a reasonable degree of certainty. The growth assumptions were dramatically shaken during the 1970s. The energy crisis brought about an economic recession that significantly reduced municipal revenues while boosting welfare-related spending. Business and industry left many cities in search of lower taxes. City tax bases were further eroded as middle- and upper-class residents fled to the suburbs. Attempts by cities to regain some of the lost revenue through higher taxes generally backfired by causing further exodus of the middle class and industry.[40]

Amidst economic recessions, growing welfare expenses, and eroding tax bases, virtually all cities have been affected by the escalating cost of providing public services.[41] Although the local government sector has remained one of the fastest growing areas of the economy for many years, the public has consistently demonstrated a resistance to higher taxes.[42] Matters were exacerbated by state and federal program mandates, which applied additional pressures on already strained revenue-expenditure mismatches for many cities.[43] However, the main factor that fueled privatization efforts was the massive reduction in federal aid. The "new federalism" as implemented during the Reagan administration, involved a review of the proper roles and responsibilities of all levels of governments as well as the public and private sectors. The idea of devolution implicit in Reagan's federalism implied that many responsibilities could be devolved to the market.[44] The cutbacks in federal aid reflected a philosophy that massive federal assistance to cities is not equitable because it siphons resources from the nation as a whole to pay for local programs. The Reagan administration believed that financing programs with a local impact should be the responsibility of the state and local governments—a position that resulted in changing a fifty-year pattern of federalism.[45]

As noted above, privatization is not a new phenomenon at the local level. What is new involves the breadth of its application. Privatization is now being used in areas once considered to be exclusively public-sector domain. Cities have privatized services across a broad spectrum of functions. These include hard services (such as garbage collection) and soft services (such as mental health care). One study reported that between 1972 and 1982, the total dollar amount of local government contract awards to private firms tripled from $22 billion to $65 billion.[46] In 1987, private firms were awarded more than $100 billion for local contracts.[47] Although the current data on the dollar amount awarded for local government contracts is not considered to be reliable,[48] it is known that the federal government spent $44 billion in fiscal year 1992 for service contracts with private firms. This figure excludes purchasing physical goods.[49] Surveys suggest that most cities (80 percent) in the United States use some form of privatization.[50] Most researchers view the widespread use of privatization as an attempt to reduce operating expenses as cities face fiscal dilemmas created by economic recessions, demographic shifts, and changing patterns of federalism.[51] This has been coupled with public pressures that make raising taxes politically unfeasible for many localities.[52] Although municipal governments use many types of privatization, the most common form is contracting out.[53] Under this arrangement, cities remain responsible for the provision of a service (which includes financing), but contract out for production and delivery. The decision to contract out seems simple, but attempting to lower the costs of municipal services through this form of privatization has ignited an intense policy debate.[54]

THE CASE FOR CONTRACTING OUT

Central to the decision to contract out are concerns relating to public-sector productivity. Even when services appear identical, private firms seem to outperform their public-sector counterparts.[55] A plethora of examples can be found that suggest government production is more costly. For instance, studies have found that public garbage collection in New York City cost twice as much as private collection and that public street repair was nearly three times as costly.[56] Such examples are abundant and paint an image of an inefficient and poorly managed public sector.

Advocates point to a large body of studies that generally confirms private production to be more efficient.[57] Proponents believe the evidence on efficiency favors the private sector because business is a superior institution for providing cost-efficient services. This is attributed to the characteristics of the competitive marketplace. Businesses must compete to generate revenues to sustain operations. Revenues must be managed efficiently to produce profits. Moreover, firms must compete with similar operations for their market share by satisfying customers' needs, wants, and expectations. Customers must be induced to make a purchase and feel satisfied with the exchange. Competition and the pursuit of profit are the key elements that force efficiency in the marketplace. Advocates contend that private business, impelled by competition and the profit motive, can provide superior goods and services more cost-efficiently than government can.[58] Proponents believe the powers of the marketplace can be transferred through contracting.[59]

The primary role of government under contracting is the performance of a "watchdog" function.[60] Government assumes responsibility for awarding and monitoring contracts. If a contractor's performance becomes unsatisfactory, a city can contract with another firm. This is assumed to be an adequate incentive to ensure firms remain both efficient and responsive. Proponents believe contracting enables cities to provide the highest level of service at the lowest cost because of the introduction of competition. It is believed that contracting works well under a certain set of conditions. These conditions include the following: (1) The work to be done is specified unambiguously; (2) A competitive climate exists or can be created and maintained; (3) The government is able to monitor the contractor's performance; and (4) Appropriate terms are included in the contract document and are enforced.[61] Advocates argue that contracting reduces direct municipal outlays (by not having to maintain large in-house departments) while sharing risks with private providers. The increased efficiency of private firms results in lower costs for taxpayers. This enables cities to maintain or increase service levels without raising taxes or imposing user fees.[62] The major advantages of contracting with private firms are summarized in Table 1.1. Most of these advantages involve efficiency, which equates to lower costs to produce services. Each of these points is found throughout the academic literature on privatization and in the popular press. Each deserves some additional attention.

The first point, *contracting harnesses competitive forces and brings the pressures of the marketplace to bear on inefficient producers*, is reflected in the nature of competitive markets (described above). Competition and the pursuit of profit are the key elements that force efficiency in the marketplace. If firms fail to compete and manage their assets efficiently, they will lose customers and eventually either improve their performance or go out of business. Bankruptcy is the penalty for poor management in the private sector. Although contracting does not replicate the marketplace, some of the forces of the market can be simulated. For example, Phoenix, Arizona, and San Diego, California, have institutionalized competitive bidding for many municipal services. Phoenix requires that many of its departments compete with private contractors for services.[63] San Diego has established a competition program that constantly reviews the performance of all services. If a service becomes available at a lower price from the private sector, their in-house department is given an opportunity to enhance its performance before contracting out is

TABLE 1.1   ADVANTAGES OF CONTRACTING OUT[64]

Contracting harnesses competitive forces and brings the pressures of the marketplace to bear on inefficient producers. It permits better management, free of most of the distracting influences that are characteristic of political organizations.

The costs of managerial decisions are felt more closely by the decision-makers, whose own rewards are often at stake.

Competition for contracts helps reveal the true costs of production and eliminates waste since contracts are granted to those offering the highest quality of service at the lowest cost.

Economies of scale can be realized by reducing the overhead and start-up costs by spreading supply over a larger area. Private firms often take advantage of economies of scale in service delivery by performing an activity in more than one locality.

Increased flexibility can be achieved in the use of personnel and equipment for short-term projects, part-time work, and specialized needs without having to maintain a municipal bureaucracy.

The performance of private contractors can serve as a yardstick for comparison of efficiency and effectiveness of services that are produced in-house. Competition from private contractors can spur municipal worker and management productivity improvements.

Avoiding public employee unions reduces personnel costs and civil service rules, which tend to escalate the cost of producing services.

Personnel costs can be reduced by not having to pay for employee benefits packages.

considered. The competition program in San Diego is based on a premise that taxpayers are not concerned with who provides a service; they are concerned that taxpayer resources are used efficiently and effectively.[65]

It [contracting] *permits better management, free of most of the distracting influences that are characteristic of political organizations,* is also related to the nature of the competitive marketplace. Decisions are supposed to be based on economics rather than politics. Contracting attempts to separate production and delivery of services from provision and financing. That is, under contracting, government remains responsible for providing and financing the service, but contracts out for production and delivery of the service. This allows vendors, such as the firms collecting garbage, to concentrate on doing their jobs efficiently. Ideally, multiple contracts should be awarded whenever possible. This forces contractors to remain competitive with other contractors performing the same task for the city. Many cities, such as New York City and Phoenix, Arizona, use multiple contractors in addition to their own sanitation departments to collect garbage.

The next point, *the costs of managerial decisions are felt more closely by the decision makers, whose own rewards are often at stake,* provides a strong incentive for private contractors to make sound decisions and manage their resources efficiently. An electric firm replacing streetlights for a city has an incentive to make the repairs in a way that fulfills the company's obligation to the city and at the same time, to manage employees, equipment, and other resources to ensure that a profit is earned. Failure to fulfill the quality and timeliness of the repairs may cause the firm to lose the contract. Failure to manage the firm's resources will lower the profits. Without profits, firms do not have the financial resources to sustain their operations. Conversely, a municipal public works department does not operate under the same set of incentives. Budgets of municipal departments are secured through a political process that has little to do with, and is far removed from, the service being produced. In the case of replacing streetlights, the public works department does not have to manage its internal affairs to make a profit (there is nothing comparable to profit found in the public sector). Replacing streetlights is simply another task included in a wide variety of functions performed by the department that is included in the public works budget and, often, the true cost of performing the task is not known, which leads directly into the next point.

Privatization advocates argue that *competition for contracts helps reveal the true costs of production and eliminates waste since contracts are granted to those offering the highest quality of service at the lowest cost.* One of the most interesting findings of studies on refuse collection conducted in the 1970s was that cities often did not know the real cost of collecting garbage. For example, how much does it cost to stop the truck and collect the garbage at each house or business? What is the cost per ton of garbage? These studies will be examined in Chapter 2. Partly due to so many studies being performed, most cities are now well aware of the cost of collecting trash in their jurisdictions. When contractors bid to provide a service, they must know the true cost (or at least the approximate cost). This provides measurement standards that can be tested. For example, if several companies bid that they can repair streets for a specific amount of money ($X per mile at a certain level of quality) not only are the true costs of the task revealed, but also a standard is set that can be verified. In the private sector, the actual costs of production are well known. For example, Ford Motor Company can tell you exactly the cost of producing the popular Ford Explorer. Hilton Hotels knows exactly the cost of setting up a hotel room, which includes the supplies, labor, construction costs, utilities, and so forth per room. Both can also tell you the amount of profit that is made off each unit. However, the *true* costs of services are not always known in the public sector.

Economies of scale can be realized by reducing the overhead and start-up costs by spreading supply over a larger area. Private firms often take advantage of economies of scale in service delivery by performing an activity in more than one locality. The key element of this point is what economists refer to as *economies of scale*. Simply stated, economies of scale refer to creating larger markets or service areas to lower the costs of providing some service. This contributes to lowering the cost of services for a variety of reasons. For example, one of the arguments for city-county consolidations has historically been that economies of scale would be created (by the consolidation itself), thus allowing services to be delivered more efficiently. In the case of city-county consolidations, the consolidated district could eliminate overlap and replication of services, such as having to maintain police and sheriff departments. One law enforcement department could be created that serves the entire jurisdiction. It has long been believed this reduces the cost of government without sacrificing quality. In the case of contracting, many contractors provide their services to multiple jurisdictions. Even if the market is too small to create an economy of scale in a single jurisdiction, many firms can offer the service at a lower cost because they serve other jurisdictions. For example, the Rural Metro is a private fire fighting company that has long provided fire protection to cities in the Phoenix area. Because the Rural Metro operates in other cities across the nation, their costs are often lower than a public fire department operating in one city. Why could there be a difference? One reason involves purchasing equipment. The Rural Metro purchases more fire trucks and equipment than a small town (or more than some cities or towns). It is the same reason that Wal-Mart can offer lower prices than a small retail store. For example, Wal-Mart may purchase 100,000 televisions in a single order because it operates stores in communities nationwide, while the small retail store may purchase 50 televisions per year because it only serves customers in a small town. Thus, Wal-Mart is in a position to negotiate with television manufacturers for a lower price per unit.

Economies of scale also involve the point at which the price per unit of some service becomes less expensive. For example, the cost of providing a service is not constant. The price for collecting garbage in a jurisdiction may be about $3.00 per household up to 100,000 households but the cost then begins to drop. After 100,000 households, the cost per ton of garbage collected may significantly decrease. But at some point the cost begins to level off. Further reductions in cost must then be made through other changes, such as the technological changes in equipment that reduce the costs of such items as labor or fuel. Private firms are generally believed to do a better job at utilizing other methods, such as implementing new technologies to reduce costs, due to competition.

Economies of scale also vary from one jurisdiction to the next. Many factors can have an effect on the cost of collecting garbage, such as population density and level of service. It might be less costly to collect garbage in areas where most people live in either condominium or apartment complexes and place their household garbage in dumpsters than in areas where most people live in traditional houses and leave their garbage in cans along the side of the street.

The next point suggests that *increased flexibility can be achieved in the use of personnel and equipment for short-term projects, part-time work, and specialized needs without having to maintain a municipal bureaucracy.* This point is simple and straightforward. Cities have short-term, seasonal projects, and specialized needs that can be contracted out. This eliminates the need to maintain a full, in-house department. Functions such as trimming trees and landscaping maintenance are tasks that many cities have contracted out, which reduces the need to maintain personnel and related equipment in the public works department. Moreover, all cities must tow vehicles (parking violations are a problem found in virtually all cities), but do they need to maintain their own tow trucks? Apparently not: More than 90 percent of cities contract out for vehicle towing.[66] Specialized needs, such as managing civic centers, are another area. For example, the first year Denver, Colorado, contracted out management of the Colorado Convention Center, the city saved $500,000.[67] Winchester, Virginia, privatized its city office-supply system, replacing it with a stockless supply system. The system functions with virtually no overhead costs by coordinating with suppliers. The city saved $17,000 in the first year of operation and employees gave the system a 100 percent approval rating over the in-house system used in the past.[68]

A point that is commonly cited as an advantage is that the *performance of private contractors can serve as a yardstick for comparison of efficiency and effectiveness of services that are produced in-house.* This point is related to having the true costs of services revealed (discussed earlier). Even critics of privatizing services have noted that a positive result of privatization is that it has created pressure for public agencies to enhance their performance.[69] If a public department knows what the cost of performing a task is in the private sector, it has a yardstick to gauge its own performance. One of the tasks of San Diego's competition program is to make sure that it knows the costs of performing services by relevant area businesses and its own departments. Once it has determined that a service can be contracted out for a lower price, it gives its in-house department the opportunity to improve its performance. If this information were not available, the city would not have a reference point to judge its own performance. Thus, *competition from private contractors can spur municipal worker and management productivity improvements*. This has occurred regularly in Phoenix, Arizona, where most in-house departments must place bids that are equal to or lower than competitive bids from private contractors.[70]

Avoiding public employee unions reduces personnel costs and civil service rules, which tend to escalate the cost of producing services, and *personnel costs can be reduced by not having to pay for employee benefits packages*, have been among the most controversial aspects of the privatization debate. The most adamant opponents of privatization have been public employee unions. There is little argument to claims that unions, public or private, raise the costs of producing services. The increased costs come in two forms, labor and benefits. Unions usually demand "across-the-board" pay increases that often reward unproductive employees along with those that are productive. Public employee unions also have secured good benefits for public workers, which have become increasingly expensive in the public and private sectors.[71] Privatizing services in a way that replaces public workers reduces personnel costs because the private firm is not bound by arduous civil service rules, such as grievance procedures, and private-sector benefit packages are not usually as generous for lower- to middle-range workers. Union supporters have argued that the only goal of privatization is to lower cost regardless of the consequences, such as causing public employees to lose their jobs. There are hidden costs when employees lose their jobs, such as unemployment and welfare benefits. However, the impact of privatizing services on public employees is not as severe as critics suggest. The evidence suggests that public employees are not usually permanently displaced due to contracting. One study of more than 9,600 federal workers, who lost their jobs in the Department of Defense because of contracting, found that only 300 (less than 5 percent) were left without employment and drew public assistance. A study by the Government Accounting Office (GAO) found that the cost of public assistance was minimal (approximately $200,000 in relation to the savings from contracting [more than $65 million]).[72] At the local level, cities often handle workforce reduction through early retirements and lateral transfers. For example, when Charlottesville, Virginia, had to reduce its public works department (from 28 to 23 employees) due to contracting, all of the reductions were handled through early retirements.[73]

THEORETICAL FOUNDATIONS

The theoretical foundations for privatization are provided by a variety of economic schools. The two most prominent are *market theory* (which deals with the nature of competitive markets) and *public choice theory* (which deals with the nature of monopolies and nonmarket decision making).[74] It is important to understand the essence of these theories because they provide the underlying theoretical assumptions that make privatization a superior method for delivering services. When privatization advocates point to the superiority of the market, they are referring to the competitive elements of capitalism where efficiency is mandated by necessity for a firm to survive.

MARKET THEORY

The characteristics of the competitive market are relatively simple and well known. Market theory is based on an idealized model in which firms seek to maximize profits, are small relative to their industries, and where no restrictions exist to prevent firms from entering or exiting any industry. Although firms seek to maximize profits, their ability to inflate prices is guarded by competition. Consumers are well informed (referred to as *perfect information*) and have defined preferences about alternative goods and services (the idea of *preference orderings*). The consumer is supreme in the competitive market. Firms must compete with similar operations for their "market share." Competition forces efficiency in the market. Efficiency is also guarded by business's ability to enter or exit markets.[75] If firms make unusually high profits, new firms will enter the market until profits return to a normal level. Price in the market is based on a combination of production cost, supply, and demand. The efficient use of resources, which is guarded by the inherent incentives in the market, provides it with supremacy over other models. In the real world, market configurations can range from perfect competition to monopolies, but it is the idealized model to which all other models are compared. Market theory is generally associated with *private goods*, the types of goods that are easy to exclude others from using (this is in contrast to *public goods*, which are goods that are difficult to exclude others from using, such as street lighting in a city). Few local services are considered to be "purely" public goods.[76] A general consensus exists among scholars that public or private organizations can provide and produce most local services. Outcomes in the market are judged by efficiency, which may be thought of as a contest among various ways of performing a task or producing a service. If the market can provide a service at a lower cost than government, or if it can provide a superior service at the same cost, then the market is considered more efficient.[77]

Why does this ideal model enter into discussions about public services? Market theory provides an alternative arrangement with a long, successful record of generating goods and services efficiently, and it is believed that some of the market's power can be transferred through contracting. To illustrate the success of the marketplace we can find numerous examples in the private sector. These include technology industry, such as the computer firms, where competition is intense and the cost of computer hardware and software has become more affordable over the years. We can look at boulevards in cities lined with businesses such as McDonald's, Burger King, Pizza Hut, and others competing with each other, offering a choice of products at competitive prices. Or, look at the soft drink industry and the intense competition between rivals such as Coca-Cola and Pepsi.[78] From the perspective of market theory, this is healthy behavior. Consumers are provided with quality products at competitive prices, and most importantly, choice. Consumers will vote in the marketplace by selecting among competing choices, say a Ford versus a Chevrolet, or an RCA television instead of a Sony television, or an IBM computer instead of a Dell, and so on. Choice is a key element in market theory because the behavior of firms without competition is similar to any monopoly. Market theory sees a variety of choices among competing products as critical in forcing efficiency in the marketplace. Ultimately, private firms would like to have 100 percent of the market of their industries, but competitive markets provide inherent protections against this because other firms will be attracted to and enter the industry in pursuit of profit. The penalty in the marketplace for failing to maintain a competitive orientation and managing resources efficiently is bankruptcy, something that is rare in the world of government.

The problem with government lies in the nature of government itself. Government is not an economically driven institution where efficiency is necessary for survival; it is a *political* institution designed to *govern*. Moreover, government is a monopoly and monopolies are inherently inefficient due to the lack of competition. There is no incentive for public managers to keep looking over their shoulders to see if the competition is gaining ground because there is no competition. Financing for public services is secured through a political process that is not directly connected to the actual services being produced. Agencies of government operate by securing funding through the public budget process to perform a function. Markets connect the cost of producing something to the income necessary to sustain operations. The connection is provided by the price charged to customers who decide whether to make a purchase. This is not the case with government because the revenues that sustain government activity usually come from taxes, which are considered to be a nonprice source (meaning the value of output is separated from the cost of production).[79] This makes government organizations more likely to use indicators such as budget size to measure performance. This causes internal standards and incentives structures to reward personnel for justifying costs rather than reducing them.[80] Thus, the inefficiency of municipal services is not because of bad commissioners, mayors, managers, or workers. It is a natural consequence of a monopoly system.[81]

PUBLIC CHOICE THEORY

Public choice theory has had an enormous impact on the privatization debate.[82] Public choice theory poses the question: What is the motivation of public managers? Is it self-interest or the public's interest? From a theoretical position, they provide a rationale that suggests public managers will take action that is in their own self-interest. This is the same rationale for motivation of managers in the competitive marketplace, but the incentive structures of public organizations and the consequences of public managers' actions are very different in the public sector. To understand their rationale, one must have some understanding of the underlying theory on which public choice theory is built. The theory is called *rational choice*.[83] Rational choice is a simple and parsimonious theory. The theory assumes that all individuals are rational actors (defined by economists as self-serving egotists) who respond to incentives and disincentives to maximize their own self-interest or satisfaction (the term used by economists is *utility*). Thus, the rational actor will respond to the cost-laden choices in a way that satisfies his or her self-interest. Applied to the public bureaucracy, bureaucrats will behave in a way that is in the public's interest only if it is also in their own self-interest. Serving some greater good (or the public interest) is secondary to serving one's self-interest.

Thoroughly grounded in laissez-faire individualism and free-market economics, public choice theory argues that the competitive marketplace produces goods and services efficiently while public monopolies are viewed as inefficient.[84] Inefficiency is viewed as an inherent characteristic of public bureaucracies because of the incentive structures that encourage empire building and overproduction of services.[85] Because government agencies are service monopolies, public employees will behave in ways that promote their own interests at the expense of the public's interest in efficiency. Thus, it is believed that the incentive structures of public agencies encourage public personnel to advance their powers, budgets, and agency staffing levels.[86]

The theory also explains why government budgets tend to grow. The theory holds that self-interest leads to benign results in the marketplace but creates pathological patterns of behavior in political organizations,[87] mainly in the form of various free-rider and rent-seeker problems.[88] The theory holds that coalitions of citizens (interest groups) join together seeking special advantages. Individuals with concentrated interests in increasing public expenditures literally take a free ride on those with diffuse interests in lower taxes. The iron triangles that develop work against the public at large while serving those with concentrated interests in increasing public expenditures. Public choice theory believes that in the public sector the citizens (who are mainly members of interest groups) will demand too many services since increased quantities are not regulated by direct increased costs for those people receiving the services.[89] In situations where the public at large is paying to benefit the few, the cost of services to the individual becomes so inexpensive that demand increases. This results in an excessively large demand for services and a bloated, overly expensive, and wasteful government.[90]

The theory's powerful impact on the privatization debate rests in its ability to explain why government cannot be efficient. Public choice theory does not attribute the blame for inefficiency to public managers and public employees who are simply behaving as rational choice theory predicts. It attributes the problem of inefficiency in government to the natural characteristics of monopolies that create incentives that cause public employees and managers to behave in ways that are counterproductive to the goal of efficiency. The theory makes many recommendations but the main one relating to privatization is to separate governmental financing from governmental production of public services, which can be accomplished through contracting.[91] Public choice theory argues that altering the delivery arrangements of public services (by contracting with private vendors) will enhance efficiency and slow the pace of government growth.[92]

The theoretical foundations of privatization have had a powerful impact on the privatization debate.[93] The thrust of the theories discussed above may be summed up as *markets* versus *monopolies*. The theories focus on the positive attributes of the competitive marketplace and highlight the inherent inefficiency found in public monopolies. In reality, the choice of markets or monopolies may be a choice between two imperfect alternatives.[94] In summary, advocates of privatization argue that government should take advantage of cost-saving potentials by turning over services to private firms. Privatization is seen as a way of improving efficiency while offering new opportunities for private businesses. Ideally, this will result in greater satisfaction for the people served.[95] Government can benefit from the powers of the marketplace and free itself to govern by allowing private firms to provide services.

THE CASE AGAINST CONTRACTING OUT

Critics of privatization have a tough argument to make. How can one argue against efficiency? The private sector also enjoys a reputation for good and efficient management. Thus, the arguments against contracting do not usually focus on efficiency. Critics have preferred to emphasize issues relating to equity and public accountability. The strongest opposition to privatization comes from the orthodox school of public administration in academia and public employee unions in the governmental sector.[96] According to the orthodox school of public administration, democracy is realistically achievable only if power is concentrated so that it can be held accountable. Otherwise, responsibility blends into the social surround.[97] Public administration tends to accept the institutions that have emerged to govern and seeks to make them more efficient and effective.[98] In other words, citizens of a city elect a mayor and city council and hold them accountable if the city is poorly managed. It is the mayor and city council's responsibility to ensure that the city operates. Usually, a city manager is hired who in turn hires an executive staff that actually manages the various municipal departments. If citizens are dissatisfied, they can vote the mayor and council members out of office at the next election.

Rejecting the notion of diffused authority, public administration tends to be more concerned with institutional continuity and public accountability. Government must be concerned with more than efficiency. They emphasize that public institutions are the principal vehicles for expressing common and public concerns. Strong public institutions are necessary to govern and the basic assumptions of public choice theory are rejected. The idea that behavior of public managers can be explained by a parsimonious theory that sees all people as self-serving egotists is not only unrealistic, but is a silly proposition on face value. Public managers and workers are not viewed as the self-serving, budget maximizing bureaucrats described in public choice. To the contrary, most public managers are sincere, well-trained professionals who are committed to professionalism and high standards in the public sector. Moreover, their activities do serve the public interest.[99] In the view of the orthodox school of public administration, public choice theory creates an enfeebled, even nonexistent state that may have served eighteenth century needs in America, but such a state is not capable for dealing with the awesome tasks the nation faces in the twenty-first century.[100] The whole theory is based on erroneous assumptions and a blind faith in the perceived superiority of private business. If private management were in fact so superior and private businesses so efficient, why do most new businesses fail? Markets are an appropriate arena for fast-food chains, hotels, and grocery stores to compete with each other but not the appropriate arena for providing essential public services or making political decisions.

The problem of public accountability is seen as a critical issue. Critics of privatization have asserted that it is more difficult for the public to hold contractors responsible than elected officials or bureaucrats when there are problems with service.[101] *Sector blurring*, a term that refers to mixing responsibility for the provision of services between the public and private sectors, is viewed as a threat to the accountability of legitimate political institutions.[102] The orthodox school of public administration argues that the public needs to have a clear perception of who is providing and responsible for services. Since sector blurring results in distortion by breaking down the division between the public and private sectors, this group does not see most forms of privatization as desirable. The roots of public administration are viewed as being embedded in public law (rather than economics) and the argument that most public-sector functions can be handled by the private sector is rejected.[103] The orthodox school of public administration believes that privatization is based on the erroneous assumption that the public and private sectors are fundamentally alike and both subject to the same set of incentives and disincentives.[104]

Public administration advocates claim the public sector cannot be compared to private business. Governments function in a political environment whereas private firms exist in a competitive, economic milieu.[105] Since the objective of private firms is to maximize profits, firms may skimp on service quality. Moreover, contractors will cut corners by hiring inexperienced, transient personnel at low wages, by ignoring the contract, or by providing inadequate supervision. This is a common problem for local governments. For example, Phoenix, Arizona, has contracted out janitorial services for many of its buildings since 1978. The city uses several contractors. In one building, the city terminated contracts with three different contractors in one year because of the poor quality of service.[106] It was a costly and time-consuming process to secure new contracts. In the interim, the city had to use its own employees. Contracting out requires that contractors be closely monitored.[107] In the case of Phoenix, the city implemented new guidelines with stronger incentives for contractors to live up to quality levels specified in the contracts. Public employee unions maintain that often a new level of bureaucracy is created to monitor contracts that offset any savings that might be realized through contracting.[108]

The possibility that a contractor may be unable to complete a job or adequately provide a service is a major concern. Critics emphasize that unlike government, contractors often go bankrupt or cease operations. This is also a problem for cities. In the case of a New Jersey city that shut down its own sanitation department and contracted its entire garbage collecting services to a single firm. The city even donated its garbage collecting equipment to the firm. The firm went bankrupt and sold off all of its equipment, including the equipment that had been donated by the city. This created a sanitation nightmare and caused the city to turn to the state for help.[109] Moreover, inadequate competition is more profound than advocates of contracting admit. For many services, such as fire protection, few contractors exist in most localities. If a city privatizes its fire department and sells off its equipment, imagine the problems that would result if the firm it contracted with goes bankrupt. The city is vulnerable and accountable. Government simply cannot afford to operate in a state characterized by this type of instability. Public bureaucracy may have its own set of problems, but it serves as a protection against the unpredictable fluctuations inherent in the marketplace. Public administration proponents generally hold that the public and private sectors are fundamentally alike in all unimportant respects.[110] Business is mainly concerned with satisfying market segments. Government must provide public services in an equitable fashion and must remain accountable to the public for its actions.[111] According to the orthodox school of public administration, the context in which government services are provided should be determined in the political arena, not in the competitive marketplace.

A major concern with contracting is corruption. Critics argue in the absence of adequate competition, relationships can develop between those granting contracts and contractors that are not in the best interest of the general public. This is illustrated in the case of Union City, New Jersey, where many of the city's contracts were awarded to companies that were owned by the mayor.[112] When cozy relationships develop between a city and private contractors, monitoring contractors can be neglected, which can lead to high costs and lower quality services.[113] Those who favor contracting tend to ignore impressive examples of inefficiency, corruption, and waste in the American experience with defense contractors, construction projects, and health care that have been privately produced with public money.[114] Privatization's opponents view contracts as one of the most common and lucrative sources of corruption in government.[115] Although the abuse has been diminished by public bidding and other techniques designed to improve the integrity of the process, private contractors doing business with governments are still one of the sources of campaign funds, and of support, for shady politicians. The history of municipal contracting is filled with scandals and corruption. One need only read the history of Albany, New York, under Mayor Daniel O'Connell's administration to be reminded. One journalist claimed that Albany should be officially named "Contracting-Out City, U.S.A."[116] because virtually every service imaginable, with the exception of the fire and police departments, had contracts with private companies. A 1972 investigation by the state (and a number of criminal trials) revealed the enormous magnitude of the waste and corruption associated with the city's contracts and procurement practices.[117]

Displacement of public employees is another concern. That is, what happens to public workers when they lose their jobs because of privatization? One study estimates that between 1980 and 1987, contracting caused 1.5 million state and local jobs to be transferred to the private sector.[118] Critics argue that displacement of public workers causes expenditures to increase for public assistance, job training, and unemployment compensation. Critics contend that increases in these expenditures can offset any savings realized through contracting.[119] The Labor Research Association conducted a study of the wage fluctuations that occur when employees shift from public jobs to the private sector. Although the study stresses regional differences exist, the findings indicate average wages decrease 39 percent when federal workers shift to private-sector, nonunion jobs.[120] At the local level, the disparity is less profound, 4.9 percent. However, the study revealed that union employees really lose in the benefits category, especially in health care benefits.[121] Public employee unions are one of the leading critics of privatization because they stand to lose their jobs if services are contracted out or devolved to the market. Pressure from public employee unions has led to a variety of policies that help protect public workers even when services are privatized. For example, Los Angeles adopted a formal "no-lay-off" policy many years ago. Similar policies have become common in many cities (and even the federal government). In short, a "no-lay-off" policy promises that no employee will be laid off due to privatization or contracting. Usually, the city handles this through internal transfers, normal attrition, or voluntary early retirements for those who qualify.[122]

Another issue involves contractors bidding low to be awarded a contract and recouping the initial losses in the future. This practice, known as "lowballing," is a major concern to public employee unions. They argue the practice causes public employees to lose their jobs while misrepresenting the actual costs to government and taxpayers.[123] Lowballing does occur. For example, soon after Garden Grove, California, contracted out for its street sweeping, the contractor requested to renegotiate the contract because of significant increases in the cost of labor and fuel. Although no public employees lost their jobs, this created a problem for the city because it could not quickly perform the service in-house or secure another contractor who could adequately perform the service for the entire city. However, the city ultimately resolved the issue by dividing the city into districts and contracting with smaller contractors that were capable of handling the smaller districts.[124] Unions have stressed that lower costs of private provision can often be explained by a reduction in the quality of services.[125] Clearly, it is possible that a reduction in quality would explain lower costs. For example, if a public sanitation department collected residential garbage twice per week and the service was then contracted out to a private vendor who collected garbage only once per week, the cost would be lower. However, this problem generally involves concerns regarding contract compliance and monitoring rather than a tendency for contractors to deliberately lower the level of service.[126]

Critics also contest the idea that contracting helps slow the growth of government. They argue government's role in society continues to grow although fewer public employees may be hired to deliver services. For example, contracting has often been used to circumvent hiring freezes while expanding programs and services. From this perspective, contracting is seen a facade. It masks government's true size and scope while serving to maintain a myth of less government.[127] Some have argued that contracting is actually a disguised form of public employment since thousands of jobs exist because of government contracts.[128]

THE THEORY OF MARKET FAILURE

Interestingly, critics of privatization also turn to economics for theoretical support. With respect to market theory, privatization's opponents acknowledge the accomplishments of the market but associate its evolution with a variety of negative consequences such as macroeconomic instability, microeconomic inefficiency, and social inequity.[129] Thus, the deficiencies of the market require government to intervene to enhance efficiency and social equity.[130] This view is based on an idealized model, but one of an informed, efficient, and humane government that is capable of correcting the deficiencies of the market. Moreover, the government possesses the expertise to take action that serves the public interest.[131] The theories of market failure and public goods are used to justify government provision. These theories focus on the shortcomings of the market. Critics turn to welfare economics to incorporate concerns about equity.

Market failure occurs in a variety of ways. In the real world, markets tend to be less perfect than the idealized model used in market theory. Market imperfections include *imperfect information*, meaning consumers may not have good information about products or prices. The lack of information affects *preference orderings*, which makes it difficult for consumers to make competent decisions about purchases. For example, firms often do not disclose adequate safety information about products. This was the case with certain Chevrolet trucks, which had a tendency to explode in certain types of common, side-impact collisions due to the location of the fuel tank. General Motors was well aware of this problem but never divulged the information until it was revealed in a lengthy lawsuit. Would sales have been as strong for Chevy trucks if consumers knew that the gas tanks exploded so easily upon a side-impact collision? Or, would millions of consumers have preferred the safer Ford trucks at the time if they had perfect information?[132] Moreover, firms cannot move from one industry to another because of barriers like large capital investments that are needed to enter an industry. This is evidenced by the tendencies for oligarchies (domination by a few large firms) to develop, which make it difficult for new firms to enter the market. How easy is it to start a new airline? The costs to enter the airline industry are colossal. Delta Airlines, the nation's third largest air carrier recently ordered several billions of dollars worth of jets to upgrade its fleet. It is an understatement to say this serves as a disincentive for new firms to enter the highly competitive airline industry. The concept of "increasing returns to scale" refers to costs continuing to decline as production volume increases. This phenomenon provides an advantage for large-scale producers, such as firms on the scale of General Electric or General Motors. Moreover, the "boom and bust" effects associated with markets undermine attaining *Pareto Optimality* (a state of perfect efficiency, according to economists).

Public goods also represent a form of market failure. Everyone shares these goods simultaneously and no one can be excluded from sharing the benefits. Generally, it is not possible to stop nonpayers (free riders) from consuming public goods. Examples include sidewalks, street lighting, and national defense. Individuals must be compelled to pay through taxation for these services and government must intervene to combat free riders (those who avoid paying, yet still enjoy the benefits of public goods).

Market failure also occurs because of *externalities*. Externalities are the spillovers produced by industry and can take the form of benefits or costs. Where business activity produces spillovers, efficiency is distorted because external benefits or costs are excluded from production calculations. When externalities take the form of benefits, too little will be produced. Conversely, when externalities are net costs, too much will be produced. Pollution is a classic example of a negative spillover. Education is an example of an activity that produces a positive spillover. Since the market tends to produce too much pollution and too little education, a rationale exists in these activities for government to intervene (regulate pollution) or assume responsibility for production for a service, such as education. According to one critic, such inadequacies in the market will produce too many cigarettes and too little health care.[133]

Natural monopolies represent another example of market failure. Natural monopolies occur in situations where a single firm can provide a service more economically. Examples typically include various types of utility services such as providing electricity or distributing natural gas. At the municipal level, natural monopolies often include water and sewerage service. One frequently cited example took place in England during the 1700s. The experiment involved Parliament opening London's water supply to the market. Private firms were allowed to compete in open competition. This resulted in some streets having as many as three separate waterlines operated by three different companies. The firms ultimately formed cartels and the price of water became more expensive than it was under government control.[134] Thus, the market failed. Natural monopolies are considered to be temporary until technology enables viable alternatives. For example, the breakup of the Bell system in telecommunications occurred when technology enabled long-distance telephone service to be handled more competitively. Since the breakup of the Bell system, consumers have several highly competitive firms for long-distance telephone service, such as AT&T and MCI (which recently purchased one of its large competitors, Sprint). Moreover, these companies face competition from new technology industries such as cellular telephone companies like Cellular One and Internet providers. Thus, the once natural monopolistic telecommunications industry is no longer considered a natural monopoly. At the local level, cable television was once considered a local monopoly. It was cheaper to grant a franchise (a form of monopoly) to providers for a city or sections of a city. Philadelphia was among the first cities to open up competition and allow multiple cable companies to operate throughout the city. The result was lower costs for consumers and expanded service over the standards found in other cities. The cable industry also received new competition from satellite dish companies, such as digital television disks that could be placed in a window. Thus, in time, it is believed that natural monopolies will eventually become part of the competitive marketplace. Until then, natural monopolies remain an aspect of market failure.

The term market failure usually is concerned with deviations from competitive equilibrium and Pareto-efficient outcomes.[135] Even perfectly functioning markets can fail to meet socially acceptable standards of equity. One clear feature of capitalism is that it produces winners and losers. That is, some are left out of the wealth generated by capitalism. In welfare economics, distributional equity is a shortcoming of the market. In freely functioning markets, the principal devices that deal with equity are philanthropy and charity. These devices are inadequate for equitable redistribution in the modern world. It is also acknowledged that trade-offs between efficiency and equity must be determined by a social consensus in the political arena. Since the ability to pay determines who receives services in the market, some groups (namely, the disadvantaged and poor) are excluded. This provides justification for government intervention to remedy problems relating to equity.[136]

In summary, critics do not suggest that cities should not consider privatization. They caution that privatization has its shortcomings. Moreover, they stress that there are other concerns, such as equity and public accountability that cities must balance with efficiency. Over time the debate has tempered to some degree and privatization is viewed as a technique that is available to cities to use in appropriate situations, usually on a case by case basis. Recent developments, including performance measurement in public organizations and the reinventing government movement, are more palatable for critics. These ideas are more consistent with the beliefs of the orthodox school of public administration, which tends to accept the institutions that have emerged to govern and prefers to work to make them more efficient and effective.

TWO IDEALIZED MODEL CITIES

What kind of *ideal* city would the orthodox school of public administration create? What is their perfect model? And, how would it differ form the *ideal* city that proponents of privatization would create? Advocates and opponents of privatization disagree over the appropriate methods cities should use for delivering services. The implications of their arguments paint two very different models for cities to emulate. Advocates prefer a market approach whereas critics stress the need for nonmarket provision. The contractual city places its emphasis on efficiency whereas the full-service city is concerned with balancing efficiency with equity and accountability.[137]

Advocates of privatization ask us to imagine a city where the provision of most public services are either contracted out or completely privatized—a city without traditional operating departments. All basic services are available to citizens but are provided by private firms. Firms must competitively bid for contracts to provide services. Services that can be returned to the market are discontinued from public provision. City Hall primarily performs administrative functions. It administers and monitors contracts, collects revenues, and transfers payments to vendors.

The rationale for this model assumes the market is better suited for providing services. Citizens are better served because firms have a monetary incentive to provide quality services. A state of affairs emerges where everyone is better off. Taxes are low, the public bureaucracy becomes less prominent, and services are provided efficiently. Government spends its time governing rather than producing services. The competitive marketplace is envisioned as the solution. The Lakewood Cities, a group of seventy-five cities in the Los Angeles area, greatly resemble this model.[138] The Lakewood Cities (named after Lakewood, California) contract out for most of their basic services.[139]

Conversely, critics ask us to imagine a truly full-service city, one that produces and delivers all essential services. A chief executive officer, who oversees all department heads and is accountable to a council comprised of elected officials, directs City Hall. A professional public bureaucracy is maintained to provide services. Its employees are civil servants hired on the basis of their competence and expertise. Services are provided in an equitable manner and are funded by taxes. The city will provide whatever services its citizens' demand through the political process. An equitable and accountable city is created and one that is responsive to citizens. The city functions within the parameters of political reality. It perceives its role to be founded in public law and the democratic process. It is not guided by the mechanisms of the marketplace; its goal is not to achieve Pareto Optimality.

The two hypothetical cities incorporate the essential points of privatization's advocates and critics. In one respect, the two models could be viewed as representing an *economic* versus a *political* emphasis. While some cities do approximate the contractual and full-service models, most municipalities employ a variety of approaches to provide services. But there are some examples that do tend to appear to emulate the idealized models, such as La Mirada and La Habra in California. La Mirada (population 44,000) either contracts out or has completely privatized most of its basic services, while La Habra (population 52,000) provides most of its services through traditional public departments. Both cities are similar in size, located in the same area (southern California), are comparable fiscally, and considered to be well managed. Thus, proponents and critics of privatization have real-world examples of well-managed cities that have organized themselves as full-service and contractual cities. But why would two similar cities choose such radically different approaches for delivering services? The larger question is what factors make some cities more prone to use privatization than others? These questions will be addressed in Chapter 3, but one might suspect that a variety of factors affect the method of service provision that a city selects, including politics.

SUMMARY

This chapter has examined the cases for and against contracting out for local services. Economic recessions, demographic shifts, and changing patterns of federalism have created fiscal pressures for most cities. These pressures have forced many cities to examine alternative service delivery arrangements to reduce operating costs. Privatization proponents believe privatization is a solution to the fiscal dilemmas faced by many cities. Advocates argue that private firms can produce and deliver local services more cost-efficiently than government can. Government monopolies are considered inferior to the competitive marketplace because the incentives reward budget maximization rather than efficiency. Advocates argue cities should take advantage of the cost-saving potentials that can be realized by contracting with private firms. Contracting is viewed as a way of improving efficiency, offering new opportunities for private business, and providing greater satisfaction for the people being served. Proponents believe that most local services can be provided through private vendors. The contractual city is viewed as a desirable model for cities to emulate because of its superior efficiency.

Opponents of contracting stress that efficiency must be balanced with other equally important concerns, namely equity and public accountability. The proper blend of equity, accountability, and efficiency should be determined in the political arena rather than the marketplace. Critics argue that privatization contributes to sector blurring, causes public employees to lose their jobs, and increases the risk for corruption. The full-service model is viewed as superior because it is capable of balancing efficiency with equity and public accountability. Contracting with private firms to provide local services poses a problem for critics because they believe neither equity nor public accountability should be sacrificed in the pursuit of cost-efficiency. Local governments remain responsible for provision of services but contract with private firms to produce and deliver the services. Theory suggests that profit-seeking firms should be more productive than government organizations. In the next chapter, the relative efficiency of public and private provision of services is examined.

NOTES

1. International City/County Management Association, *Service Delivery in the 90s: Alternative Approaches for Local Governments* (Washington, D.C.: author, 1989), p. 4.
2. The concepts of efficiency, equity, and accountability are examined in Chapter 2. At this point, one may think of efficiency as referring to delivering a service of equal or better quality for a lower price. Equity refers to ensuring that services are provided fairly to all citizens of a city; for example, ensuring that snow is removed from of the streets of both poor and wealthy neighborhoods. Accountability is a term concerned with who is held responsible if a service fails. That is, who is held accountable if snow is not removed from poor neighborhoods but is removed from wealthier areas?
3. Paul Starr, "The New Life of the Liberal State: Privatization and the Restructuring of State-Society Relations," in *Public Enterprise and Privatization*, ed. John Waterbury and Ezra Suleiman. (Boulder, CO: Westview Press, 1990), pp. 22–54.
4. Paul Starr, "The Meaning of Privatization," in *Privatization and the Welfare State*, ed. Sheila Kammerman and Alfred Kahn (Princeton, NJ: Princeton University Press, 1988), pp. 15–48.
5. The idea of reinventing government refers to removing rules, bureaucratic red tape, and other cumbersome procedures, thereby freeing public officials to take

action. In short, the era of reinvention seeks to create a results orientation in government (in lieu of a process orientation). Creating an action- or results-based orientation has a price attached. Rules and red tape are partly used to enhance process and public accountability. Removing these cumbersome procedures, which help slow down the pace of action in government, runs the risk of losing accountability and other checks and balances. The idea became popular after David Osborne and Ted Gaebler published *Reinventing Government* (New York: Addison-Wesley) in 1989.

6. The term *devolution* refers to shifting responsibility (and sometimes the burden of financing) for services once held by the federal government to state and local governments. Devolution began under President Nixon in the late 1960s and continues under the current administration. See D. Brammer, "Privatization of Programs and Services: An Increasingly Popular Option for State and Local Governments," *Public Administration Survey* 44 (Oxford, MS: Public Policy Research Center, University of Mississippi, 1997), pp. 1–4. Also, see Charles Mahtesian, "The Privatizing Daley," *Governing: The Magazine of States and Localities* (April 1994), pp. 26–33.

7. Orange County invested in a risky endeavor known as *derivatives*. Derivatives are financial instruments that "derive" their value from underlying assets such as stocks, bonds, futures, or mortgages. Derivatives change as the value of the underlying assets change. Moreover, derivatives do not constitute ownership, but merely promise to convey ownership. In the case of Orange County, their financial investor was investing in derivatives that were tied to interest rates. In short, the investor was borrowing money from stocks, bonds, and mortgages to bet on the direction of interest rates. He lost the bet and Orange County became one of the largest public bankruptcies in our nation's history. It should be noted that Orange County did recover from the disaster but it took years to become financially sound again. For a more detailed account of Orange County's bankruptcy, see Sallie Hoffmeister, "Too Many Questions, But Too Late," *New York Times*, 6 December 1994, p. D-2. Also, see John Peterson, "Orange County Aftermath," *Governing: The Magazine of States and Localities* (November 1995), pp. 77–87.

8. Fred Barnes, "The City that Privatized Everything," *Wall Street Journal*, 17 May 1989, p. A-19.

9. Paul Johnson, "City Privatization Plan Trims Bureaucratic Fat," *Asheville Citizen-Times*, 1 February 1991, p. A-10.

10. Ron Moe, of the Library of Congress, considered privatization to be the most influential concept of the 1980s. See Ron Moe, "Exploring the Limits of Privatization," *Public Administration Review* 47 (November/December 1987), pp. 453–459.

11. James Bennett and Manuel Johnson, *Better Government at Half the Price* (Ottawa, IL: Carolina House, 1981), p. 19.

12. See A. K. Sen, "Rational Fools: A Critique of the Behavioral Foundation of Economic Theory," *Philosophy and Public Affairs* 6 (1966), pp. 317–344. See also, Paul Starr, "The Limits of Privatization," in *Prospects for Privatization*, ed. Steve Hanke (New York: Academy of Political Science, 1987), pp. 124–137.

13. See Touche Ross, *Privatization in America* (Washington, D.C.: author, 1987).

14. Robert Poole, "The Local Privatization Revolution," *The Heritage Lectures* (Washington, D.C.: The Heritage Foundation, 1990).

15. See Robert Poole, *Cutting Back City Hall* (New York: Universe Books, 1981).

16. Much of local government contracting involves intergovernmental contracts. Although it is considered to be an alternative form of service delivery arrangement, it is technically not a form of privatization. Perhaps the best example of intergovernmental contracting is found in many of southern California's Lakewood Cities. For a thorough discussion of the Lakewood Plan, see Gary Miller, *City by Contract* (Cambridge, MA: MIT Press, 1981).

17. Democracy and capitalism are the larger concepts that are part of the privatization debate. Privatization illustrates part of the interaction that occurs between democracy and capitalism. Democracy creates public institutions to handle the government's business, such as national defense or airline safety, or transportation systems. Capitalism is synonymous with our economy. However, capitalism is more interwoven with government than popular myth would have it. Government and capitalism are often portrayed as rivals involved in an ideological tug-of-war; countervailing forces that keep each other in check. But government and capitalism interact on a daily basis to provide services at all levels of government. National defense involves various government institutions and agencies and large private contracts with firms such as Boeing that engineer and develop the machinery of national defense. America has a long history of preferring private ownership with government oversight. Airlines in the United States are private corporations that fall under numerous public safety regulations. Legislatures appropriate money for highways, city streets, bridges, or subway systems that are usually constructed by private firms.

 Democracy establishes the structures and conditions for governing and capitalism generates wealth in the economy by providing products and services for consumers, including government. Capitalism also provides a taxable base to fund government activities. Democracy needs capitalism to create a healthy, vibrant economy, and capitalism needs democracy to provide structure and stability. But the appropriate size and scope of the public and private sectors was not resolved in the twentieth century. Privatization is part of this debate because it threatens a long pattern of government expansion into many aspects of American life, including the economy. This debate continues in the new century.

18. National Academy of Public Administration, *Privatization: The Challenge to Public Management* (Washington, D.C.: author, 1989), p. vii.

19. Ibid.

20. John Donahue, *The Privatization Decision: Public Ends, Private Means* (New York: Basic Books, 1989), p. 5.

21. Ibid. pp. 5–6.

22. National Academy of Public Administration, *Privatization: The Challenge to Public Management*, p. vii.

23. See E. S. Savas, *Privatization and Public-Private Partnerships* (New York: Seven Bridges Press, 2000), for a thorough discussion of the various forms of privatization. Also see Savas' classic book, *Privatization: The Key to Better Government* (Chatham, NJ: Chatham House Press, 1987).

24. Peter Drucker is credited with providing the first comprehensive description of privatization, although he referred to the concept as *reprivatization* in the *Age of Discontinuity* (New York: Harper-Collins, 1969). Robert Poole shortened the term *reprivatization* to *privatization* in 1976. See Robert Poole, *Cut Local Taxes without Reducing Essential Services* (Santa Barbara, CA: Reason Press, 1976).

25. Milton Friedman, *Free to Choose: A Personal Statement* (New York: Harcourt Brace, 1980). Also, see Friedman's classic work about free-market economies in *Capitalism and Federalism* (Chicago: University of Chicago Press, 1962).

26. Charles Wolf, *Markets or Governments: Choosing between Imperfect Alternatives* (Cambridge, MA: MIT Press, 1988), p. 2.

27. Peter Drucker, *The Age of Discontinuity* (Boston: Harper & Row, 1969), pp. 233–234.

28. For example, for many years the private sector operated subways, utilities, and many other services in cities. Largely due to the corruption of the political machines that controlled many of the nation's cities and granted favors to the private firms that ran various services, such as transportation systems, services were gradually taken over by the public sector to ensure greater public accountability. See Bernard Ross and Myron Levine, *Urban Politics: Power in Metropolitan America*, 2nd ed. (Itasca, IL: Peacock Publishers, 2000), Chapters 5, 8, and 15. Also, see Dennis Judd and Todd Swanstrom, *City Politics: Private Power and Public Policy* (New York: Harper Collins, 1994), especially Chapters 1 and 2, which discuss the transition from private cities to public, municipal corporations. Part Four of this book contains a detailed discussion about how the private city appears to be returning. For an analysis of New York City's experience with its subway system, see James Ramsey, "Sell the New York City Subway: Wide-eyed Radicalism or the Only Feasible Solution?" in *Prospect for Privatization*, ed. Steve Hanke (New York: Academy of Political Science, 1987), pp. 93–103.

29. See Stuart Butler, *Privatizing the Federal Budget: A Strategy to Eliminate the Deficit* (New York: Universe Books, 1985); and Drucker, *The Age of Discontinuity*.

30. Starr, "The Meaning of Privatization," pp. 124–137.

31. See William Colman, *State and Local Government and Public-Private Partnerships* (New York: Greenwood Press, 1989).

32. Richard Musgrave, *The Theory of Public Finance: A Study in Political Economy* (New York: McGraw Hill, 1959), pp. 5–6.

33. Evelyn Brodkin and Dennis Young, "Making Sense of Privatization: What Can We Learn from Economic and Political Analysis?" in *Privatization and the Welfare State*, ed. Sheila Kammerman and Alfred Kahn (Princeton, NJ: Princeton University Press, 1988), p. 122.

34. See Bernard Ross and Myron Levine, *Urban Politics: Power in Metropolitan America*, 5th ed. (Itasca, IL: Peacock Publishers, 1996), pp. 84–87.

35. Brodkin and Young, "Making Sense of Privatization: What Can We Learn from Economic and Political Analysis?" p. 123.

36. Montana's welfare program is called Families Achieving Independence in Montana (FAIM) and is almost completely a contracted operation. See "21st Century Delivery of Human Services in Montana," a report prepared by the Department of Social and Rehabilitation Services (October 1993), State of Montana, Helena, MT 59604. The source of some of the information came from an interview with Frank W. Clarke, Chair, Department of Social Work, University of Montana, Missoula, MT, 21 March 2000. Professor Clarke has performed evaluations on the pilot programs that led to Montana's privatized welfare system.

37. Jonathan Walters, "The Welfare Bonanza," *Governing: The Magazine of States and Localities* (January 2000), pp. 34–36.

38. Donahue, *The Privatization Decision: Public Ends, Private Means*, p. 131.

39. Charles Levine, "Cutback Management in an Era of Scarcity: Hard Questions for

Hard Times," in *Intergovernmental Personnel Notes* (Washington, D.C.: Office of Personnel Management, 1978), p. 316.

40. Irene Rubin, *Running in the Red* (Albany, NY: State University of New York Press, 1981).

41. D. Fisk, H. Kiesling, and T. Muller, *Private Provision of Public Services: An Overview* (Washington, D.C.: Urban Affairs Institute, 1978).

42. Robert Lee, *Public Personnel Systems* (Rockville, MD: Aspen Publishers, 1987), p. 5. Also, see Lyle Fitch, "Increasing the Role of the Private Sector in Providing Public Services," in *Improving the Quality of Urban Management*, ed. Willis Hawley and David Rogers (Beverly Hills, CA: Sage Publications, 1974); and Richard Gustley, *Municipal Public Employment and Public Expenditures* (Lexington, MA: Lexington Books, 1974).

43. David Ammons, *Municipal Productivity: A Comparison of Fourteen High-Quality-Service Cities* (New York: Praeger Press, 1984), Chapters 1 and 2.

44. Wolf, *Markets or Governments: Choosing between Imperfect Alternatives*, pp. 7–8.

45. Pearl Kamer, *Crisis in Urban Finance: A Case Study of Thirty-Eight Cities* (New York: Praeger Press, 1983), p. 2. The Bush and Clinton administrations did little to alter the pattern of devolution. See Ann Bowman and Richard Kearney, *State and Local Government: The Essentials* (Boston: Houghton Mifflin, 2000), pp. 41–43.

46. National Council on Employment Policy, *The Long-Term Employment Implications of Privatization* (Washington, D.C.: Dudek, 1989), p. 8.

47. Stephen Moore, "Privatization in America's Cities: Lessons For Washington," *The Heritage Foundation Backgrounder* no. 652 (Washington, D.C.: The Heritage Foundation, 1988), p. 2.

48. See Savas, *Privatization and Public-Private Partnerships*, p. 74.

49. General Accounting Office, *Public-Private Mix: The Extent of Contracting Out for Real Property Management Service in the GSA*, Report GAO/GGD-94-126BR (Washington, D.C.: author, 1994), p. 2.

50. Touche Ross, *Privatization in America* (Washington, D.C.: author, 1987), p. 3. This study suggested that 80 percent of the surveyed cities contracted out for some services. More recent surveys also suggest that most cities use some form of privatization. See R. Miranda and K. Andersen, "Alternative Service Delivery Arrangements, 1982–1992," in *Municipal Yearbook* (Washington, D.C.: International City/County Management Association, 1994), pp. 26–35. It should be noted that Miranda and Andersen found that aside from contracting, local governments did not appear to use many of the other alternative service delivery arrangements included in the International City/County Management Association's surveys.

51. E. Blaine Liner, *A Decade of Devolution* (Washington, D.C.: Urban Affairs Institute, 1989). See also Irene Rubin, *Running in the Red* (Albany, NY: State University of New York Press, 1981). Despite the economic expansion associated with the late 1980s and early 1990s, many cities continued to exhibit tenuous financial portfolios throughout the 1990s. See W. Pammer, "The Future of Municipal Finances in an Era of Fiscal Austerity and Economic Globalization," in *Municipal Yearbook* (Washington, D.C.: International City/County Management Association, 1992), pp. 3–11. Also, see R. Waste, *Independent Cities: Rethinking Urban Policy* (New York: Oxford University Press, 1998); and Michael Pagano, *City Fiscal Conditions 1995* (Washington, D.C.: National League of Cities, 1996). *City Fiscal Conditions* is a regular National League of Cities' publication and is available for a variety of years.

52. Irene Rubin, "Municipal Enterprises: Exploring Budgetary and Political Implications," *Public Administration Review* 48 (January/February 1988), pp. 542–550. Also, see Gary Miller, *City by Contract*; and Stephen Moore, "Contracting Out: A Painless Alternative to the Budget Cutter's Knife," in *Prospects for Privatization*, ed. Steve Hanke, pp. 60–73.

53. International City/County Management Association, *Service Delivery in the 90s: Alternative Approaches for Local Governments* (Washington, D.C.: International City/County Management Association, 1989). Also, see James Ferris and Elizabeth Graddy, "Contracting Out: For What? With Whom?" *Public Administration Review* 46 (July/August 1986), pp. 332–345. Also, see James Ferris, "The Decision to Contract Out," *Urban Affairs Quarterly* 2 (December 1986), pp. 289–311.

54. One of the most notable advocates of privatization since the beginning of the debate in the mid-1970s has been the Reason Foundation, which maintains an excellent Web site at <http://www.reason.org>.

55. Ammons, *Municipal Productivity: A Comparison of Fourteen High-Quality-Service Cities*, p. 15.

56. Reported in Randall Fitzgerald, *When Government Goes Private* (New York: Universe Books, 1988), p. 7. See also, E. S. Savas, *Privatizing the Public Sector* (Chatham, NJ: Chatham House Press, 1982); and E. S. Savas, "Intracity Competition between Public and Private Service Delivery," *Public Administration Review* 41 (January/February 1981), pp. 46–52.

57. There are many studies that have been conducted over the past thirty years that have found private production of an array of services to be more efficient than government production. Many of these studies are included in Chapter 2. Some examples include: David Davies, "The Efficiency of Public versus Private Firms: The Case of Australia's Two Airlines," *Journal of Law and Economics* 14 (1971), pp. 149–165; Louis de Alessi, "The Economics of the Evidence," *Research in Law and Economics* 2 (1980), pp. 1–47; Louis de Alessi, "Managerial Tenure under Private and Government Ownership in the Electric Power Industry," *Journal of Political Economy* 82 (May/June 1974), pp. 645–653; Roger Ahlbrandt, "Efficiency in the Provision of Fire Services," *Public Choice* 16 (fall 1973), pp. 1–15; Leland Neuberg, "Two Issues in the Municipal Ownership of Electric Power Distribution Systems," *Bell Journal of Economics* 6 (1977), pp. 303–323; Barbara Stevens, "Scale, Market Structure, and Cost of Refuse Collection," *Review of Economics and Statistics* 60 (1977), pp. 438–448; Robert McGuire and Robert Ohnsfelt, "Public versus Private Water Delivery: A Critical Analysis of a Hedonic Cost Approach," *Public Finance Quarterly* (July 1986), pp. 339–350; and Barbara Stevens, "Scale, Market Structure, and Cost of Refuse Collection," *Review of Economics and Statistics* 60 (1977), pp. 438–448. These and many other studies are included in Appendix A.

   One study summarized the findings of 50 empirical studies that compared the relative efficiency between public and private operations. In 40 of the 50 studies, private provision was found to be more efficient. See Thomas Borcherding, Werner Pommerehne, and Fred Schneider, *Comparing the Efficiency of Private and Public Production: The Evidence from Five Countries* (Zurich, Switzerland: Institute for Empirical Research, University of Zurich, 1982).

58. J. F. Leiber, *Private Means-Public Ends* (New York: Praeger Publications, 1982), p. 3.

59. See Savas, *Privatization and Public-Private Partnerships*, Chapters 4 and 7.

60. Ruth DeHoog, *Contracting Out for Human Services* (Albany, NY: State University of New York Press, 1984), p. 5.

61. Savas, *Privatization: The Key to Better Government*, pp. 109–110.

62. For a more thorough discussion of contracting, see Savas, *Privatization: The Key to Better Government*, pp. 108–115; and Savas, *Privatization and Public-Private Partnerships*, Chapter 7.

63. See Fitzgerald, *When Government Goes Private*, pp. 59–61.

64. This table is not intended to be all-inclusive. There are many other advantages associated with contracting. The information included in the table was adapted from Savas, *Privatization: The Key to Better Government*, p. 112; DeHoog, *Contracting Out for Human Services*, pp. 6–8; Moore, "Privatization in America's Cities: Lessons for Washington," p. 5; D. Fisk, H. Kiesling, and T. Muller, *Private Provision of Public Services* (Washington, D.C.: Urban Affairs Institute, 1979), p. 7.

65. The mission statement of San Diego's Competition Program can be viewed online at the city's Web site. The address is <http://www.sannet.gov/competition.shtml>.

66. See International City/County Management Association, *Service Delivery in the 90s: Alternative Approaches for Local Governments*, p. 4.

67. Thom Connors and Dick Shaff, "Three Cities Reduce Government Subsidy of Public Assembly Facilities," *Nation's Cities Weekly* 18 (August 14, 1995), pp. 9–10.

68. Evelyn Terry, "Stockless Supply System Saves Winchester Time, Money," *Virginia Town & City* 31 (February 1996), p. 16.

69. See Harry Hatry, "Privatization Presents Problems," in *Annual Editions: State & Local Government*, 5th ed., ed. Bruce Stinebrickner (Guilford, CT: Dushkin Press, 1989), pp. 220–221.

70. Surveys suggest that most cities do not have a good program for measuring their own performance against firms in the private sector. See Lawrence Martin, "A Proposed Methodology for Comparing the Costs of Government versus Contract Service Delivery," *Municipal Yearbook 1992* (Washington, D.C.: International City/County Management Association), pp. 12–15.

71. Benefits packages, which include items like health insurance, retirement, sick leave, etc., are a major cost for both private companies and governments. The cost of these packages can be 20 or 30 percent (sometimes even more) of a worker's base salary. Generally, public sector benefits packages are better than their private sector counterparts. Many private companies have trimmed back their packages, opting for less generous health care and retirement systems.

72. Stephen Moore, "Contracting Out: A Painless Alternative to the Budget Cutter's Knife," in *Prospects for Privatization*, p. 68.

73. David Parsons, "Talking Trash: Charlottesville Refuse Collection Competition Pays Dividends," *Virginia Town & City* 30 (December 1995), pp. 8–10.

74. It should be noted that public choice theorists focus on many other issues unrelated to privatization, such as voting behavior. The schools involved in the privatization debate are known as the Indiana School (University of Indiana; the principal scholars include Vincent and Elinor Ostrom) and the Chicago School (University of Chicago; the principal scholars include Milton Friedman, Gordon Tullock, William Niskanen, and James Buchanan).

75. In market theory, a state of perfect efficiency (Pareto Optimality) exists when resources are allocated in such a way that no one's position can be improved

without a loss to someone else. In other words, this may be thought of as a state of equilibrium where any movement comes at the expense of another firm.

76. Vincent Ostrom and Elinor Ostrom, "Public Choice: A Different Approach to the Study of Public Administration," *Public Administration Review* 31 (March/April 1971), pp. 203–216. Also, see Mark Schneider, *The Competitive City* (Pittsburgh, PA: University of Pittsburgh Press, 1989).

77. Charles Wolf, *Markets or Governments: Choosing between Imperfect Alternatives*, p. 18.

78. In reality, the marketplace is not exactly as the ideal market just described. For example, economists have long noticed a tendency for oligarchies (the few or the best) to develop. That is, after an industry matures, only a few firms are left and they compete with each other. This is reflected in the number of automobile makers, the number of fast-food chains, the number of airlines, or hotel corporations. In these and many other industries, only a handful of companies survived. At one time there were many airlines, hotel companies, and automobile manufacturers. But as the market matured, most either were absorbed by their competitors or went bankrupt.

79. Charles Wolf, *Markets or Governments: Choosing between Imperfect Alternatives*, Chapter 1.

80. Ibid.

81. See Randall Fitzgerald, *When Government Goes Private*, p. 7.

82. For an excellent analysis of public choice theory, see Vincent Ostrom, "Some Developments in the Study of Market Choices, Public Choice, and Institutional Choice," in *The Handbook of Public Administration*, ed. Jack Rabin, W. B. Hildreth, and Gerald Miller (New York: Marcel Dekker, 1989), pp. 861–882.

83. Rational choice has developed over a long period of time in economics. Several variations of the theory exist. Rational choice is a parsimonious theory that has been prominent in the privatization debate. For a thorough analysis of rational choice, see Alexander Rosenberg, *Philosophy of Social Science* (Boulder, CO: Westview Press, 1988), Chapters 3–6.

Anthony Downs was among the first scholars to bring rational choice to political science. His example helps explain why public choice theory has emerged in the privatization debate. Downs was motivated by an anomaly that he noticed in economics, specifically in the field of public finance and welfare economics. In these areas government action is a key variable and economists had been successful in using theories based on rational choice to analyze the impact of alternative public policies. Based on their analyses, economists could recommend policies (that were based on rational choice models) to government decision makers. Downs complained that economists had not succeeded in explaining which policy recommendations government officials would actually follow. Instead, economists were content to indicate which policies *should* be used and assume that government officials would implement them. Given the assumptions of rational choice, Downs argued that there is no reason to believe that government officials would follow the recommendations of economists. Like other individuals, government officials must be self-serving, rational actors and it must be assumed that they will make policy as a means of satisfying their own interests. It cannot be assumed that public officials are a special case and will maximize the public interest. Such an assumption would contradict the underlying theories on which the recommendations themselves were predicated. If government could act in a nonmaximizing manner, the same could be true for others and the predictions of the whole theory would be called into question. In short, Downs argued that public officials are also rational actors and will follow the recommendations of economists only if those recommendations happen to be in their own interest. By the mid-1960s, public choice theory was well developed and raising similar questions about the action of government. With regards to privatization, rational choice predicts that government will resist privatization because officials seek to satisfy their own interests, which include budget maximization, empire-building, protecting the turf of their agency, and so on. For a thorough discussion of public choice theory, see Vincent Ostrom, "Some Developments in the Study of Market Choice, Public Choice, and Institutional Choice," in *The Handbook of Public Administration*, ed. Jack Rabin, W. B. Hildreth, and Gerald Miller (New York: Marcel Dekker, 1989), pp. 861–882.

84. William Niskanen, *Bureaucracy and Representative Government* (Chicago: Aldine Atherton, 1971). Also, see Thomas Borcherding et al., *Budgets and Bureaucrats* (Durham, NC: Duke University Press, 1977); and Gordon Tullock, *The Politics of Bureaucracy* (Washington, D.C.: Public Affairs Press, 1965).

85. Robert Bish and Vincent Ostrom, *Understanding Urban Government* (Washington, D.C.: American Enterprise Institute, 1973).

86. James Buchanan, "Why Does Government Grow?" *Budgets and Bureaucrats*, pp. 13–14; and Gordon Tullock, "Why Politicians Won't Cut Taxes," *Taxing and Spending* (October/November, 1978), pp. 12–14. Also, see E. S. Savas, "Municipal Monopolies versus Competition in Delivering Urban Services," in *Improving the Quality of Urban Management*, ed. H. W. Hawley and D. Rogers (Beverly Hills, CA: Sage Publications, 1974), pp. 473–500.

87. Milton Friedman, *Tyranny of the Status Quo* (New York: Basic Books, 1984). Also, see Dennis Mueller, *Public Choice* (London: Cambridge University Press, 1979).

88. The concept of rents is often associated with government bureaucracy. Rents occur when agents are paid more than the public should have spent for a service. In the public bureaucracy, rents come in the form of fringe benefits, pleasant working conditions, undemanding workloads, and job security. Economists refer to these as *nonpecuniary rents*. See Donahue, *The Privatization Decision: Public Ends, Private Means*, pp. 91–94.

89. Rubin, *Running in the Red*, p. 7.

90. Ibid.

91. Buchanan, "Why Does Government Grow?" p. 15.

92. Privatization finds support in another economic theory that focuses on government failure. The theory holds that nonmarket failure results from the distinct characteristics of nonmarket supply and demand. As noted in the text, markets link the costs of producing something to the income necessary to sustain operations. This link is provided by the price charged to consumers. This link does not exist in nonmarket activity. In the absence of this link, the value of the output is separated from the cost of production. This results in misallocation of resources and disequilibrium between supply and demand. Nonmarket failure also is linked to the internal operations of government organizations. Because government operations are typically monopolies, adequate incentives are lacking to develop internal standards that are efficient. In private firms, inefficient internal operating practices affect profits. Internalities are the standards that

apply within organizations to guide, regulate, and evaluate organizational performance. In market organizations, the internal system must be connected to the external pricing system. In nonmarket organizations, internalities are disconnected with the external purpose of the organization. Nonmarket organizations are likely to use budget size as an indicator of performance due to the political context in which they exist. Performance of personnel is then evaluated in terms of either expanding the budget or protecting it from cuts. Thus, the incentives within nonmarket organizations are to reward personnel for justifying costs.

Charles Wolf has written extensively on this theory. See Charles Wolf, "A Theory of Nonmarket Failure: Framework For Implementation Analysis," *Journal of Law and Economics* (April 1979), pp. 107–140; Charles Wolf, "A Theory of Nonmarket Failures," *Public Interest* 55 (1979), pp. 114–133; and Charles Wolf, *Markets or Governments: Choosing between Imperfect Alternatives*, Chapter 1. Also, see Francis Bator, "The Anatomy of Market Failure," *Quarterly Journal of Economics* 72 (1958), pp. 351–379

93. It should be noted that the theory of property rights has impacted the theoretical framework for privatization. The theory treats the modern package of property rights as one of the various possible configurations. Public institutions represent an alternative property rights arrangement to private ownership. Property rights theory is also grounded in the rational choice tradition. The theory explains differences in the behavior of organizations entirely on the basis of the individual incentives created by the structure of property rights. Like public choice, property rights theory assumes that individuals seek to look after their own self-interest. The theory holds that property will be cared for in proportion to the amount the individual stands to gain from tending it. Conversely, the more diluted property rights become, the less motivated the individual will be to use the property in an efficient manner. Private ownership concentrates rights and rewards whereas public ownership dilutes them. This is often referred to as the *tragedy of the commons* dilemma. As an example, most citizens will not pick up trash on a city's sidewalk or in a public park even if they are taxpayers of the jurisdiction, but they will pick trash off their lawns at home. This illustrates the simple idea of diluted property rights. Since property rights are diluted in public ownership, it is argued that public bureaucracies will perform less efficiently than private enterprises. Private businesses have concentrated property rights; therefore, businesses have an incentive to manage their assets efficiently.

It is believed that the market provides the necessary incentives to keep management in line. Stockholders have the ability to monitor corporations and show their dissatisfaction with management by selling their stocks if returns are too low. This could further depress the price of stocks and cause managers to lose their jobs. This incentive does not exist in public bureaucracies since citizens have no transferable property rights. In other words, they cannot sell their portion of the bureaucracy to demonstrate dissatisfaction. Moreover, government bureaucracies cannot be taken over by those who believe their assets can be used more efficiently. Thus, property rights theory believes that the general public would be better served if public organizations and their assets were privately owned and forced to meet the test of profitability. The theory recommends privatization in general because it alters the ownership characteristics and introduces competitive markets in areas traditionally controlled by the political process. For a complete discussion of property rights theory, see Louis de Alessi, "Property Rights and Privatization," in *Prospects for Privatization*, pp. 24–35; Armen Alchian, "Some Economies of Property Rights," *Politico* 30 (1965), pp. 816–829; Brodkin and Young, "Making Sense of Privatization: What Can We Learn from Economic and Political Analysis?" in *Privatization and the Welfare State*, pp. 121–156; and Harold Demsetz, "Toward a Theory of Property Rights," *American Economic Review* 57 (1967), pp. 347–359. Also, see Garret Hardin, "The Tragedy of the Commons," *Science* 162, pp. 1245–1248.

94. The theme of Charles Wolf's book, *Markets or Governments: Choosing Between Imperfect Alternatives*, is the choice between imperfect alternatives for providing public services.

95. Ann Chase, "Privatization: Who, What, and How," *Governing: The Magazine of States and Localities* (May 1992), pp. 53–54.

96. The larger public unions have been the most vocal in the debate, in particular, the American Federation of Government Workers and the American Federation of State, County, and Municipal Employees. The American Federation of State, County, and Municipal Employees maintains an excellent Web site in opposition to privatization, including case studies about contracting failures and an on-line version of the latest edition of *Government for Sale*. The material is linked on their home page at <http://www.afscme.org>.

97. Dwight Waldo, *The Enterprise of Public Administration* (Novato, CA: Chandler and Sharp, 1980), p. 110.

98. Louise White, "Public Management in a Pluralistic Arena," *Public Administration Review* 49 (November/December 1989), p. 524.

99. No clear definition of the public interest exists that is agreed upon by scholars. Although the term is commonly used, it is also controversial due to the lack of an accepted definition. For our purposes here, the public interest refers to actions that place the interest of the public (or society as a whole) above individual interests. However, determining what this truly means has always been problematic. The concept of the public interest will be discussed more thoroughly in Chapter 5.

100. Richard Stillman, "Ostrom on the Federalists Revisited," *Public Administration Review* 49 (January/February 1987), p. 83.

101. Ira Sharkansky, "Policy Making and Service Delivery on the Margins of Government: The Case of Contractors," *Public Administration Review* 40 (March/April 1980), pp. 116–123.

102. Barry Bozeman, *All Organizations are Public* (San Francisco: Jossey-Bass, 1987); Ronald Moe, "Exploring the Limits of Privatization," pp. 453–460; and Paul Starr, "The Limits of Privatization," in *Prospects for Privatization*, pp. 124–137.

103. Moe, "Exploring the Limits of Privatization," p. 453.

104. Ibid.

105. George Downs and Patrick Larkey, *The Search for Government Efficiency: From Hubris to Helplessness* (Philadelphia, PA: Temple University Press, 1986).

106. International City/County Management Association, *Service Delivery in the 1990s: Alternative Approaches for Local Governments*, p. 129.

107. For an excellent guideline for contracting, see John Temper Marlin, ed., *Contracting Municipal Services: A Guide to Purchase from the Private Sector* (New York: John Wiley & Sons, 1984). Also, the International City/County Management

Association (ICMA) has numerous publications available that provide detailed guidelines for contracting out services. The ICMA's address is 777 North Capitol Street, NE, Suite 500, Washington, D.C. 20002-4201. The ICMA's Web site is <http://www.icma.org>.

108. See the American Federation of State, County, and Municipal Employee Web site at <http://www.afscme.org>.

109. For many examples of privatization failures at the local level, see John Hanrahan, *Government for Sale* (Washington, D.C.: American Federation of State, County, and Municipal Employees, 1986).

110. Graham T. Allison, "Public and Private Management: Are They Fundamentally Alike in All Unimportant Respects?" in *Public Administration: Concepts and Cases*, 3rd ed., ed. Richard Stillman (Boston: Houghton Mifflin, 1983), pp. 453–467.

111. Ted Kolderie, "Two Different Sides of Privatization," *Public Administration Review* 46 (July/August 1986), pp. 285–286.

112. Phillip Fixler and Robert Poole, "Status of State and Local Privatization," in *Prospects for Privatization*, ed. Steve Hanke (New York: The Academy of Political Science, 1987), p. 174. For many other examples of failures in contracting out local services, see John Hanrahan, *Government for Sale: Contracting Out, The New Patronage* (Washington, D.C.: American Federation of State, County, and Municipal Employees, 1977).

113. DeHoog, *Contracting Out for Human Services*, p. 12.

114. Starr, "The Limits of Privatization," pp. 124–137.

115. Lyle Fitch, "Increasing the Role of the Private Sector in Providing Public Services," in *Improving the Quality of Urban Management*, ed. Willis Hawley and David Rogers (Beverly Hills, CA: Sage Publications, 1974), pp. 501–559.

116. This comment should be credited to Lyle Fitch, which is cited in DeHoog, *Contracting Out for Human Services*, p. 12.

117. For a full discussion about the corruption with contracting in Albany, see Hanrahan, *Government for Sale: Contracting Out, The New Patronage*, Chapter 1. Albany has a long and interesting history and is often used as a classic example to illustrate the workings of political machines. For a more in-depth study of Albany, see Alexander Callow, Jr., *The Tweed Ring* (New York: Oxford University Press, 1966).

118. National Council on Employment Policy, *The Long Term Employment Implications of Privatization* (Washington, D.C.: Dudek, 1989), p.1.

119. See John Hanrahan, *Government for Sale*, Chapter 1.

120. International City/County Management Association, *Service Delivery in the 90s: Alternative Approaches for Local Governments*, p. 5.

121. Ibid.

122. Phillip Fixler, Jr. and Robert Poole, "Status of State and Local Privatization," p. 176.

123. See Hanrahan, *Government for Sale*, Chapter 1. Also, see American Federation of State, County, and Municipal Employees, *Passing the Bucks: The Contracting Out of Public Services* (Washington, D.C.: author, 1983).

124. Phillip Fixler, Jr. and Robert Poole, "Status of State and Local Privatization," p. 173.

125. DeHoog, *Contracting Out for Human Services*, pp. 6–10.

126. It should be noted that evaluations of the performance of contractors and satisfaction with the service have tended to favor privatization. For example, a nationwide study conducted by Ecodata, Inc., for the Department of Housing and Urban Development, investigated a variety of municipal services and concluded

that cities with the lowest cost of delivery tended to have the highest levels of quality. See Barbara Stevens, "Comparative Study of Municipal Service Delivery," a report prepared for the Department of Housing and Urban Development by Ecodata, Inc. (1984).

127. Elinor Brilliant, "Public or Private: A Model of Ambiguities," *Social Science Review* (September 1973), p. 39.

128. Lee, *Public Personnel Systems*, p. 8.

129. See John Kenneth Galbraith, *The Age of Uncertainty* (Boston: Houghton Mifflin, 1977), Chapter 1. Also, see John Kenneth Galbraith, *The Affluent Society* (Boston: Houghton Mifflin, 1958), Chapters 1–2.

130. Wolf, *Market or Governments: Choosing between Imperfect Alternatives*, p. 3.

131. Ibid. p. 3.

132. In fairness to General Motors, many of their competitors have had similar problems, such as the famous Ford Pinto in the 1970s. In the case of the Pinto, the fuel tank tended to explode in rear-end collisions. Similar examples can be found throughout many industries. It should also be noted that economists concede the lack of perfect information on which consumers base their choices. Economists recognize that consumers must often deal with imperfect information but argue that enough information exists to make choices in an environment that includes risk and uncertainty.

133. For an excellent discussion about the failures of the market, see John Kenneth Galbraith, *The Age of Uncertainty*.

134. Steve Hanke and Stephen J. K. Walters, "Privatizing Waterworks," in *Prospects for Privatization*, pp. 104–113. Also see Pedro Schwartz, "John Stuart Mill and Laissez-faire: London Water," *Economica* 33 (February 1966), pp. 71–83.

135. Wolf, *Markets or Governments: Choosing between Imperfect Alternatives*, p. 28.

136. For a simple and interesting discussion about natural monopolies, public goods, and other forms of market failure, see Robert Heilbroner and Lester Thurow, *Economics Explained: Everything You Need to Know About How the Economy Works and Where It's Going*, 4th ed. (New York: Simon & Schuster, 1998), Chapter 13. For a good discussion of the modern economy and its consequences for government, see Peter Drucker, *Post-Capitalist Society* (New York: Harper Collins, 1993).

137. Randall Fitzgerald provides an excellent discussion about full-service versus contractual cities. See *When Government Goes Private*, pp. 56–78.

138. For a complete discussion of the Lakewood Cities, see Miller, *City by Contract*. Also, see City of Lakewood, *The Lakewood Plan*, 3rd ed. (Lakewood, CA: author, 1961). Privatization's proponents often cite *The Lakewood Plan*, although most of the contracting has historically been intergovernmental contracting.

139. Although most of the contracting is intergovernmental contracting with counties and the City of Los Angeles, private contracting is well developed and common in the Lakewood Cities.

The Evidence on Efficiency
and the Use of Privatization by Cities

One of the most enduring issues in government reform has been the be-lief that public bureaucracies should function like businesses.[1] Early in the twentieth century, reformers argued that government should emulate private businesses to enhance both efficiency and effectiveness. Contemporary reformers, such as the *reinventing government movement*, also argue that government should learn from private enterprise and become more results-oriented, which in their view would enhance efficiency. The idea of adopting "businesslike" techniques is epitomized with privatization, especially with contracting out for services. Employing private firms to deliver services enables government to purchase the practices of private enterprise while minimizing the things found in government that are believed to inhibit efficiency.[2]

Economic theory suggests that private enterprise should be more efficient than government. But how much more efficient are private businesses than government at delivering public services? And how well does privatization perform once it has been adopted? It is generally assumed that once privatization has been adopted and properly monitored, performance will be consistent. While this may appear to be a straightforward question, the evidence used to gauge privatization's performance usually points to the numerous studies that have compared producing a service in the private sector against producing a similar service in the public sector. Longitudinal efficiency studies, which examine privatization's performance over time, would appear to be the best way to gauge the performance of privatization. Such studies are common but are usually performed by local jurisdictions or for an agency.[3] There are many examples of "before and after privatization" cost comparisons. For example, a study of Los Angeles County's contracts over an eight-year period concluded that the county saved $182 million over what it would have cost to provide the services with the county's own employees.[4] A comparative study of urban bus systems found that the cost savings after contracting ranged from a low of 29 percent in Miami to a high of 50 percent in New Orleans.[5] Such comparisons are critical to understanding the long-term consequences and performance of privatization. But most of the evidence on efficiency does not involve "before and after" privatization studies. Most of the evidence involves straightforward comparisons between the public and private sectors. Over the years economists have developed an impressive body of studies that compare the efficiency of public versus private provision of services. The services range from collecting garbage and operating wastewater treatment facilities, to managing hospitals. This chapter provides an overview of the evidence on the efficiency of public and private organizations performing similar tasks.[6] The chapter also looks at the amount of privatization used by municipal governments. However, before reviewing the evidence on efficiency, the concepts of efficiency and effectiveness need to be clarified.

THE CONCEPT OF EFFICIENCY

Simply stated, efficiency is the ability to produce a product or service in a cost-effective manner. Whether operating a bus system or manufacturing computers, efficiency is being able to provide a service or product at a specified level of quality, at a lower price. For example, if one firm can produce a computer and another firm can produce a computer of equal or better quality for less money, then the second firm is more efficient. Examples are easy to find in the marketplace. Efficiency can be illustrated in what occurred in the personal computer market during the late 1980s and early 1990s. For years personal computers were very costly and the International Business Machines Company (IBM) dominated the market. Other competitors emerged and took advantage of new technologies and processes that lowered the cost of production and the price for consumers. This in turn forced IBM to also reduce the cost of its computers. In short, many of the manufacturers of IBM "clone" computers became more efficient than IBM. Although the price of a product is determined by a variety of factors aside from efficiency of production, such as supply and demand, price remains the ultimate factor in the marketplace. Companies must do whatever is necessary to keep costs under control. That is, the company must control transportation and shipping costs, materials, and labor to compete with other companies. It must ultimately get its computers into stores like Best Buy and Circuit City at a competitive price. It is more difficult to force efficiency in the public sector because no true competition exists. With whom does a city compete?[7] Cities can simulate competition or attempt to compare themselves to similar cities, which is often difficult to do.[8] Thus, efficiency in the public sector relies on the self-discipline of government (including political institutions like city councils that control budget appropriations) and the demands of voters, which is usually inadequate and not comparable to the incentives that force efficiency in the marketplace. Moreover, it is possible that the demands of citizens contribute to inefficiency rather than efficiency by demanding too many services while at the same time resisting efforts to raise taxes.[9] Internal measures of efficiency are used in both the private and public sectors, but direct competition *forces* efficiency in competitive markets regardless of how it is measured.

Efficiency is generally defined as a ratio measuring related outputs (the product or service) to inputs (the materials, labor, and so forth) used to make the product. In other words, inputs are the resources used to produce a good or service. A municipal refuse collection operation uses inputs such as personnel and equipment (such as garbage trucks and fuel) to collect garbage. All of the costs associated with producing the service must be taken into account to determine the actual cost of operations. Outputs are the units of goods or services produced from the inputs. A typical efficiency measurement for refuse collection is cost per household, which is simply the ratio of production costs divided by the total number of households served. For example, if the total cost of collecting residential garbage were $100,000 and 50,000 houses were served, the cost per household would be $2.00. Efficiency for government services has been defined as *a relative measure based on previous performance levels or performance levels of other government agencies*.[10] If the cost of performing a given service is lower this year than it was last year, it is common to assume that efficiency has increased. The lower cost may be attributable to a variety of reasons such as an improved maintenance program that results in less downtime for vehicles, using more efficient routes to collect garbage, or the purchase of better equipment that requires fewer employees and uses less fuel. Conversely, increases in costs are considered to indicate decreases in efficiency.

Such comparisons usually require qualification. The tendency to accept increases or decreases in costs as an indication of efficiency is common but potentially misleading. Obviously, changes in costs could be attributed to other factors such as crews deliberately taking more time to collect garbage or falsified records. A production system is considered to be more efficient if it has a lower per unit output cost than another system. If the annual cost for collecting garbage in Atlanta is $12.00 per household and $16.00 in Orlando during the same year, the difference in relative efficiency may be attributable to an array of factors. These include physical differences between the two cities or in the type of equipment used, labor market differences, variation in the quality of service provided, managerial techniques, pay incentive plans, or accounting practices. If one attempts to compare the efficiency between cities, great care must be taken to ensure that all critical variables are taken into account to develop a meaningful comparison.[11] This is often difficult to do in the public sector because so many factors are involved, including politics. Moreover, as noted above, garbage collection is not sold in stores like Wal-Mart. It is easier to compare the output for items like televisions or lawn mowers because of the convenience of pricing. Efficiency, in both the public and private sectors, takes output as a given without questioning the output's benefit.[12] Efficiency measurements are only concerned with the manner in which resources are combined into final products.[13] Thus, efficiency is a rather narrow concept that assumes lower cost is desirable when similar goods or services are produced.[14]

Effectiveness is a measurement of *goal attainment*. It is usually expressed as a ratio relating observed output to the desired output for a given time period. It can be thought of as how well established goals are achieved. If a refuse collection operation planned to collect garbage from 50 households per hour but was only able to collect it from 40 households, the operation is 80 percent effective. It is important to note that an operation can be effective without being efficient. If the refuse collection operation planned to collect 50 households' garbage but actually collected 150, it is 300 percent effective but may be achieving these results at three or four times the cost per household of other comparable operations. The usefulness of measurements of effectiveness greatly depends on establishing meaningful output targets. Government has often been criticized for not balancing these two often-competing goals. That is, government can be effective at achieving it's goals, such as providing public transportation such as buses for its citizens. However, public transportation is often inefficient when buses operate on routes with few passengers. Conversely, the private sector is forced to balance the two concepts in order to survive in the marketplace.

Both of these concepts have been significant in the debate on privatization. Proponents of privatization believe that private firms are more efficient in production and more effective in attaining organizational goals because of the different incentives faced by private ownership and competition. That is, private firms must perform the service and generate a profit.

THE EVIDENCE ON EFFICIENCY

Assuming that efficiency is better in the private sector, how much more efficient are private operations than government operated services? And in which services has privatization been the most successful? Generally, private firms appear to outperform their public sector counterparts in most hard services, such as collecting garbage, while the gap appears to be narrower in soft services like hospitals. There are some exceptions where efficiency between public and private organizations performing similar services appears comparable. What does the evidence say about public accountability and equity? Few systematic studies have been conducted on accountability and equity, and the efficiency issue has dominated and continues to dominate the privatization debate. Moreover, when contracting out for services, accountability and equity are not usually significant issues because government remains responsible for financing. That is, cities buy the services and set the conditions of the contract and the performance and quality levels. Thus, we will begin with an overview of the evidence pertaining to efficiency.

One of the most frequently cited examples used to illustrate the performance of privatization is not about a municipal service; it is a comparison of the performance of two airlines in Australia.[15] One of the airlines was a government operation and the other a private corporation. Efficiency was compared between the two operations over time, which provided a longitudinal dimension. The government imposed mandates on both airlines in an attempt to ensure equality of operations. The mandates went to considerable length. For example, each airline was required to use similar aircraft and fares were heavily regulated.[16] Despite the severe regulatory restrictions, the relative efficiency of the two airlines was different.[17] Efficiency indicators were 2 to 12 times higher for the privately owned airline. This pattern was consistent over a ten-year period. The better efficiency of the private airline was attributed to the characteristics associated with property rights. The comparison of the two airlines has been widely cited to illustrate the virtues of private ownership and show that private firms can perform at twice the efficiency of publicly managed organizations.[18] Is it possible that private companies could outperform public municipal departments to this degree?[19]

FIRE PROTECTION

The Rural Metro, a private, employee-owned company, has served Scottsdale, Arizona, for more than sixty years.[20] The company builds many of its own fire trucks and has introduced numerous innovations to the field of fire suppression, including a fire-fighting robot.[21] To compare efficiency between public fire departments and the Rural Metro, a model was developed to explain fire service costs based on factors such as region, population density, the number of fire stations, number of fire trucks, the number of volunteer and professional firefighters, and the nature and value of structures in the area. Data from the Seattle metropolitan area was used to construct and test the model.[22] The model was then used to estimate the cost of public fire protection in Scottsdale, Arizona. The study estimated that the cost of having a public fire department in Scottsdale would have been $7 per capita. The Rural Metro was providing fire protection to Scottsdale for $4 per capita. The increased efficiency was attributed to technological and managerial innovations and the firm's ability to spread its overhead cost.[23]

Direct comparisons between the performance of the Rural Metro and other fire departments in the Phoenix area have usually been favorable for the Rural Metro. Comparisons have examined the dollar loss from fires, response times, and firefighter salary ranges for towns in the Phoenix area. With the exception of Scottsdale, all jurisdictions in the Phoenix area had public fire protection and similar residential patterns, yet Scottsdale had the fastest response times and the lowest loss per capita from its fires, $5.74 versus an average of $7.60 for the others. The private Rural Metro also paid its workers higher salaries than the public departments.[24]

The Rural Metro has been used to suggest that private fire fighting firms are more efficient than public operations. However, only a small number of studies have actually been conducted on this function because few private, for-profit operations exist. Most fire protection is provided through either publicly operated departments or volunteer jurisdictions. The lack of comparable studies makes it impossible to determine if these findings would hold true in other similar cases. In fact, there are cases that raise doubts about for-profit fire fighting firms' ability to reduce costs enough to get cities to change. Fire protection is one of the most essential services provided by cities. For example, when Westminster, California, decided to contract out its fire protection, the Orange County Fire Authority won the bid; the Rural Metro came in second.[25] Cities seeking to increase efficiency in fire protection find limited evidence suggesting private sector superiority, and most municipalities continue to use publicly operated fire departments.[26]

REFUSE COLLECTION AND BASIC MUNICIPAL SERVICES

Collecting garbage is considered to be an ideal task to study public versus private provision, and no local service area has received more attention. Most American cities (approximately two-thirds) have some version of private garbage collection. The arrangements include open competition among firms, exclusive franchises, and contracts with municipal governments. Nearly half of the cities in the United States exclusively use private collection while about one-third of all cities grant monopolies to their municipal sanitation departments. The role of the private sector has increased greatly in recent years. In 1964, only 18 percent of cities in the United States contracted with private firms for refuse collection.[27] In 1997, 49 percent of American cities were contracting with private firms.[28]

Many studies have been conducted on collecting garbage.[29] Most studies follow a similar pattern; efficiency is compared among various types of service delivery arrangements.[30] Efficiency is typically defined in terms of cost of service per household or cost per ton of collection. A lower cost of service is assumed to indicate a greater degree of efficiency. Tables 2.1 and 2.2 (on page 44) provide findings that are typical of efficiency studies on collecting garbage. Contracting with private firms has been consistently the most efficient method. Open competition is typically the most expensive method. Open competition has been found to be about a third *more* costly than contracting with private firms. This is noteworthy considering the theoretical foundations of market theory. That is, notwithstanding natural monopolies, open competition is usually considered to be the superior method for producing goods and

TABLE 2.1   ANNUAL COST PER HOUSEHOLD FOR GARBAGE COLLECTION

Type of Collection	Mean	Ratio Mean/ Contract Mean	Number of Cities (315)
Municipal	$32.08	1.15	102
Contract	27.82	1.00	68
Franchise	29.74	1.07	59
Private	44.67	1.61	86

Source: Adapted from E. S. Savas, "An Empirical Study of Competition in Municipal Service Delivery," *Public Administration Review* 37 (November/December 1977), pp. 717–724.

services. This has been a surprising and consistent finding by most studies. Why would open competition fail to be the most efficient method in this service area? Having vendors run door-to-door seeking the business of citizens could cause vendors to run their trucks all over town on many inefficient routes. Recall the example of London's experience with water provision in Chapter 1 where private vendors ran water pipes all over the streets in open competition with each other.

Municipal departments tend to collect garbage more often than private contractors do and there is more backdoor service.[31] The size of cities also seems to affect efficiency. There appears to be little difference between municipal and contract collection for cities with populations less than 50,000 but in cities with more than 50,000 residents, contract collection is typically less costly. In these cases, municipal collection is typically 25 percent to 40 percent more expensive.[32]

For private firms, the figures included in Tables 2.1 and 2.2 are based on the prices charged rather than production costs. It is generally conceded that if the performance of private firms were based on production costs rather than the actual price charged, private companies would be even more efficient. Private firms must make a profit; therefore, their production costs must be substantially lower than the price charged to customers. Thus, comparisons often are examining the price charged by private firms against the production costs of cities.[33]

TABLE 2.2   REFUSE COLLECTION: COST PER TON

Type of Collection	Cost per Ton
Municipal	$28.28
Private Contract	25.78
Private Franchise	28.23
Private Competitive	38.54

Source: Adapted from E. S. Savas, "Policy Analysis for Local Governments," *Policy Analysis* 3 (winter 1977), p. 66.

Most inquiries into garbage collection have found contracting to be more efficient than alternative methods (see Appendix A, Refuse Collection, for a summary of the major studies).[34] With the exception of one study, there appears to be a consensus that private contracting is the most efficient method of collecting garbage.[35] Considering some of the problems that plague municipal departments, it is understandable why private contractors have better efficiency ratings in trash collection.[36] Municipal sanitation departments must contend with almost twice the absentee rate of private firms (12 percent versus 6.5 percent).[37] They employ larger collection crews (3.26 workers versus 2.15) and spend more time servicing each household (4.35 man-hours versus 3.27).[38] Also, where public collection agencies face rival private firms, public operations appear to be more efficient than in cities where publicly run collection departments have an exclusive monopoly.[39] Garbage collection appears to be a case where "limited or controlled competition" works best. That is, contractors appear to be more efficient when operating in exclusive zones where they are assured all of the business. They appear to be less efficient when placed into open competition with other firms competing in the same areas. This is likely attributable to open competition forcing companies to operate many unprofitable routes to compete.

It is also noteworthy to mention that the garbage collection industry has changed during the past twenty years, when most studies were conducted. Prior to the 1980s, smaller firms, at least by contemporary standards, dominated garbage collection. Today, large corporations like Allied Waste and BFI (Browning-Ferris Industries) play a much larger role.[40] Companies like BFI often have their own landfills, possess the most modern equipment, and operate nationwide (and often internationally). It is possible that future studies might reveal different findings since large corporations may be better suited to deal with head-to-head competition with competing firms.

The consistent finding that private contracting is the most efficient method of collecting garbage has led to considerable discussion. Many of the traits associated with competitive markets appear to apply. Contractors must compete to secure bids and often demonstrate the kinds of behavior associated with competitive enterprise. When contractors provide garbage collection in more than one city, it enables them to take advantage of any technological advances developed in other locations. Moreover, ownership provides an incentive to control costs. Refuse collection usually involves small economies of scale, does not require any type of sophisticated technology, and involves only a moderate capital investment in relation to most industries. Cities often have multiple firms competing for contracts and most cities do not grant exclusive contracts to a single firm. Thus, locating a new contractor if a service level become unsatisfactory is less of a problem than with many other services, such as fire protection (which does require a large investment and considerable training of employees).[41] Accountability remains with cities because they hire the contractors, and citizens can easily monitor contractors by reporting disruptions in service.

TABLE 2.3   COST ADVANTAGES FROM PRIVATIZATION[42]

SERVICE	PRIVATE CONTRACT SAVINGS
Asphalt overlay	96%
Janitorial Service	73
Traffic signal maintenance	56
Street cleaning	43
Garbage collection	42
Turf maintenance	40
Tree maintenance	37

Source: Barbara Stevens, "Comparing Public- and Private-Sector Privatization Efficiency: An Analysis of Eight Activities," *National Productivity Review* (autumn 1984), p. 401.

Similar findings appear to be the norm for most municipal services. Private contracting appears capable of saving cities considerable amounts of money. Every municipal service imaginable has been the focus of studies and the results have consistently revealed that private provision is more efficient for most services.[43] The figures shown in Table 2.3 are typical of the findings of numerous studies that have examined local services.[44] Public and private provision is often compared by looking at such factors as scale of service, level of service, quality of service, physical conditions, and organizational arrangement. The increased efficiency of private contractors is usually attributed to better managerial practices and the use of innovative technology.[45]

WATER UTILITIES

Public versus private provision of various municipal utilities has also drawn the attention of economists. Private corporations own the vast majority of public utilities in the United States. These private firms differ from other businesses. Utility companies are obligated to serve everyone who asks for their services and utilities usually require a very large capital investment in relation to the revenues they receive. Philadelphia was the first municipality to have its own waterworks system, which was operational in 1801.[46] Cities began investing in water and sewerage systems in the nineteenth century largely due to widespread epidemics caused by mixing sewerage with drinking water. However, cities tended to form authorities and boards that dealt with a crisis, then receded from view after the crisis had passed. A positive philosophy about the responsibility of government to provide for the general welfare of its citizens simply did not exist in the eighteenth and nineteenth centuries.[47] Few cities made serious attempts to provide clean water until the 1850s and outbreaks of yellow fever, typhoid, and cholera were common. By the beginning of the Civil War, about seventy towns had waterworks systems owned by eighty different private companies.[48] Thus, most municipal waterworks systems at that time were privately owned. By the late nineteenth century, a growing middle class began demanding integrated water and sewerage systems.[49] Over time, cities would begin to develop their own waterworks systems and authorities but most cities and towns are still serviced by privately owned systems.[50] Currently, there are more than 54,000 water utility systems in the United States, which include 22,609 municipality-owned or government-owned water and sewerage systems, and nearly 30,000 privately owned water systems.[51] Most of the privately owned systems are technically called "investor-owned public utilities."[52]

One would expect that private enterprise should be more efficient than public enterprises because the private owner stands to gain enhanced wealth from improvements in efficiency, reductions in cost, and the like. In most cases, waterworks is considered to be a natural monopoly. That is, a single provider can usually conduct production more efficiently than several firms competing in the same area. Part of the reason is based on a theory that is fairly simple and well understood in the waterworks industry. A water pipe's capacity is roughly proportional to its cross section area. The cost is roughly proportional to a pipe's circumference. If the cross section area of a pipe is doubled, the circumference is less than doubled. Thus, doubling the volume of the water to be sent between any two given points less than doubles the cost—that is, it cuts costs roughly in half. Since the average cost is declining, having more than one firm providing water in any single area results in wasteful duplication.[53]

Since waterworks tend to be monopolies, does it matter whether a public waterworks authority or a privately owned company pumps water into our cities? Interestingly, the findings of major studies are inconclusive; they suggest that private firms are no more efficient than public operations at pumping and distributing water into the nation's cities and towns (see Appendix A, Water Utilities, for summaries of the major studies).[54] Of eight major studies conducted on water utilities, only two studies have found private provision to be more efficient. Most of the studies found no significant difference between public and private provision of water. However, it should be noted that these studies do not take all possible conditions into account. For example, it is possible that for large cities, municipal provision may be the least-costly method while in smaller cities and towns, private provision may be the best method to use. For example, two cities that are comparable in size (Asheville, North Carolina, and Missoula, Montana) use opposite service delivery systems for water. Asheville uses a metropolitan water authority (government owned and operated) whereas Missoula uses a utility that is privately owned.[55] Based on these studies, it is not possible to determine in which settings public versus private water provision would work best. Chapter 4 includes a number of examples in which private water provision has proven to be less costly than municipal provision, but these are case studies rather than extensive and sophisticated analyses of the waterworks industry versus municipal waterworks. As a generalization, one must conclude that the evidence is inconclusive. Most cities are serviced by municipal water systems.

ELECTRIC POWER UTILITIES

What type of organization functions the most efficiently for producing electric power? The history of electric utilities in American cities is filled with corruption. In cities like Detroit, it was well known that council members often sold their votes to the private electric utility owners, which in turn resulted in higher costs for citizens, while aldermen filled their pockets with cash. Hazen Pingree, the mayor of Detroit in the 1890s, was one of the first reform-oriented mayors to take on the powerful utilities of his city, namely Detroit Electric Light and Power Company and Detroit Gas Company. After a tumultuous battle, the mayor won. As a result of his victory, Detroit began operating a municipal electric plant to operate the city's streetlights in 1895. Over time, other reform-oriented mayors and citizen groups cleaned up much of the corruption caused by political machines and their relationship with utility companies. In many cases, like Detroit, cities began their own electric power utilities in the name of accountability to help correct the corruption so rampant in many cities.[56]

Like water and sewerage, provision of electric power is considered to be a natural monopoly. That is, it is more efficient for one producer to serve a specific area rather than have many competing companies going door-to-door for business. Provision of electricity comes in several organizational forms, including investor-owned organizations, public utilities (which include municipally owned and operated electric power systems), and cooperatives. Several other variations exist, but they are less relevant to the discussion here.[57] There are 239 investor-owned utilities in the United States, which possess about 77 percent of the nation's electric power generating capacity. Because they are considered to be natural monopolies, investor-owned utilities operate in a heavily regulated environment. However, the environment is slowly changing due to passage of the Energy Policy Act of 1992 (EPACT) that marked the beginning of deregulation of the electric power industry. There are 912 cooperatives (co-ops), which operate to provide at-cost electric service to the consumer-owners. A co-op's net margin above expenses and reserves does not belong to the utility; it belongs to the individual consumer-owners of the co-op. The margins must either be used to improve or maintain operations, or be distributed to those who use the co-op's products or services. Investor-owned utilities that are not cooperatives are operated to maximize profit for the shareholders. Additionally, there are 2,019 public utilities, which include municipally owned and operated electric systems. Also included in the publicly owned group are 10 federally owned and operated systems. Despite the progress and ongoing attempts to deregulate this industry, most electric utilities still function as natural monopolies.[58]

Utilities may be unique because they are natural monopolies. Those who examine the efficiency of utilities tend to compare public and private management under a unique set of incentives and constraints imposed by regulation.[59] Public and private management is compared in this unique environment, and in the case of natural monopolies, the utility companies cannot compete for customers in their exclusively defined jurisdictions. Utilities are local monopolies and theory suggests that if unconstrained, they will charge too much for their services. Thus, they are regulated.[60] Since utility regulators set prices to ensure an established profit is not exceeded, some have suggested this type of regulation creates an excessive incentive to invest in capital equipment.[61] This hypothesis has been confirmed in empirical studies.[62]

Most studies of electric utilities (see Appendix A, Electric Utilities, for a summary of major studies)[63] have controlled for organizational form to enable the cost of production to be determined between public and private operations. The electric utility studies that are listed in Appendix A used similar data sets, employed sophisticated methodologies, and were published in well-respected journals. None of these studies found private power companies to be more efficient than publicly operated electric utilities.[64] Like the case with water utilities, it appears to make little difference whether the municipalities or private firms provide power. Most power utilities do not face direct competition. However, there are some exceptions.[65] In cases where power utilities face competition, competition appears to contribute to an average cost reduction of 11 percent whether the utilities are publicly or privately operated. The implication supports claims that monopolies, public or private, tend to be less efficient than organizations facing competition. Although deregulation may change the dynamics of the electric power industry, the evidence on efficiency provides little justification for cities to privatize their electric utilities.

SUMMARIZING THE EVIDENCE ON EFFICIENCY

It is fair to generalize that the evidence on efficiency is favorable toward privatizing municipal services. Utilities, such as water and electricity, are the exception rather than the norm for efficiency comparisons between public and private operations. Literally hundreds of efficiency studies have been conducted in the United States and Europe and the evidence generally favors private production for most services (see Appendix A for a sample of a variety of municipal service areas). But critics have not been completely sold on the evidence on efficiency and have suggested that we remain skeptical about the potential savings associated with various forms of privatization.[66] Critics stress that the evidence on efficiency should lead only to a cautious, conditional endorsement of privatization.[67] It is also fair to generalize that the evidence suggests that better efficiency comes from *competition* rather than from the *privateness* or *publicness* of organizations.[68] Although in many cases privatization does produce significant savings, the magnitude of the savings may not be as overwhelming as is often reported.[69] Nonetheless, a general consensus exists that privatization can save money in most services and that private operations are generally more efficient than their public-sector counterparts.[70]

THE USE OF PRIVATIZATION BY CITIES

Local governments have demonstrated a willingness to experiment with privatization. The question is: How much privatization do cities actually use?[71] Table 2.4 reveals a relative consistency in the use of contracting between 1982 and 1997 by local governments for the services included in the table (see Appendix B for an expanded table that includes many more services). Can this be interpreted as meaning that the use of contracting, and perhaps other forms of privatization, has been overstated? Probably not, but it can be interpreted as suggesting that the pace at which privatization was growing over the past twenty years may have slowed. Aside from contracting, which is the most common form of privatization used by local governments, cities appear to make little use of the other alternative-service delivery arrangements included in the surveys.[72] Despite the widespread attention that privatization has received, public employees still provide most public services.[73] Why would cities not adopt privatization on a wholesale basis? Like old habits, old service delivery patterns may be difficult to change.[74] Inertia coupled with established relationships and routines may be formidable barriers to privatization.[75] Although highly touted and publicized, local officials must deal with other factors that are not included in efficiency studies, namely politics.[76] There is a difference between academic studies and theories and real-world implementation. In other words, what looks great on paper and makes for great discussions in the classroom may not work in the real world of city governments.[77]

Although the figures in Table 2.4 suggest that the use of privatization may have stabilized, examples of cities experimenting with many forms of privatization are not difficult to find.[78] Privatization is commonly used by local governments and has always been part of the municipal landscape. The evidence presented here simply suggests that the use of contracting by cities appears to have been relatively stable over the past twenty years.[79]

REGIONAL PATTERNS OF PRIVATIZATION

Do regional patterns of privatization exist? That is, do some areas of the country use more privatization than others do? Many believe that privatization is more widely used in the West because of the effects of Proposition 13. It is

TABLE 2.4 PRIVATIZATION OF SELECTED LOCAL SERVICES, 1982–1997

SERVICE	LOCAL GOVERNMENTS CONTRACTING OUT			
	1982	1988	1992	1997
Vehicle towing and storage	80%	80%	85%	83%
Legal services	49	55	49	53
Residential refuse collection	35	36	38	49
Tree trimming and planting	31	36	32	37
Solid waste disposal	28	25	32	41
Street repair	27	36	30	35
Traffic signal maintenance	26	27	25	24
Ambulance service	25	24	37	37
Bus system operation	24	26	22	30
Labor relations	23	33	49	53
Data processing	23	17	9	15

Sources: *Service Delivery in the 90s: Alternative Approaches for Local Governments* (Washington, D.C.: International City/County Management Association, 1989) and Elaine Morley, "Local Government Use of Alternative Service Delivery Approaches," *Municipal Yearbook 1999* (Washington, D.C.: International City/County Management Association), pp. 34–44.

also believed that "newer" or "growing" cities have a greater incentive to expand the use of the private sector in service delivery, which also leads one to associate privatization with the West.[80] Some evidence suggests that privatization is more prevalent in the West,[81] but most of the evidence has generated mixed findings.[82] There are a variety of reasons for not finding consistent regional patterns.[83] Factors that may cause privatization, such as fiscal stress or fast-growing populations that can overload local services, can cause similar behaviors. For example, areas with growing populations may experience an overload effect and turn to privatization to expand services because of the demands placed on roads, schools, and other infrastructure. Population growth has been common in Sunbelt states, especially the Southwest. Many cities in the Southwest, such as Phoenix, Arizona, have made extensive use of privatization. Indianapolis, Indiana, is also a large city that is considered to be one of the leading innovators in privatization, but it is not located in a Sunbelt state. Indianapolis has turned to privatization mainly to reduce its budget rather than handle the problems associated with a rapidly growing population. The most plausible explanation (which will be addressed in Chapter 3 more thoroughly) is that population shifts, fiscal stress, political culture, and politics can take on a variety of combinations that cause cities to privatize services. Fiscal stress has long been considered the primary impetus for privatization and fiscal stress does not adhere to regional boundaries. Thus, no distinct regional patterns may exist.

THE ATTITUDES OF LOCAL OFFICIALS REGARDING PRIVATIZATION

Municipal privatization affects local officials, who ultimately determine whether to privatize services. How do local official feel about privatization (see Table 2.5)? In the late 1980s, local officials believed that cost savings were the main advantage of privatization. Eighty percent of the local officials believed that privatization would be a primary method for providing local government services and facilities in the future.[84] Fifty percent of local governments, whose motivation for contracting out with private firms was to cut costs, did, in fact, save money by using privatization.[85] Local officials felt the primary disadvantages associated with privatization were loss of control, politics, and doubt about the actual benefits over time.[86] The primary reasons that cities consider privatization have not changed much over the past decade. For example, a 1998 survey that asked local officials why they consider privatization found potential cost savings still to be the main reason (see Figure 2.1).[87]

Evidence suggesting cities can realize 96 percent savings by contracting out for street repair or 20 to 50 percent by contracting for wastewater treatment is appealing to municipal governments facing fiscal pressures. While the debate continues among ideologues and academics, local governments continue to experiment with privatization. In the real world of cities, fiscal pressures are real and local officials appear willing to experiment with privatization if it can help remedy fiscal problems.[88]

SUMMARY

The evidence on efficiency generally favors privatization but in some services has generated mixed findings. In some functions, such as garbage collection and most basic municipal services, the evidence appears to favor

TABLE 2.5   LOCAL OFFICIALS' OPINIONS ABOUT
THE ADVANTAGES OF CONTRACTING OUT MUNICIPAL SERVICES

	RESPONDENTS LISTING THESE ADVANTAGES
Cost savings	74%
Solves labor problems	50
Shares risks	34
Higher quality of service	33
Provides services otherwise not available	32
Shorter implementation time	30
Solves local political problems	21
No advantages	3

Source: *Privatization in America* (New York: Touche Ross, 1987), p. 5.

FIGURE 2.1   WHY DO CITIES PRIVATIZE?

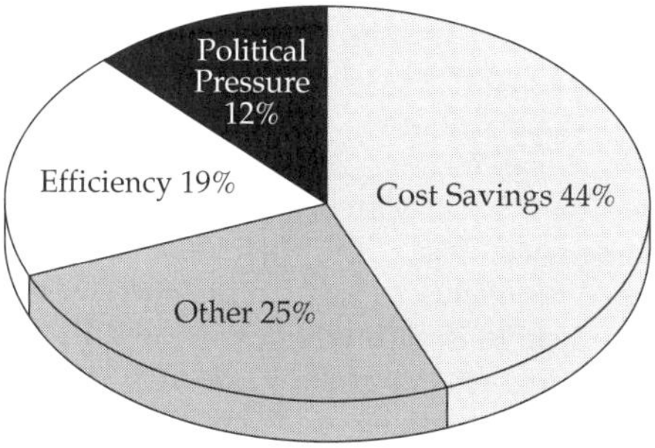

Political Pressure 12%

Efficiency 19%

Cost Savings 44%

Other 25%

Source: Bethany Barber, "Privatization: Not Just Garbage," *Recycling Times* (September 1, 1998).

private contracting. In other areas, such as utilities, private production seems no more efficient than government operations. Popular discussion of privatization often assumes the inevitability of increased efficiency. Although local governments commonly use privatization, the use of contracting appears to have remained relatively stable between 1982 and 1997. Moreover, there are no discernable regional patterns for using privatization. Local officials appear willing to consider privatization, but they have not adopted privatization on a wholesale basis.

Proponents of contracting have tended to cite studies that compare the cost of producing similar services in the public and private sectors. Critics point out that many of the studies commonly cited are not actually about contracting out or pure privatization; they simply compare the cost of producing something in the public sector against a similar service in the private sector. Although such comparisons are necessary, they do not address actual contractual relationships with government or how a contractor will handle a service over time.[89] It is often assumed that contractors will behave the same when contracting with a government as they would in a competitive market, but studies have not confirmed this behavior. Although "before and after" studies of privatization appear favorable, the relative stability of contracting between 1982 and 1997 suggests that local governments are skeptical about privatization's promise of superior efficiency.[90]

Critics have not been completely sold on the evidence on efficiency and have remained skeptical about the potential savings associated with various forms of privatization. Critics stress that concerns about public accountability and equity are not adequately addressed. Although in many cases privatization does produce significant savings, the magnitude of the savings may have been overstated.[91] Nonetheless, a consensus exists that privatization does, in fact, save money in most services and that private organizations are more efficient than their counterparts in the public sector.

NOTES

1. This is referred to as the *public-private dichotomy* in the discipline of public administration. For a good review of the debate surrounding this concept, see Brian Fry and Lloyd Nigro, "Five Great Issues in the Profession of Public Administration," in *Handbook of Public Administration*, 2nd ed., ed. Jack Rabin, W. Bartley Hildreth, and Gerald J. Miller (New York: Marcel Dekker, 1997), pp. 1163–1222.

2. Examples of incompetence, waste, and inefficiency abound. For example, in the mid-1980s, the state of Pennsylvania was paying nearly $500,000 in subsidies to the Pittsburgh and Lake Erie Railroad, which was used by an average of 250 commuters a day. At this rate, the state could have bought each rider a new car every three years. In another case, a citizen of Prince William County, Virginia, received a legal notice about his overdue taxes. The notice stated that if the taxes were not paid promptly, the county would take legal action. The amount in question was one cent. For an excellent comparison of government and business, see George Downs and Patrick Larkey, *The Search for Government Efficiency: From Hubris to Helplessness* (Pittsburgh, PA: University of Pittsburgh Press, 1986). The theme of their book is that government is not as poorly managed as commonly thought, and businesses are not as well managed as is generally believed.

3. Studies have examined costs before and after privatization occurred, but costs are not always coupled with the quality of the contracted work or other performance factors. Longitudinal studies have been conducted in many areas that do not involve municipal services. For example, studies have examined productivity, profit, and other performance measures in industries after privatization, and the effects on the national economy. Most of these are international studies involving countries such as Great Britain, New Zealand, and Australia. Generally, the results have been favorable toward privatization for most industries. For a summary of these studies, see Graeme Hodge, *Privatization: An International Review of Performance* (Boulder, CO: Westview Press, 2000), pp. 177–180.

4. It should be noted that this study did not include any findings about the quality of the contracted work. E. S. Savas presents a number of these studies (which include studies that did account for quality of services) that are favorable toward privatization in *Privatization and Public and Private Partnerships* (New York: Seven Bridges Press, 2000), pp. 149–153.

5. E. S. Savas, *A Comparative Study of Bus Operations in New York City*, Report FTA NY-11 0040-92-1 (Washington, D.C.: U.S. Department of Transportation, 1992). Also, see Savas, *Privatization and Public and Private Partnerships*, pp. 151–152.

6. Economists have conducted numerous studies examining virtually all types of services. This chapter only includes a sampling of services. Appendix A contains a long list of studies and the major findings that have been conducted over the years. While extensive, the list does not include all of the studies that have been published.

7. Theory does suggest that cities compete with each other on some levels, but the general lack of direct competition is what has caused economists to make so many direct comparisons of efficiency between public and private operations performing similar tasks.

8. Some cities have simulated a form of internal competition. For example, a city may be divided into zones to collect garbage and the performance of each zone can be

compared. If proper incentives are used, such as pay increases for the managers and employees of the most efficient zones, it is possible to simulate competition to some degree. Comparing cities to other cities is common. However, it is usually difficult to ascertain meaningful comparisons because cities vary greatly. Just because cities may appear similar in areas such as population, population density, region, form of government, and so forth, it does not mean that meaningful efficiency comparisons are possible. Cities are unique entities and no two cities are exactly alike.

9. Public choice theory, discussed in Chapter 1, suggests that citizens will demand too many services when the cost of services appears inexpensive. That is, because citizens do not always feel the true costs, they demand more service. Examples are not hard to find. In some garbage collecting studies, it was found that city crews would pick up virtually anything left by the curb. Once the service was contracted, the private firms agreed to pick up only specific types of garbage. This often led to citizens complaining about the private service. In some cases, cities returned to the publicly operated service and increased service levels, which should have also increased the cost per household. A similar scenario occurred in Warren, Michigan, in the late 1960s. See John Hanrahan, *Government for Sale, Contracting Out, the New Patronage* (Washington, D.C.: American Federation of State, County, and Municipal Employees, 1977), pp. 71–73.

10. Downs and Larkey, *The Search for Government Efficiency: From Hubris to Helplessness*, p. 8.

11. Meaningful comparisons are critical. For example, the U.S. Postal Service has been the subject of many jokes for its perceived lack of efficiency and often blatant incompetence. Citizens often view the post office being staffed with lazy, overpaid workers. Most Americans have had experiences with the post office in which packages did not arrive in a reasonable time, poor service was received from postal employees, and so forth. For example, in the early 1990s during the debate over nationalizing health care, critics often asked whether we wanted to use the post office as a model to deliver health care. This was intended as satire, but it was very effective because most of us relate inefficient service with the post office and it did not seem like a good model to emulate, even if it was not a fair comparison. Most often, the Postal Service is compared to private companies like United Parcel Service (UPS) or Federal Express, which usually appear to be far more efficient and reliable than the postal service. However, when the U.S. Postal Service is compared to postal services operated by other countries, such as Japan, Germany, or France, one finds that the U.S. Postal Service is very efficient. In fact, studies have shown that the U.S. Postal Service moves more letters and tons of packages more cost effectively than any other postal service in the world. See Downs and Larkey, *The Search for Government Efficiency: From Hubris to Helplessness*, p. 17.

12. Ibid, pp. 7–8.

13. John Ross and Jesse Burkhead, *Productivity in the Local Government Sector* (Lexington, MA: Lexington Books, 1974), p. 14. Also see, Frederick Hayes, *Productivity in Local Government* (Lexington, MA: Lexington Books, 1977).

14. Productivity should also be mentioned here. Productivity is generally considered to be "… a systematic measure of efficiency with which physical inputs, land, labor, and capital, are converted into physical outputs—goods and services." See Ross and Burkhead, *Productivity in the Local Government Sector*, p. 11. It is usually

expressed as a ratio of units of physical output to one or more of the inputs associated with that output. Little consensus exists on a concrete definition of productivity. It is difficult to differentiate efficiency from productivity because they are often used synonymously in the literature. Definitions range from single measures like relating labor to output, to broad conceptualizations that incorporate efficiency and effectiveness. Generally, productivity is simply a more precise method of measuring efficiency. Ross and Burkhead provide an excellent discussion of this problem in *Productivity in the Local Government Sector*.

15. David Davies, "The Efficiency of Public versus Private Firms: The Case of Australia's Two Airlines," *Journal of Law and Economics* 14 (1971), pp. 149–165.

16. Ibid.

17. The efficiency measures used were tons of freight and mail carried per employee, number of paying passengers per employee, and revenue per employee. The private airline averaged carrying more than twice the amount of freight and mail per employee, the number of paying passengers was 20 percent higher, and the average revenue per employee was $9,627 versus $8,428.

18. Recall from Chapter 1 that private ownership concentrates property rights while public ownership dilutes property rights. The criticisms levied against the study are typical of case studies; conclusions based on nonrandom samples of two have their limitations. Although this study does not focus on local services, it has been widely used to illustrate the advantages of private ownership and often appears in discussions about local governments. See Downs and Larkey, *The Search for Government Efficiency: From Hubris to Helplessness*, p. 37. Downs and Larkey argue that, "the airline case may present a golden opportunity to explore the consequences of property-rights variation, it would be overly optimistic to generalize too broadly from the results. Conclusions based on a nonrandom sample of two have their limitations.… There is no way of knowing whether the performance of the two airlines is "typical" of that to be expected from their respective sectors. What we have here is not a "test" but a provocative case study."

19. Caves and Christensen conducted a similar study but reached a different conclusion from Davies. Their study examined two Canadian railroads in two different time periods. In the earlier time period, the private railway was more efficient. In the latter time period, the two railways had comparable efficiency. See Douglas Caves and Lauritis Christensen, "The Relative Efficiency of Public and Private Firms in a Competitive Environment: The Case of Canadian Railroads," *Journal of Political Economy* 88 (1980), pp. 958–976.

20. Police and fire protection are among the most crucial services provided by cities. In the area of police protection, privatization is almost nonexistent with the exception of some support functions. This is largely attributed to constitutional concerns and legal restrictions. In fact, the least privatized area for cities fall into the area of public safety, which include both police and fire departments. Few private fire fighting companies exist and the Rural Metro is definitely an exception. Of course, volunteer fire departments are extremely common, but virtually all cities maintain their own fire departments.

21. Randall Fitzgerald, *When Government Goes Private* (New York: Universe Books, 1998), p. 77.

22. Roger Ahlbrandt, "Efficiency in the Provision of Fire Services," *Public Choice* 16 (1973), pp. 1–15.

23. The Rural Metro also provides fire protection to several other jurisdictions. See John Donahue, *The Privatization Decision: Public Ends, Private Means*, p. 71.

24. Randall Fitzgerald, *When Government Goes Private*, p. 78.

25. Westminster case illustrates the hard fought battles between public employees and cities. In this case, an intergovernmental arrangement was used, which saved the city about $11 million over the five-year contract term. This case is available on the Reason Foundation's privatization database located at <www.privatization.com> under fire protection services.

26. About 90 percent of all fire departments in the United States are composed either entirely or mostly of volunteers. These departments protect 42 percent of the population mainly located in rural or suburban areas. However, most cities maintain their own fire departments.

27. John Donahue, *The Privatization Decision: Public Ends, Private Means* (New York: Basic Books, 1989), p. 58.

28. This finding is included in the International City/County Management Association's 1997 survey on alternative service delivery approaches used by local governments. The survey is available from the ICMA, 777 North Capitol Street, NE, Suite 500, Washington, D.C. 20002. The findings are summarized in the *Municipal Yearbook*. See Elaine Morley, "Local Government Use of Alternative Service Delivery Approaches," *Municipal Yearbook* (Washington, D.C.: International City/County Management Association, 1999), pp. 34–44.

29. E. S. Savas, "An Empirical Study of Competition in Municipal Service Delivery," *Public Administration Review* 37 (November/December 1977), pp. 717–724. This study is one of the most impressive studies ever conducted on collecting garbage, and one of the most widely cited. It examined a sample of 1,378 communities, and then 315 localities were analyzed intensively.

30. Typical service delivery arrangements include municipal provision, contracts, franchises, private provision, and self-help. *Municipal provision* is having trash collected by public sanitation departments. *Contract provision* refers to contracting with private firms, not with other governments. *Franchise collection* entails granting private vendors an exclusive right to operate in a specified jurisdiction or area. *Private provision* refers to open competition with citizens able to select from competing firms. *Self-help* simply places the burden on households to dispose of their own garbage.

31. Collecting garbage comes in a variety of levels of service. For example, backdoor service refers to having the crews pick up residential garbage cans literally on the backdoors, patios, and so forth of residents. Curbside is the most common form, where residents place their garbage cans at the curb to pick up on the day of collection. Service levels can also vary on the frequency of collection, once- or twice-per-week.

32. Savas, "An Empirical Study of Competition in Municipal Service Delivery," p. 68.

33. Another widely cited study found private contracting to be the most efficient method of collecting garbage, but also revealed some interesting findings about economies of scale. The study attempted to measure the average household's collection costs and gathered data from on-site localities to avoid the often-inconsistent accounting systems used by local governments. The factors examined in the study included organizational form, cost of labor, quantity of garbage collected, frequency of collection, proportion of backyard to curbside pick-ups, population density, and

weather conditions. The study was extensive and evaluated 340 collection operations. The study concluded that economies of scale did make a difference. Operations that served fewer than 20,000 residents tended to be less efficient. Economies of scale get smaller above populations of 20,000 and the cost curve flattens at a scale of about 50,000 residents. Costs tend to rise with the level of service—backyard pickup costs roughly a third more than curbside and twice-a-week collection costs about one-quarter more than once-a-week pickup. The study found that population density and weather conditions did not have a significant impact on costs. Open competition was found to be a more costly method of collecting garbage. See Barbara Stevens, "Scale, Market Structure, and Cost of Refuse Collection," *Review of Economics and Statistics* 68 (1977), pp. 438–448.

34. The major refuse collection studies include: Werner Hirsch, "Cost Functions of an Urban Government Service: Refuse Collection," *Review of Economics and Statistics* 47 (1965), pp. 87–92; Peter Kemper and John Quigley, *The Economics of Refuse Collection* (Cambridge, MA: Ballinger Press, 1976); John Collins and Bryan Downes, "The Effects of Size on the Provision of Public Services: The Case of Solid Waste Collection in Smaller Cities," *Urban Affairs Quarterly* 12 (March 1977), pp. 333–347; E. S. Savas, "An Empirical Study of Competition in Municipal Service Delivery," *Public Administration Review* 37 (November/December 1977), pp. 717–724; Barbara Stevens, "Scale, Market Structure, and Cost of Refuse Collection," *Review of Economics and Statistics* 60 (1977), pp. 438–448; James Bennett and Manuel Johnson, "Public versus Private Provision of Collective Goods: Garbage Collection Revisited," *Public Choice* 34 (1979), pp. 55–64; James McDavid, "The Canadian Experience with Privatizing Residential Solid Waste Collection Services," *Public Administration Review* 45 (September/October 1985), pp. 602–608; and Simon Domberger, S. A. Meadowcroft, and D. J. Thompson, "Competitive Tendering and Efficiency: The Case of Refuse Collection," *Fiscal Studies* 7 (November 1986), pp. 69–87.

35. The study that found free markets to be the most efficient method of collecting garbage examined Fairfax County, Virginia. In parts of the county, garbage is collected by a public department while in other sections, private firms compete in an open market. Out of the 29 firms operating in the county, only one charged more than the public department. The solid waste disposal department operated by the county charged an average of $127 per year while the private firms charged an average of $87. This study received widespread methodological criticism and remains a unique case. See James Bennett and Manual Johnson, "Public versus Private Provision of Collective Goods: Garbage Collection Revisited."

36. Downs and Larkey, *The Search for Government Efficiency: From Hubris to Helplessness*, pp. 32–34.

37. Ibid.

38. Ibid.

39. James McDavid, "The Canadian Experience with Privatizing Residential Solid Waste Collection Services," pp. 602–605.

40. Allied Waste's purchase of BFI provides some evidence that large corporations are playing a larger role in waste collection and management. Allied Waste was the second-largest solid waste collection corporation in the world at the time this book went to press. For more information about this industry, visit <http://www.solidwaste.com>.

41. Donahue, *The Privatization Decision: Public Ends, Private Means*, p. 67.

42. The study that produced these findings used regression analysis to explain cost. Multiple regression analysis is a statistical technique for estimating the relationship between a continuous dependent variable and two or more continuous independent variables. In its most simple form, regression analysis is used to examine data plotted along an X (horizontal) axis and Y (vertical) axis, to find the line that best fits the data.

43. The most thorough and widely cited study on local services in the United States was conducted by Barbara Stevens. Like her earlier study of garbage collection, the data were collected on-site rather than from municipal budgets. See Barbara Stevens, "Comparing Public- and Private-Sector Productivity Efficiency: An Analysis of Eight Activities," *National Productivity Review* (autumn 1984), pp. 395–406. The study focused on the Los Angeles metropolitan area, which is comprised of roughly 121 cities. Twenty cities and eight basic functions were studied intensely. Public and private provision were compared by looking at such factors as scale of service, level of service, quality of service, physical conditions, and organizational arrangement. The major findings of the study are provided in Table 2.3. The increased efficiency of private contractors was attributed to astute managerial practices and the use of innovative technology.

    The study was one of the most systematic and detailed research efforts ever conducted on municipal services. It is also one of the most thoroughly scrutinized and criticized. Critics have attacked the study on methodological grounds, especially on the limited geographical scope. The study only included cities in the Los Angeles area; an area where government contracting with private firms is well established and ample competition exists. It has been argued that many aspects were downplayed, mainly because the study was funded by the U.S. Department of Housing and Urban Development during the Reagan administration. Some believe the study was carefully written to minimize the administration's tough stance taken against labor. See Donahue, *The Privatization Decision: Public Ends, Private Means*, p. 145.

44. One of the most thorough collections of municipal privatization studies can be found in E. S. Savas, *Privatization and Public-Private Partnerships* (New York: Seven Bridges Press, 2000).

45. It should be noted that most privatization studies on efficiency have been contested. For a discussion about the problems associated with efficiency studies, which are primarily technical or methodological problems, see Donahue, *The Privatization Decision: Public Ends, Private Means*, pp. 140–145; and Werner Hirsch, "Contracting Out by Urban Governments: A Review," *Urban Affairs Review* 30 (January 1995), pp. 458–472.

46. Sam Bass Warner, Jr., *The Private City: Philadelphia in Three Periods of Its Growth* (Philadelphia, PA: University of Pennsylvania Press, 1968), pp. 107–109. It should be noted that historians appear to disagree over which city had the first public waterworks system and the exact dates. Boston is thought to have had the first "crude" water system, although few records still exist for confirmation. The first towns to make a civic effort to have waterworks with pumps were Schaefferstown and Bethlehem, Pennsylvania. But these were not truly public systems. New York City built a reservoir in 1774. Some accounts place Baltimore as having waterworks in 1804 and Philadelphia's system beginning in 1819 rather than 1801, as reported in the text. See Edward Hungerford, *The Story of Public Utilities* (New York: Aron Press, 1972), Chapter 16.

47. Dennis Judd and Todd Swanstrom, *City Politics: Private Power and Public Policy* (New York: Harper Collins, 1994), pp. 42–44.
48. Blake McKelvey, *The Urbanization of America* (New Brunswick, NJ: Rutgers University Press, 1963), p. 13.
49. Ibid, p. 90.
50. Charlie Tyer conducted a study on cities and towns in South Carolina who owned their own utilities. His study found that cities with their own electrical utilities increased spending on municipal services and subsidization of property taxes by substituting utility fees from city customers and noncity customers for taxes. Cities with municipally owned water and sewerage systems followed similar practices. See Charlie Tyer, "Municipal Enterprises and Taxing and Spending Policies: Public Avoidance and Fiscal Illusions," *Public Administration Review* 49 (May/June 1989), pp. 249–256.
51. The American Water Works Association (6666 Quincy Avenue, Denver, CO 80235, 303-794-7771), provided the data reported here. For a discussion about privatization of government-owned waterworks systems, see Steve Hanke and Stephen J. K. Walters, "Privatizing Waterworks," in *Prospects for Privatization*, pp. 104–113.
52. Investor-owned public water utilities operate in the same manner as investor-owned electric utilities. They are called "public utilities," are considered to be natural monopolies, and operate under heavy regulation. However, they seek to maximize returns for investors. In addition to the government-owned and privately-owned water utilities, there are roughly 4,000 other water utilities that do not report to the Environmental Protection Agency. For additional information, contact the American Water Works Association, The AWWA maintains an elaborate Web site about the water industry at <www.awwa.org>. From this Web site, one can access any water utility system in the nation, public or private. The AWWA also maintains an elaborate database about the water utilities. There are other major associations in the waterworks industry, such as the Association of Metropolitan Water Agencies and the National Rural Water Association. Both maintain Web sites at <www.amwa-water.org> and <www.nrwa.org>, respectively.
53. For the complete discussion about the natural monopoly phenomena in the waterworks industry, see Steve Hanke and Stephen J. K. Walters, "Privatizing Waterworks," in *Prospects for Privatization*, pp. 107–110.
54. The relative cheapness and efficiency of service, coupled with local conditions, are the chief factors to be considered in deciding between public and private ownership. Sufficient methods of financing municipally owned undertakings must also be planned so as not to increase municipal debt beyond prudent limits. In addition, recent changes in federal tax laws have made it more difficult for municipalities to raise capital for the acquisition of utility property through tax-exempt financing. Although these and other relevant concerns exist, the evidence suggests that public and private efficiency in the provision of water is comparable.

    The major water utility studies included in Appendix A are: Patrick Mann and John Mikesell, "The Determinants of the Choice Between Public and Private Production of Publicly Funded Service," *Public Choice* 54 (1987), pp. 197–210; Mark Crain and Asghar Zardkoohi, "A Test of Property Rights Theory and the Firm: Water Utilities in the United States," *Journal of Law and Economics* 21 (October 1978), pp. 395–408; Thomas Bruggink, "Public versus Regulated Private Enterprise in the Municipal Water Industry: A Comparison of Costs," *Quarterly Review of Economics and Business* 22 (1982), pp. 111–125; Susan Feigenbaum and Ronald Teeples, "Public versus Private Water Delivery: A Hedonic Cost Approach," *Review of Economics and Statistics* 65 (1983), pp. 89–107; Ronald Teeples, Susan Feigenbaum, and David Glyer, "Public versus Private Water Delivery: Cost Comparisons," *Public Finance Quarterly* 14 (1986), pp. 351–366; and Patricia Byners, Shawn Grasskopt, and Kathy Hayes, "Efficiency and Ownership: Further Evidence," *Review of Economics and Statistics* 68 (1986), pp. 958–976.

55. Missoula and Asheville are comparable in size, but Asheville has a much larger surrounding area and extensive suburbs. Thus, the metropolitan water district for Asheville is much larger than Missoula's. The Missoula area is served by several water companies.

56. For a more in-depth summary of the situation with Mayor Pingree and the Detroit utilities, see Judd and Swanstrom, *City Politics: Private Power and Public Policy,* pp. 69–72. Also, see John Hilgram, *Strangers in the Land: Patterns of American Nativism, 1960–1925* (New Brunswick, NJ: Rutgers University Press, 1955), pp. 54–55.

57. There are several other categories, such as nonutilities, which generate power for their own use and sell any excess power to the wholesale market. There is also a new category called "power marketers," which buy and sell electricity but do not own or operate generation, transmission, or distribution facilities. See *The Changing Structure of the Electric Power Industry 1999: Mergers and Other Corporate Combinations,* Report DOE/EIA-0562 (99) (A report prepared for the Energy Information Administration, Office of Coal, Nuclear, Electric and Alternative Fuels, U.S. Department of Energy, Washington, D.C.), p. 4.

58. It should be noted that the electric power industry is undergoing major structural changes as we begin the new century. Deregulation is a significant part of the larger privatization movement and as technology continues to develop, it is impossible at this writing to predict what lies ahead for the electric power industry. For more information about this industry, contact the Energy Information Administration in Washington, D.C., at 202-586-8800, or visit their Web site at <www.eia.doe.gov>. This agency maintains a rich source of information, including articles and databases about the electric power industry, and many other energy-based utilities, from the national perspective and state-by-state.

59. Donahue, *The Privatization Decision: Public Ends, Private Means,* pp. 76–77.

60. Ibid, p. 77.

61. H. Averch and L. L. Johnson, "Behavior of the Firm under Regulatory Constraints," *American Economic Review* (December 1962), pp. 1052–1070.

62. Robert Spann, "Rate of Return Regulation and Efficiency in Production: An Empirical Test of the Averch-Johnson Thesis," *Bell Journal of Economics* 5 (spring 1974), pp. 38–52.

63. The major electric power utility studies conducted are: Robert Meyer, "Publicly Owned versus Privately Owned Utilities: A Policy of Choice," *Review of Economics and Statistics* 57 (1975), pp. 391–400; Dennis Yunker, "Economic Performance of Public and Private Enterprise: The Case of U.S. Electric Industries," *Journal of Economics and Business* 28 (1975), pp. 60–68; Leland Neuberg, "Two Issues in the Municipal Ownership of Electric Power Distribution Systems," *Bell Journal of Economics* 6 (1977), pp. 303–323; Donn Pescatrice and John Trapani, "The Performance and Objectives of Public and Private Utilities Operating in the United States," *Journal of Public Economics* 13 (1980), pp. 259–276; R. Fare, S. Grasskopt, and J. Logan, "The

Relative Performance of Publicly Owned and Privately Owned Electric Utilities," *Journal of Public Economics* 26 (1985), pp. 89–107; and Scott Atkinson and Robert Halvorsen, "The Relative Efficiency of Public and Private Firms in Regulated Environment: The Case of U.S. Electric Utilities," *Journal of Public Economics* 29 (1986), pp. 281–294.

64. It should be noted that a few studies have been conducted that have found differences between public and private provision of electricity. See Charles Wolf, *Markets or Governments: Choosing between Imperfect Alternatives* (Cambridge, MA: MIT Press, 1988) Appendix B, p. 193.

65. Walter Primeaux, "An Assessment of X-Efficiency Gained through Competition," *Review of Economics and Statistics* 59 (1977), pp. 105–108. In this study, forty-nine cities that faced direct competition were matched against comparable cities with electric utilities that did not have competition.

66. Ruth DeHoog, *Contracting Out for Human Services* (Albany, NY: State University of New York Press, 1984), p. 10. Critics point out that many of these studies are not actually about contracting out or pure privatization; they simply compare the cost of producing something in the public sector against a similar service in the private sector. Although such comparisons are necessary, they do not address actual contractual relationships with government or how a contractor will handle a service over time. It is assumed that contractors will behave the same when contracting with a government as they would in a competitive market. Although studies that examine the effects of privatization have generally found that privatization continued to generate savings, critics have remained skeptical. For examples of the performance of privatization over time, see Graeme Hodge, *Privatization: An International Review of Performance*.

67. See Donahue's conclusion in, *The Privatization Decision: Public Ends, Private Means*.

68. See Hodge, *Privatization: An International Review of Performance*, Chapter 10.

69. Werner Hirsch, "Contracting Out by Urban Governments," *Urban Affairs Review* 30 (January 1995), pp. 458–472. In this article, Hirsch raises concerns about the efficiency of privatization being overstated.

70. The paradigm used in privatization research on efficiency has been a microanalytical approach. That is, the focus has tended to be on specific services like garbage collection or street repair. It is assumed that any cost savings realized through private contracting will be transferred to the larger functional area or government or returned to taxpayers through some mechanism, such as lower taxes or at least slower tax increases. This assumption poses an interesting problem. Microanalyses ignore the possibility that savings might not be transferred. For example, case studies often cite examples of savings realized through private contracting, but note that few public employees lost their jobs. Although innovative programs may effectively transfer displaced public employees to other available positions, it cannot be assumed that the savings will be passed along to taxpayers. The attention accorded to examining services overshadows efforts to examine the impact on broader functional areas. Clearly, the microanalytical approach has provided insight about the efficiency of specific public services, but the need for macroanalyses also exists. Very little research has been conducted on functional areas in cities. Examining the larger effects of private contracting at the bureau level could enhance our understanding about privatization. For example, one effort to examine cities at the bureau level found very little difference in efficiency or overall cost savings

between cities that used privatization extensively and those that used very little privatization. See Robert Stein, *Urban Alternatives: Public and Private Markets in the Provision of Local Services* (Pittsburgh, PA: University of Pittsburgh Press, 1990) for a discussion about why the saving realized through privatization may not be passed along to taxpayers. Also, see Jeffrey D. Greene, "Does Privatization Make a Difference? The Impact of Private Contracting on Municipal Efficiency," *International Journal of Public Administration* 17 (1994), pp. 1299–1325. This study examines the impact of privatization at the bureau level of cities.

71. This has been examined in several serious inquiries that have recorded the incidents of various forms of privatization in the local government sector. The findings of these studies are interesting and often contrary to the expectations of privatization advocates. The International City/County Management Association (ICMA) has conducted the most in-depth series of surveys on local government privatization, although the ICMA refers to their surveys as alternative service delivery approaches. Four surveys have been conducted since 1982, which provide an excellent source for gauging the amount of privatization used by cities. Surveys were conducted in 1982, 1988, 1992, and 1997. The methodologies were similar in all of the surveys. Surveys were mailed to all cities with populations over 10,000 and to all counties with populations over 25,000. A sample was drawn (one in eight in the 1997 survey) from cities and counties with populations under 10,000. In the 1982 survey, 1,780 cities and counties responded (39 percent), while 1,681 (35 percent) responded to the 1988 survey. In 1992, the ICMA received 1,504 (31 percent) survey responses from cities and counties and in 1997 the response rate was 32 percent (1,586 responses). The ICMA surveys recorded privatization incidents for cities and counties. More cities responded than counties in all of the surveys. Generally, roughly three-fourths of the responses were from cities in the surveys. The ICMA recognizes that certain biases exist in their data due to the methodology employed. The data sets are available in various data formats for researchers and there also are a variety of publications available from the ICMA, 777 North Capitol Street, NE, Suite 5000, Washington, D.C. 20002.

Over the years, the surveys have included numerous services. For example, the 1997 survey included 62 services included within eight broad functional areas. The functional areas included in the 1997 survey were public works, public utilities, public safety, health and human services, parks and recreation, cultural and arts programs, and support functions. However, it should be noted that the methodology used by the ICMA involved sending surveys to all local governments with populations above a specified number, usually 25,000, and sending surveys to a certain percent of local governments below a specified population (below 10,000 for earlier surveys and below 25,000 for the more recent surveys). As one would suspect, the response rates were relatively low to most of the surveys. One might ask, how has the use of privatization changed among cities that responded to each survey? This method would allow one to compare the same cities across time. Chapter 3 includes a study that examined how the use of privatization increased among only the ICMA-surveyed cities that responded to surveys across a ten-year period.

72. Rowan Miranda and Karlyn Andersen, "Alternative Service Delivery in Local Government, 1982–1992," *Municipal Yearbook* (Washington, D.C.: International City/County Management Association, 1993), pp. 26–35.

73. Elaine Morley, "Patterns in the Use of Alternative Service Delivery Approaches," *Municipal Yearbook* (Washington, D.C.: International City/County Management Association, 1989), p. 40. Also, see Elaine Morley, "Local Government Use of Alternative Service Delivery Approaches," *Municipal Yearbook* (Washington, D.C.: International City/County Management Association, 1999), pp. 34–44.

74. Ibid, p. 41.

75. Elaine Morley, "Local Government Use of Alternative Service Delivery Approaches," pp. 40–42.

76. Ibid, pp. 41–43. Similar findings were also reported by Miranda and Andersen, "Alternative Service Delivery in Local Government, 1982–1992," pp. 34–44.

77. It should be noted that all forms of privatization were not included in the ICMA surveys. However, contracting was included and it is the primary form of privatization used by American local governments.

78. The Reason Foundation maintains a database about the use of privatization. Many of these examples can be accessed on their Web site at <www.reason.org>. This is also the main subject of Chapter 4.

79. For a compilation of the cost savings reported from many studies, see John Hilke, *Cost Savings from Privatization: A Compilation of Study Findings* (Los Angeles, CA: Reason Foundation, 1993). It should be mentioned that the wave of efficiency studies has run through several waves. Many studies were conducted during the 1970s, then another wave during the late 1980s. By 1994, most efficiency studies had been completed and few studies have been published in academic journals since that time.

80. Morley, "Patterns in the Use of Alternative Service Delivery Approaches," p. 41.

81. Touche Ross Company, *Privatization in America* (New York: author, 1987).

82. See Carl Valente and Lydia Manchester, *Rethinking Local Services* (Washington, D.C.: International City/County Management Association, 1984). Also, see Morley, "Patterns in the Use of Alternative Service Delivery Approaches"; Miranda and Andersen, "Alternative Service Delivery in Local Government, 1982–1992"; and Morley, "Local Government Use of Alternative Service Delivery Approaches." Also, see Mercer/Slavin, Inc. *Findings of a National Survey of Local Government Contracting Practices* (Atlanta, GA: author, 1987).

83. There are many reasons to suspect that regional patterns may exist. For example, political cultures vary and could account for differences in the use of privatization. This phenomenon will be examined in Chapter 3.

84. Touche Ross Company *Privatization in America* (New York: author, 1987). This survey was sent to 5,718 cities and counties from which 1,086 local governments (19 percent) responded.

85. Irwin David, "Privatization in America," *Municipal Yearbook* (Washington, D.C.: International City/County Management Association, 1988), pp. 43–55.

86. The results of surveys conducted by other organizations have been fairly consistent with the findings shown in the table. Several of the ICMA surveys on alternative service delivery arrangements included questions about the attitudes local officials held about privatization.

87. This chart is included in Bethany Barber, "Privatization: Not Just Garbage," *Recycling Times* (September 1998). The article is available on line at <http://www.wasteage.com>. The information was based on a survey conducted in 1998 by Orlando, Florida-based R. W. Beck (a consulting firm) that was an update to the *1996 National Privatization Survey*.

88. Privatization case studies abound in the academic literature and in the popular press. The Reason Foundation maintains a Web site that is filled with examples. It is located at <www.reason.org>. The use of privatization by cities will be further discussed in Chapter 3.

89. Ruth DeHoog, *Contracting Out for Human Services* (Albany, NY: State University of New York Press, 1984), p. 10.

90. Ibid. Also, see James Bennett and Manuel Johnson, "Public versus Private Provision of Collective Goods: Garbage Collection Revisited," *Public Choice* 34 (1979), pp. 55–64.

91. Hirsch, "Contracting Out by Urban Governments."

Examining Various Dimensions
of Municipal Privatization

The evidence on efficiency is very favorable toward privatization for most services. Thus, for the past twenty-five years economists and proponents have extolled the virtues of the superior efficiency of privatization, and academics from political scientists and public administration have countered with arguments based on concerns such as public accountability and equity for poor citizens. The efficiency issue has dominated the debate and continues to dominate most discussions about privatization.[1] Despite the widespread attention privatization has received, the concept remains as controversial as ever in the new century.

The attention given to efficiency has caused many areas to be ignored. For example, we know a lot about the relative efficiency of public and private firms performing similar tasks, but we know less about the long-term consequences of privatizing services, or the behavior of contractors over time. We know that privatization is commonly used by most local governments, but very little is known about the types of cities that tend to use privatization. Privatization is frequently offered as a remedy for fiscal stress, but even if cities save money by using privatization, will the savings be passed along to taxpayers? Or, will the city use the savings to expand other services? Although economists and privatization proponents have had much to say about efficiency, less has been said about the types of cities that use privatization. Thus, less is known about the fiscal, social, economic, political, and demographic characteristics of communities that privatize services. In particular, the political dynamics of the decision to privatize have received little attention. Numerous questions arise that indirectly pertain to the efficiency issue. For example, what makes some cities more prone to use privatization than others do? What types of cities actually use privatization? Are they generally fiscally stressed or fiscally healthy cities? Do politics really matter? Or, is the decision to privatize municipal services usually based on economics? Also, the amount of privatization used by cities can be examined further. That is, the "How Much Privatization?" question deserves more attention. This chapter examines the questions that relate to aspects of municipal privatization aside from the arguments about efficiency.

EXPLAINING VARIATIONS IN THE USE OF PRIVATIZATION

The use of privatization varies greatly among cities. For example, privatization has not been widely adopted in Asheville, North Carolina (population 62,000). After an eleven-year debate, the city privatized only part of its garbage collection.[2] Ecorse, Michigan (population 14,000) was revived from bankruptcy after privatizing virtually all of its services.[3] Phoenix, Arizona, institutionalized privatization by requiring many municipal departments to compete for contracts in a competitive bidding process against private contractors.[4] This has caused Phoenix to use publicly operated department and many private contractors to provide municipal services to control costs.

These examples represent three very different types of cities that use privatization in varying degrees. Asheville is a mid-sized, fiscally sound southern city; Ecorse is a small town located in fiscally depressed Wayne County, Michigan; and Phoenix is among the nation's largest cities situated in one of the Sunbelt's fastest-growing areas. These cities appear to share very little in common in terms of general characteristics. Thus, one might conclude that the differences in the use of privatization could be attributed to these cities dissimilar characteristics. However, even when cities appear comparable, significant differences exist in the degree that privatization is used. For example, La Mirada, California (population 44,000) either contracts out or has completely privatized most of its basic services, while nearby La Habra (population 52,000) provides most of its services through traditional publicly operated departments. Both cities are similar in size, located in the same area of southern California, and comparable fiscally. Why would two similar cities choose such radically different service-delivery arrangements? What factors make some cities more prone to use privatization than others?[5]

There are many reasons that a city might privatize its services. The response from most local officials is simple: Privatization is considered and often adopted because it saves money. But, it is doubtful that local officials want to save money just for the sake of saving money. There must be some impetus that forces them to consider privatization. Even in the world of private business, managers seldom seek to save money without some incentive. In the private sector, the incentives include having to cut costs to generate a profit for the company to keep their jobs, and prudently using resources to get a monetary reward such as a bonus. Unlike many managers of private businesses, public managers do not get an end-of-the-year bonus, although it is possible that a good management record may provide public managers with a favorable performance appraisal that enables them to get pay increases or promotion in the future. In the public sector, the budgetary process provides an incentive not to save money. Most public budgets appropriate funds to provide services for a specified amount of time, and the funds must be spent by the end of the fiscal year. Any money left over does not carry over into the next year, but is returned to the general fund. In other words, in the public sector, one either spends the money or loses it. Moreover, public managers face internal pressures from their own departments and public employee unions who tend to resist efforts to privatize services.[6] In light of these disincentives, why would public managers consider privatization?

At the municipal level, department heads work for a city manager hired by the city council, and members of the council must be elected. City council members are politicos. Most importantly, city council members generally do not like to raise taxes and privatization is often viewed as a way to maintain or even expand services without raising taxes. Pressure from a city council could provide a strong impetus to consider privatization. Of course, local officials might want to privatize to provide lucrative contracts for their friends in the private sector, a case that is probably more common than one might think.[7] Clearly, there are many reasons that appeal to common sense for considering privatization and there also are incentives to resist privatization, such as pressure from public employee unions.

Fiscal pressures likely serve as a significant impetus to privatize regardless of the cause of the financial stress. The causes of fiscal pressures can range from reductions in federal or state aid, shortages of revenue caused by economic recessions, demographic shifts in the population from city to suburbs that decrease tax revenues, or even poor city management. Local officials consider and often respond to fiscal pressures by privatizing or utilizing intergovernmental arrangements to provide services.[8] However, despite the fiscal problems associated with the 1980s, cities did not appear to adopt privatization to the degree that many believed would occur. Recall from Chapter 2 that the level of contracting with private firms, the most common form of privatization used by local governments, remained relatively stable between 1982 and 1997.[9] Why did some cities privatize many services while others did not? There are a variety of potential explanations.

The popular image of a city that turns to privatization to save money is one of an economically depressed city on the brink of fiscal disaster, such as the case of Ecorse, Michigan (the city that privatized virtually all of its services to relieve its fiscal woes). Drawing generalizations about the evidence is risky because privatization can be found in all types of cities. There are many examples like Ecorse and Orange County, California, that have used privatization to relieve fiscal stress. And there are examples of smaller, suburban cities that use privatization extensively and are not fiscally stressed, such as Lakewood, California.[10] Due to the sheer scope and size of their operations, large cities spend more money on privatization than smaller cities. For example, the private contracts to collect garbage in New York City are colossal compared to the entire budgets of most cities, but these contracts represent a small portion of New York's municipal budget. Conversely, the budget of Lakewood, California, is almost entirely used to pay for contracts. Thus, the breadth of privatization among services and the percent of the budget used to pay contractors are greater in Lakewood. The term used to refer to the breadth of privatization among services is *privatization level*.

It is plausible that certain types of cities are more likely to use privatization than others are. One explanation involves a city's location. That is, whether a city is a *central*, *suburban*, or *independent* city. The Census Bureau's system of classification includes these three major types of cities.[11] The categories are based on the geographic location of cities within standard metropolitan statistical areas (referred to as SMSAs). Central cities are the core (or primary) cities in SMSAs. Suburban cities are other cities in SMSAs (they are usually located near central cities, often literally in the suburbs) and independent cities are incorporated cities not located in SMSAs.

There are a variety of distinctions between cities related to location. Central cities generally have broad scopes of functional responsibility.[12] That is, they provide a full range of services because they tend to be large or major cities. For example, most large cities like New York City, Chicago, Atlanta, and Seattle are all classified as central cities. However, many smaller cities are also considered central cities because they are the primary city for a defined geographic area.[13] For example, Asheville, North Carolina, is classified as a central city for its SMSA because it is the primary city in western North Carolina. These cities tend to be the center of commerce and other functions such as health care and transportation (such as airports) for their area. Because they are larger and provide an expanded set of functions relative to smaller cities and towns in the area, they tend to have well-developed municipal bureaucracies that likely would oppose privatization. This could keep the use of privatization low relative to the total services provided through traditional departments. Thus, a rationale exists for finding less privatization used by central cities.[14] Although central cities often expend more money to pay for contracted services, such as collecting garbage in Chicago, privatization levels tend to be much lower in central cities regardless of their size.[15]

Conversely, suburban cities are located near central cities. The market for local services tends to be well developed in most metropolitan areas.[16] This is because many cities and communities are located near the larger city, which creates a much more concentrated population. Where large amounts of people and businesses are concentrated, more services are needed. Examples of suburban cities include Irving, Texas, in the Dallas area; Tempe, Arizona, in the Phoenix, area; Anaheim, California, which is part of the greater Los Angeles area; and, Quincy, Massachusetts, which is located in the suburbs of Boston. Because of their close proximity to central cities and the abundance of services provided by central cities, suburban cities have the luxury of choice for the way they deliver services. That is, they can provide services through their own departments, utilize intergovernmental arrangements with the central or other cities in the area, or contract with private for-profit or nonprofit firms. Thus, one finds a basis for expecting to find more privatization in suburban cities.[17] Privatization levels tend to be the highest in suburban cities.[18]

An analysis of the Lakewood Cities provides a political rationale that suggests suburban cities would have an incentive to use privatization.[19] The Lakewood Cities are a group of suburban cities that developed in the greater Los Angeles area that include many wealthy communities. The redistributive effects of municipal policies may create tensions between the wealthy and poor. Poor residents need redistributive policies, for example, various kinds of welfare services such as public housing. To avoid redistributive policies, wealthy residents may try to limit the scope of functional responsibility of their cities to minimal services. It is plausible that suburban cities, especially those with residents that have high personal incomes, would have a greater propensity toward privatization. Stated differently, wealthy communities may have a greater tendency to use privatization to ensure that they do not have to provide the whole gamut of welfare-related benefits that are provided by most central cities. In short, this is a policy of exclusion that has a similar effect to zoning, which is often intended to protect the interests of wealthier residents. Generally, privatization levels are higher in suburban cities with wealthier than average residents.[20] Moreover, many socioeconomic characteristics are encompassed in wealth. For example, wealthy residents tend to be well educated and therefore more likely to be active in the political process. They also are typically politically conservative. This seems plausible since conservatives tend to support privatization.

Independent cities can take many forms since they are not located in SMSAs, but they are usually smaller cities or towns. They often are located in more remote locations far away from metropolitan areas such as Seattle or the Bay Area of California. For example, Missoula, Montana, is classified as an independent city, although it is considered to be the center of commerce and health care for a large area of western Montana.[21] Because independent cities are more isolated and usually have fewer residents and industries, they may lack the tax base to provide the full range of services typically provided by central cities. It is possible that privatization might be more widely used by independent cities because of lack of financial resources. Currently, there is no evidence to support the belief that privatization levels are different from central or suburban cities.[22]

There are also demographic factors, such as changes in population that may affect the use of privatization. Demographic shifts can have different short- and long-term effects on cities. Tax bases tend to erode as cities lose residents and industry. Conversely, as cities gain residents and industry, tax bases increase. On a larger scale, it is well known that in the 1970s, the demographic shifts from the northeast and Midwest to the Sunbelt drained the resources of Snowbelt cities while populations and economies in the Sunbelt grew. However, these different effects may cause similar behaviors. Population growth in the South and West may have an "overload" effect, thus serving as an impetus to privatize. For example, Arizona has experienced tremendous population growth since the late 1970s and has made extensive use of privatization. In the northeast and industrial Midwest, the adverse fiscal conditions caused by population loss could also cause cities to privatize. Examples include Chicago and Indianapolis. Both cities have developed extensive privatization plans to combat fiscal problems. By the 1990s, much of the northeast and industrial Midwest had been rebuilt and was no longer considered to be the "Rust Belt." Changes in the economy and the ability of state and local officials to attract new industries to their area helped these two regions recover and once again prosper. But privatization was widely used during the hard times for these areas despite the presence of powerful public-employee unions.[23] Privatization levels appear to be higher in cities located in areas with rapidly growing populations, such as Sunbelt states like Arizona, or, in areas where the population grew rapidly during the past few decades, like California.[24] There appears to be little difference in the fiscal health of cities that make extensive use of privatization and cities that use very little privatization.[25] For example, cities with very low levels of privatization are often equally as fiscally healthy as cities with very high levels of privatization. However, central cities tend to have the lowest levels of privatization while suburban cities use the most privatization.[26] (These explanations were incorporated into several studies that are summarized in Appendices C and D).[27]

Of course, there are other ways to classify and examine cities aside from central versus suburban, or based solely on fiscal matters. Since privatization is as much a political issue as it is an economic issue, classifications that incorporate politics would be helpful. Thus, we will turn our attention toward the local-level orientations of cities.

FACTORS AFFECTING THE PRIVATIZATION DECISION

What types of cities use privatization? Cities can be examined that are classified on the basis of two critical factors that likely affect the decision to privatize services: fiscal stress and politics. The fiscal environment (a city's balance between the taxes it collects and the services it provides) is one critical element for understanding the orientation of a city. Equally important is the political environment (the political realities in which city government operates).

FISCAL ENVIRONMENT

Tax and service levels of cities operate within an established equilibrium.[28] All cities have to balance their services and tax efforts within a political and social environment that is unique to each city. Fiscal systems are structured within a wide variety of constraints such as the demand for services, the level of political participation, and politically acceptable tax limits. Cities strive to attain a balance between services and taxes. This balance is not guided solely by economics, but is determined in a political process.

A tax-service imbalance (disequilibrium) occurs when the quality of services declines, when the cost of service delivery increases, or when perceived opportunities for more efficient and/or higher quality service delivery is present. Simply stated, when tax and service levels get out of balance, fiscal stress occurs. When a city's fiscal system no longer delivers an acceptable quantity and/or quality of services at a politically acceptable price, officials must find a way to balance taxes and services. Officials may respond to fiscal problems in a variety of ways. They can raise taxes to pay for services, cut service levels, or even privatize. But they must remain within the acceptable boundaries of a tax-service equilibrium that is constrained by both the fiscal system and the political environment.[29]

POLITICAL ENVIRONMENT

Fiscal pressures alone may not be enough to cause a city to actually privatize a service. The decision may be complicated by other factors that are part of the unique economic, political, and social environment of a city. Although officials have the authority to claim resources, such as taxes, to maintain service levels, theory suggests that there are inherent forces that encourage the development of revenue and expenditure structures that are in line with competing cities.[30] The presence of other cities and demands of the residents of a city are constraints that likely affect the decision to privatize.

A general understanding of a hierarchical order of cities is important here. The idea that a hierarchy of cities exists is based on the belief that cities within a specified region specialize in producing goods and services for that region. Cities with the most economic diversification tend to be dominant. Each region has a primary city, a city that is more economically diversified and functionally superior to all other cities in the region.[31] The pattern resembles a hierarchical pyramid. Some cities are functionally equal to other cities. That is, they occupy the same place within the hierarchy. They are subordinate to some cities and superior to others. Is such a concept real, or just something applicable to the classroom at universities? The fact is that this idea is very real and research has found that city officials are very aware of where their city fits into this hierarchy.[32] For example, in the southeast, Atlanta is considered to be the dominant city. Nearby Charlotte, North Carolina, and Nashville, Tennessee, are major cities, but neither is considered the primary city for the region. Of course, there are a number of major cities in the southeast that fall under Atlanta in the hierarchy. Smaller cities, such as Asheville, North Carolina, fall under Charlotte, which in turn, falls under Atlanta, and so on.

The concept of a system of cities is important because of its impact on the market for local services. It is believed that cities face competition with other cities to attract residents and industry.[33] As is the case with any market, there are buyers (residents and industry) and sellers (local governments). This market contains *voice* (or input) mechanisms through the political process, which is the ability to participate through political mechanisms and structures, such as city council meetings. It also contains an *exit* mechanism, which is the option of buyers to relocate to other jurisdictions. There is ample evidence of residents, and particularly industry, relocating to other jurisdictions. For example, during the 1970s numerous industries left northeastern cities and moved to Sunbelt states because of lower taxes and a more favorable labor climate. The twentieth century has a long history of residents of cities fleeing to the suburbs, partly to escape high taxation. This type of exodus has contributed to fiscal stress, which causes cities to consider alternative service delivery methods to control costs. For example, the powerful northeast and industrial Midwest was referred to as the Rust Belt by the end of the 1970s (although aggressive economic development helped remove the nickname by the early 1990s). Privatization is important in the market for local services because it may enable a city to offer a more attractive tax-service mix by controlling or even lowering costs. If privatizing a service reduces operating costs, the tax-service mix becomes a better value for those either already living in the city or those interested in relocating to the city. Privatization could enable a city to maintain its tax-service equilibrium or gain a competitive advantage over cities that use less efficient methods for delivering services.[34] In short, lower taxes coupled with services (such as education and protection from crime) are often a critical advantage for attracting residents and industry to an area.

A variety of factors can affect the service-delivery arrangements used by cities (see Figure 3.1 on page 74).[35] The illustration is relatively simple and straightforward. Service-delivery arrangements (whether a city uses its own publicly operated department or some form of privatization to deliver services) are influenced by the political-economic system (the combination of politics, such as the conservative or liberal characteristics of residents, and the economic condition and realities of the area). Communities can vary greatly in politics and economic circumstance. A community can be a conservative, retirement-oriented city, like many cities in Florida, or it can be a progressive-liberal-oriented city like many "college towns," such as Missoula, Montana.[36] Local economies also vary greatly. Some cities are located in booming areas, such as San Jose in the Silicon Valley in California or the Research Triangle area in North Carolina (the Raleigh-Durham-Greensboro area, which

FIGURE 3.1   TRIGGERING MUNICIPAL PRIVATIZATION

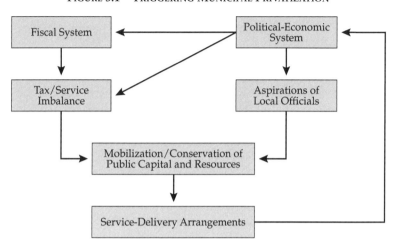

Source: Adapted from Ann Bowman and Michael Pagano, "City Intervention: An Analysis of the Public Capital Mobilization Process," *Urban Affairs Quarterly* 27 (March 1992), pp. 356–374.

also includes Chapel Hill). The fiscal system is a separate system that is influenced greatly by the economics of the city. It is comprised of such things as the budgetary process, and city finances, including revenue system (taxes), debt, and assets. The fiscal system must finance and maintain the tax-service balance (the level, quality, and quantity of services). The tax-service balance is often difficult to maintain during fiscally stressed times. Intervening are the aspirations and motivations of local officials, who seek to manage and provide direction for the city. The aspirations of local officials reflect the politics of the city. That is, their aspirations must be in tune with the will of the residents who ultimately pay for services through taxation and other costs associated with living in the city. But people run cities, and local officials sometimes have their own political and personal agendas to fulfill. The influence of local officials is a critical factor in public-policy matters of city government. After all, they are ultimately responsible for managing the city and providing leadership and direction for the future. And officials are a key part of the public-policy process. Their importance cannot be overstated here. All of these factors influence the use of public capital for services, and in turn, affect the type of service-delivery methods used by a city.

The system shown in Figure 3.1 produces two primary factors. The first factor, as discussed earlier, involves fiscal pressures that can threaten a city's revenue system and disrupt the tax-service balance. This causes officials to search for ways to adjust the imbalance. Efforts to adjust the imbalance are influenced by the political-economic system. For example, some cities, like conservative Naples, Florida, have long enjoyed the luxury of an economically advantaged area with wealthy residents. Santa Barbara, California, is another city that has enjoyed the ability to control growth and manage its tax-service mix as it sees fit because of the city's fortunate economic circumstances. Although taxes and services have to be managed appropriately in cities like Naples and Santa Barbara, officials have the advantage of resources and a strong tax base. Not all cities enjoy these economic advantages. Beaumont, Texas, is a city that prospered during the oil boom of the 1970s, but was plagued with fiscal problems after the oil boom was over.

The second factor, also discussed earlier, is politics. The politics of a city can be reflected in the aspirations of its city officials, including their aspirations regarding the position of their city in the relevant system of cities. This often involves their aspirations about economic development to help retain or enhance a city's status. As noted above, the aspirations of officials are checked by the political-economic system. That is, officials are constrained from guiding the city in a direction that is not acceptable to its citizens. Charlotte, North Carolina, is one example. After many years of rapid growth and astounding economic development, surveys began to indicate that citizens had seen enough urban sprawl and growth. In Missoula, Montana, citizens approved millions of dollars in bonds to buy up the open space around the city to control the city's growth. City officials must take action that is politically palatable to citizens regarding the appropriate balance of a variety of concerns such as efficiency, equity, and public accountability. In the case of Missoula, a mayor would likely be defeated in the next election if he or she tried to implement an economic development plan that ran counter to the desires of the city's residents. Research has confirmed politics to be a significant part of economic development and growth for a city, and that the political environment creates a character that is unique for a city.[37] Moreover, local officials are very aware of the position of their city among other relevant cities. For example, cities in the northwest are very aware of the dominance of Seattle, and cities in the Midwest are very aware of the dominance of Chicago and St. Louis.[38] These two factors produce four city-level orientations: survivalist, market, expansionist, and maintenance.[39] Privatization levels vary significantly among the four city-level orientations.[40]

CITY ORIENTATIONS AND PRIVATIZATION: TRIGGER MECHANISMS

The decision to privatize probably occurs in response to trigger mechanisms such as fiscal pressure (see Table 3.1 on page 76). Fiscal stress is present in survivalist cities and serves as the primary trigger mechanism. Mainly concerned with recouping losses, officials intervene and take whatever action necessary to survive. The political mode of these cities is likely one of panic or anxiety. These cities are likely to consider privatization for some services. Survivalist cities are not concerned with moving to a higher plane. Market cities are also fiscally stressed and not motivated to move to a higher plane among their system of

TABLE 3.1   CITY ORIENTATIONS AND PRIVATIZATION[41]

ORIENTATIONS	TRIGGER MECHANISMS
Survivalist Orientation	Fiscal stress and/or tax-service imbalance is present. Aspiration to conserve resources or recoup losses. Willing to use whatever techniques necessary to survive. Likely to use privatization. Fiscal Stress: High Activism: High
Market Orientation	Fiscal stress and/or tax-service imbalance is present. Aspiration to conserve resources. Favors the use of market forces. Likely to have high levels of privatization. Fiscal Stress: High Activism: Low
Expansionist Orientation	No fiscal stress or tax-service imbalance. Aspiration to move to higher plane among relevant cities. Not likely to have as high of levels of privatization as other typologies. Fiscal Stress: Low Activism: High
Maintenance Orientation	No fiscal stress or tax-service imbalance. No aspiration to move to higher plane among relevant cities. Takes only the action necessary to maintain its current status. Levels of privatization likely to vary. Fiscal Stress: Low Activism: Low

Source: The city-level orientations were developed by Ann Bowman and Michael Pagano in "City Interven-tion: An Analysis of the Public Capital Mobilization Process," *Urban Affairs Quarterly* 27 (March 1992), pp. 356–374.

cities. Officials take a "hands-off" approach and prefer using the private sec-tor as much as possible. Because they tend to favor market forces, market cities would likely have high levels of privatization.[42] The desire to move to a high-er plane among relevant cities is the trigger for expansionist cities. Since they are fiscally healthy and have strong local economies, expansionist cities enjoy the economic luxuries associated with growth. Expansionist cities would not have a strong incentive to privatize services because of their favorable eco-nomic circumstance. Thus, privatization levels are likely to be low. The trigger mechanism for maintenance cities is the desire to maintain the city's position within the system of cities. Although maintenance cities are not fiscally stressed, their aspiration to maintain their city's position would allow privatization levels to vary. Officials would likely privatize some services to ensure the city did not lose ground among its relevant cities.[43]

Do privatization levels vary among these distinct types of cities? (See Tables 3.2 and 3.3.) Distinct differences appear to exist between expansionist cities and the other types.[44]

Market cities had the highest levels of privatization (34.8 percent). These cities are fiscally stressed and are not concerned with moving to a higher plane among relevant cities. The high privatization levels are not surprising considering market cities' discernible preference to use private markets. This also suggests that fiscal stress is *not* the only factor. Market cities prefer to take a "hands-off" approach in economic development, which is reflected in their low economic activism scores. It appears that this preference carries over into service delivery. It is interesting that market cities have significantly higher levels of privatization than survivalist cities, which are also fiscally stressed, but very active in economic development. This suggests that the orientation of market cities (a preference to use private markets) is important in their decision to privatize. However, it should also be recognized that market cities and survivalist cities are both fiscally stressed and have the highest levels of privatization.

TABLE 3.2   PRIVATIZATION LEVELS COMPARED

ORIENTATION	PRIVATIZATION LEVEL	CASES (318 CITIES)
Expansionist	13.6	50
Market	34.8	61
Maintenance	29.4	115
Survivalist	27.4	92

Source: Jeffrey D. Greene, "City Orientations and Privatization," *Southeastern Political Review* 25 (June 1997), pp. 339–352.

TABLE 3.3   COMPARING PRIVATIZATION LEVELS IN CITY ORIENTATIONS

CITY ORIENTATION	EXPANSIONIST	MARKET	MAINTENANCE	SURVIVALIST
Expansionist	n/a	Yes	Yes	Yes
Market	Yes	n/a	Yes	Yes
Maintenance	Yes	Yes	n/a	No
Survivalist	Yes	Yes	No	n/a

Note: YES indicates that the use of privatization is significantly different; NO indicates that the use of privatization is not significantly different between the cities compared in the matrix. (Table 3.2 contains the privatization levels for the four city orientations). The test used to determine whether differences exist was a one-factor, randomized analysis of the variance (ANOVA). See Jeffrey D. Greene, "City Orientations and Privatization," *Southeastern Political Review* 25 (June 1997), pp. 339–352.

The lowest levels of privatization are found in expansionist cities (13.5 percent). Expansionist cities are fiscally healthy, are experiencing economic growth, and seek to move to a higher plane within their system of cities. These cities have both the economic resources and political will to enhance the status of their cities. The incentive to privatize is likely to be weak due to favorable financial circumstances. Thus, it is not surprising to find low privatization levels in expansionist cities. Expansionist cities use significantly less privatization than maintenance cities, which are also fiscally healthy, but concerned with maintaining their city's position in the system of cities. It is not surprising to find lower levels of privatization in expansionist cities than cities experiencing fiscal stress (market and survivalist cities).

It is interesting that the use of privatization is comparable in survivalist and maintenance cities (29.4 percent and 27.3 percent respectively) because the scenarios are opposite. Maintenance cities are not fiscally stressed and seek to maintain their city's position among relevant cities while survivalist cities are fiscally stressed and take whatever action is necessary to survive. Comparing survivalist and maintenance cities illustrates the difficulty of associating privatization solely with fiscal stress. This finding implies that fiscal stress alone may not cause a city to privatize services. The decision is likely complicated by politics. However, although one would expect the incentive to privatize to be higher in survivalist cities than in maintenance cities, there is no reason to expect the use of privatization to be low in maintenance cities. The orientation for maintenance cities suggests that officials might privatize services to maintain a city's position. Since this only focuses on a single snapshot in time, it is not possible to know what the orientation of a city was in the past. It should be noted that the orientations of cities could change due to environmental conditions. For example, a survivalist city may become a maintenance city after its fiscal condition stabilizes. It is likely that considerable movement occurs in the larger universe of cities between these two orientations.

Thus, we have another method to examine variations in the privatization levels of cities. The orientations provide four distinct patterns of behavior that incorporate fiscal conditions and politics. With only one exception, the use of privatization varied significantly between the orientations. The highest levels of privatization were found in cities exhibiting the market orientation—fiscally stressed cities that have a discernible preference for using private markets. Privatization levels are significantly higher in market cities than in the other three orientations. The lowest levels of privatization were found in expansionist cities—cities that are fiscally healthy and driven to enhance the prestige of their cities in the larger system of cities. The use of privatization was significantly lower in expansionist cities than in the other three orientations. The only comparison in which the use of privatization was comparable was between the survivalist and maintenance orientations.

The decision to privatize services is complex. Local officials considering privatization face a paradox. They must balance the laudable goal of cost-efficiency with other important concerns such as equity and public accountability within a political environment. The decision to privatize services is likely affected by the local environment. Fiscal stress is often believed to be the primary determinant of privatization but evidence suggests that local-level orientations may go further in explaining how much privatization a city uses. Comparing city orientations and privatization levels illustrates that fiscal stress may not be the only factor.

THE USE OF PRIVATIZATION BY CITIES REVISITED

Are cities using more privatization than in the past? Popular discussions about privatization lead one to believe that there has been a surge in the use of various forms of privatization. Newspapers often contain stories about cities experimenting with privatization in a wide range of services. Recall from Chapter 2 that some evidence suggests that the use of privatization has stabilized. Although the use of privatization is widespread and has increased since the 1970s,[45] the rate at which privatization is growing remains questionable. Thus, two questions emerge:[46] Has the use of privatization by cities actually increased?[47] If so, by how much has the use of privatization increased?[48] (See Table 3.4; also see Appendix E for a listing of individual services.)

In 1982, the average privatization level for cities (a term that refers to the breadth of privatization among services) was 12.9 percent of services.[49] By 1992, the average privatization level had increased to almost 28 percent, which is an increase of 121 percent. Regional comparisons reveal that the largest increase in privatization levels occurred in cities located in the South, which experienced a 158 percent increase. During this period, the South, like many areas in the Sunbelt, was experiencing tremendous economic and population growth. The smallest increase in the use of privatization was in the heavily unionized cities of the northeast. Clearly, the use of privatization appears to

TABLE 3.4   THE USE OF PRIVATIZATION COMPARED, 1982 AND 1992

LOCATION OF CITIES	CASES	PRIVATIZATION LEVELS (1982)	PRIVATIZATION LEVELS (1992)	SIGNIFICANT DIFFERENCE
All Cities	596	12.9	27.8	Yes
North	90	15.2	24.9	Yes
South	187	10.1	26.9	Yes
Midwest	164	12.2	28.2	Yes
West	155	14.8	29.9	Yes

Note: Privatization levels are based on responses to two International City/County Management Association (ICMA) surveys. The scores are shown as means (averages). Scores are based on the percentage of ICMA-surveyed functions in which a city used private service delivery arrangements. The scores are intended to reflect the breadth of privatization among services. See Jeffrey D. Greene, "City Orientations and Privatization," *Southeastern Political Review* 25 (June 1997), pp. 339–352.

TABLE 3.5   PRIVATIZATION DIVERSITY LEVELS COMPARED, 1982 AND 1992

LOCATION OF CITIES	CASES	PRIVATIZATION DIVERSITY 1982	PRIVATIZATION DIVERSITY 1992	SIGNIFICANT DIFFERENCE
All Cities	596	13.9	19.4	Yes
North	90	16.2	17.2	No
South	187	11.9	18.6	Yes
Midwest	164	13.2	20.0	Yes
West	155	19.7	21.0	Yes

Note: The diversity scores are reflected as the mean percentage of different privatization methods a city used within services. The types of privatization included in the scores were: contracting with private for-profit or nonprofit organizations, volunteers, self-help, franchising, and voucher systems. The International City/County Management Association surveys were modified to enable comparison. Privatization diversity refers to the use of various forms of privatization within services. See Jeffrey D. Greene, "How Much Privatization? An Analysis of the Use of Privatization by Cities in 1982 and 1992," *Policy Studies Journal* 24 (winter 1996), pp. 632–640.

have increased. Similar results are illustrated in Table 3.5, which uses a different measure of privatization. These cities appear to be using more types of privatization to provide services than in the past.[50] The increased use of privatization is also supported by numerous case studies that have been collected over the years.[51]

What do these figures mean? Over a ten-year period, cities experienced significant increases in the use of privatization using two separate ways to measure privatization. Privatization increased in both measures: the breadth of privatization among services (*privatization levels*) and the use of various types of privatization within services (*privatization diversity levels*). The larger implications suggest that privatization may be here to stay. In services in which the use of privatization was high in 1982, the use of privatization was still high ten years later. In services in which privatization was not widely used in 1982, the use of privatization had increased by 1992.[52] (See Appendix E for details about individual services.)

THE USE OF PRIVATIZATION IN A LARGE, RURAL, WESTERN STATE: THE CASE OF MONTANA

How do large rural states compare to the rest of the nation?[53] Montana is an interesting case. It is a rural, geographically large, western state with a political culture that is very resistant to higher taxes and efforts to increase the size and scope of government. In November 1998, Montana's voters passed Constitutional Initiative 75 (CI-75). The initiative required that voters approve *all* tax increases. In an unpredicted turn of events, the Montana Supreme Court overturned CI-75 in February 1999. However, resistance to taxation is simply part of Montana's political culture and another version of CI-75 may appear

on the ballot in the near future. This type of political culture makes political forces in Montana propitious to the concept of privatization. Montana's
Republican-controlled state government views privatization as a way to reduce state expenditures. The state has experimented boldly with privatization.
It has privatized part of its welfare system, health care system, prisons, and
even discussed privatizing its public university system.[54] Despite rapid growth
in the western part of the state, Montana continues to experience budgetary
shortfalls at the state and local level. It is one of only five states without a general sales tax and its statewide tax base is relatively small. Considering Montana's fiscal dilemmas and an apparent predisposition toward privatization,
one would expect the use of privatization to be common in Montana.

Table 3.6 compares the aggregate levels of privatization of Montana's local
governments with those surveyed by the International City/County Management Association (ICMA). The average privatization level was 31 percent
for Montana's cities and nearly 34 percent for counties. Privatization levels
are higher in Montana than national averages.[55] One can conclude that Montana's local governments use more privatization than the national sample of
cities and counties surveyed by the ICMA.[56]

It is possible that privatization is even greater than the data indicates.
Much of the growth in western Montana has been in counties. Montana's
counties are weak political entities whose powers are severely restricted by the
constitution and state law. Restrictions imposed by the state affect service provision. The growth in suburbs located in counties has caused a unique problem. By law, the cities cannot provide services outside their jurisdictional
boundaries. Counties cannot provide services because of restrictions imposed
by law. Thus, developers and citizens must take care of the service. For example, private water provision is common throughout Montana. This type of
development has created pressures for what might be thought of as *virtual
privatization*. That is, markets must provide services that are usually provided by governments because of restrictions imposed by law. These services
would otherwise be unavailable for residents. The weak authority of counties
is reflective of Montana's political culture and tradition.

TABLE 3.6   PRIVATIZATION LEVELS IN MONTANA'S
LOCAL GOVERNMENTS VERSUS NATIONAL AVERAGES

MONTANA CITIES	NATIONAL CITIES	DIFFERENCE	MONTANA COUNTIES	NATIONAL COUNTIES	DIFFERENCE
N=131	N=1220		N=43	N=284	
31.0	26.8	16.0%	33.8	24.8	36.2%

Note: All of the comparisons are statistically significant

Source: Jeffrey D. Greene, "Privatization Popular among Local Governments," *Montana Business Quarterly*
37, no. 4 (winter 1999), pp. 17–20.

HOW DO MONTANA'S CITIES, TOWNS,
AND COUNTIES PROVIDE SERVICES?

The most common form of service-delivery method used was by government employees for all categories. The second most common response was contracting with other governments. Despite the widespread use of privatization in Montana, public employees provide most public services. In the case of Montana, this may be attributable to the lack of economies of scale. Most towns are small, scattered geographically, and situated in rural areas. Services are limited and perhaps manageable by small, public workforces. The fact that privatization is not widely used in support functions provides support for this theory. Support functions are services in which privatization has been widely utilized nationally.

The form of privatization used most often by Montana's local governments is private contracting (see Table 3.7), which is the most popular form of privatization for local governments nationwide. The second most commonly used form of privatization is included within the "Other ASDA" category, self-help. This is not particularly surprising, considering that many of Montana's communities are relatively rural and remote. Thus, residents often are responsible for handling certain services, such as disposing of their own garbage. Most alternative service delivery arrangements, such as subsidies, volunteers, and franchises, were not widely used by Montana's local governments.

Privatization is widely included in the management portfolios of Montana's local governments. Local governments in Montana use a *mix* of service delivery arrangements, which includes various forms of privatization. As

TABLE 3.7   HOW SERVICES ARE PROVIDED BY CATEGORY
FOR MONTANA COUNTIES AND CITIES

SERVICE CATEGORY	GOVT. EMPLOYEES	CONTRACT W/GOVT.	CONTRACT W/PRIVATE	FRANCHISE	OTHER ASDAS
Public Works	67%	16%	20%	12%	16%
Pubic Utilities	56	10	20	16	15
Public Safety	52	22	7	7	18
Cultural and Arts	50	41	17	5	28
Health & Human Services	27	37	14	3	32
Parks & Recreation	74	20	14	5	7
Support Services	67	32	26	8	13

Note: The responses reflect the average percentage of local governments that used the service delivery method by category. The percentages shown will not equal 100 percent because more than one response is possible. "Other ASDAs" refers to Alternative Service Delivery Arrangements such as self-help and subsidies.
Source: Jeffrey D. Greene, "Privatization Popular among Local Governments," *Montana Business Quarterly* 37, no. 4 (winter 1999), pp. 17–20.

Montana continues to grow, it will be interesting to see which methods local governments adopt to meet increased service demands. Privatization is not a panacea, even in states like Montana with political cultures favorable toward privatizing services. In March 1999, Montana's legislature—which has tended to favor privatization in the past—cancelled a $400 million contract with the private health care corporation that handled its statewide mental health care for failing to meet performance standards (a topic that will be discussed in Chapter 4). Despite examples of the shortcomings of privatization, it is a practice that is not likely to fade. Interest in privatization in Montana and elsewhere will likely continue as long as fiscal pressures persist for local governments.

SUMMARY

The discussion in this chapter offers a different perspective about privatization from the traditional arguments about efficiency. Several questions about various dimensions of municipal privatization were presented. First, privatization levels vary greatly among cities. A variety of potential explanations were explored that include fiscal, demographic, economic, and political factors. Although fiscal pressure is probably the most significant determinant of privatization, the pattern of privatization appears to be that wealthy, suburban, fiscally healthy cities use the most privatization. This is attributed to the conservatism of suburbia, the political characteristics of wealthy residents, and the convenient location of suburban cities to larger cities that provide a full range of services. It is well known that the market for local services is well developed in most metropolitan areas, which enables suburban cities a greater selection of ways to provide their services. Moreover, privatization levels appear to be greater in Sunbelt states, including the West, that are experiencing population increases. This is attributed partly to the "overload effect," which strains local resources as more residents place demands on schools, infrastructure, such as water and sewerage systems, and police and fire protection. Growth brings many enhancements to the quality of life for an area, but it also brings the need for expanding services to handle such changes as increases in crime and residential garbage. In addition to fiscal stress, certain demographic factors go further to explain the use of privatization.

Local level, city orientations were also examined. Cities that had a preference for using the market in other policy areas appear to use more privatization than other types of cities. The two orientations with the most fiscal stress had the highest privatization levels: market and survivalist cities. Clearly, the local orientations of cities are important, and the role of politics is likely a major factor in the decision to privatize services.

Privatization is a complex and prominent issue for local governments. Privatization is often viewed as a tool that can provide public services more cost-efficiently. It is reasonable to suspect that cities are turning to privatization to take advantage of the lower costs associated with private production of services, and that privatization may be a permanent component of the municipal landscape. It is also likely that politics is coupled with economics in determining whether to privatize services. Cities across America continue to search for management strategies useful for accomplishing their responsibilities and programs and privatization appears to be widely included in the management portfolios of cities. In the next chapter, the successes, failures, and politics of municipal privatization will be examined.

NOTES

1. It should be noted that the evidence has been so convincing to economists that few efficiency studies have been conducted since the mid-1990s. A consensus exists among most economists that privatization is more efficient for most services.
2. Paul Clark, "City Garbage May Be Privatized," *Asheville Citizen-Times*, 3 February 1993, p. A-1. As of this writing, local officials at the city of Asheville have resisted efforts to privatize service. Asheville remains virtually a full-service city (as described in the idealized models discussed in Chapter 1).
3. Fred Barnes, "The City That Privatized Everything," *Wall Street Journal*, 17 May 1993, p. A-9. It should be noted that Ecorse was placed in bankruptcy by a state court and was involved in a variety of suits, including one from its own employees over the city's pension system. The court appointed someone to oversee the city's management and financial matters to try to pull it out of bankruptcy. The city literally privatized most services and erased its $4 million debt within four years.
4. Randall Fitzgerald, *When Government Goes Private* (New York: Universe Books, 1988), pp. 59–61. Phoenix has long been used as an example of successful privatization and for years has forced many of its departments to bid for contracts against private companies. Generally, this process has worked well for the city.
5. Although the efficiency issue usually dominates discussions about privatization, other issues have caught the attention of researchers. Researchers have examined a variety of factors in an effort to explain variations in the use of privatization at the municipal level. Most inquiries have focused on contracting. Researchers have examined the effect intergovernmental revenues and fiscal conditions have on the incidence of contracting. Others have sought political explanations such as the impact of interest groups, public employee unions, and political conflicts between the wealthy and poor. See Paul Courant, Edward Gramlich and Daniel Rubinfield, "Tax Limitations and the Demand for Public Services," *National Tax Journal* 32 (1979), pp. 147–159; Robert McGuire and Robert Ohnsfelt, "Public versus Private Water Delivery: A Critical Analysis of a Hedonic Cost Approach," *Public Finance Quarterly* (July 1986), pp. 339–350; and Gary Miller, *City by Contract* (Cambridge, MA: MIT Press, 1981). Empirical studies have revealed that significant relationships exist between the incidence of contracting and population size, market conditions, public employment, local fiscal conditions, and state-local relations. See James Ferris, "The Decision to Contract Out," *Urban Affairs Quarterly* 22 (1986), pp. 289–311; James Ferris and Elizabeth Graddy, "Contracting Out: For What? With

Whom?" *Public Administration Review* 46 (1986), pp. 332–345; David Morgan and Michael Hirlinger, "Intergovernmental Service Contracts: A Multivariate Explanation," *Urban Affairs Quarterly* 27 (1991), pp. 128–144; David Morgan, Michael Hirlinger, and Robert England "The Decision to Contract Out City Services: A Further Explanation," *Western Political Quarterly* 41 (1988), pp. 363–373; and P. E. Mouritzen and K. H. Nielsen, *Handbook of Urban Fiscal Data* (Odense, Denmark: Odense University, 1988). These same studies also suggest that form of government and dependence on intergovernmental revenue is not significantly related to the amount of private contracting used by cities. Researchers have also demonstrated that the diversity of a city's service delivery arrangement is related to its scope of functional responsibility and to factors such as the age of the city. See Robert Stein, *Urban Alternatives: Public and Private Markets in the Provision of Local Services* (Pittsburgh, PA: University of Pittsburgh Press, 1990).

6. One of the largest unions that represent municipal employees is the American Federation of State, County, and Municipal Employees. Their Web site clearly states the position held by most public employee unions and is located at <http://www.afscme.org>.

7. Providing lucrative city contracts to friends and associates has long been one of the concerns raised by public employee unions. And, they have a long history of examples to illustrate their concerns. Cozy relationships can easily develop between those awarding contracts and those receiving contracts. For example, see John Hanrahan's critique of Albany, New York, in *Government for Sale: Contracting Out: The New Patronage* (Washington, D.C.: American Federation of State, County, and Municipal Employees, 1977).

8. See David Morgan, Michael Hirlinger, and Robert England, "The Decision to Contract Out City Services: A Further Explanation," pp. 363–373; and P. E. Mouritzen and K. H. Nielsen, *Handbook of Urban Fiscal Data*, Chapter 1.

9. Elaine Morley, "Local Government Use of Alternative Service Delivery Approaches," *Municipal Yearbook* (Washington, D.C.: International City/County Management Association, 1999), pp. 34–44.

10. Ibid.

11. This system is called *Metropolitan Status*. It indicates a city's status vis-à-vis standard metropolitan statistical areas (SMSAs). Central cities are the core cities in SMSAs; suburban cities are other cities in SMSAs; and independent cities are incorporated cities not located in SMSAs.

12. For an excellent analysis of the functional roles and differences among cities, see Ronald Liebert, *Disintegration and Political Action: The Changing Function of City Governments in America* (New York: Academic Press, 1976); and R. D. Norton, *City Life Cycles and American Urban Policy* (New York: Academic Press, 1979).

13. The term *primary city* comes from urban economics and has a distinct definition in what is known as the *hierarchy of cities*. This will be discussed later in the chapter.

14. There are many ways to measure or gauge the amount of privatization being used by a city. The point here is not referring to the amount of money expended for contracts. Clearly, a large city could privatize its garbage collection and spend more money than a smaller city that used privatization to deliver most of its services.

15. See Appendix C for summaries of studies that have examined the effect of location.

16. Mark Schneider, *The Competitive City* (Pittsburgh, PA: University of Pittsburgh Press, 1989).

17. The use of privatization is not necessarily connected to the dollar value of contracts. For example, one contract in a large city like Chicago or New York could be worth more than the total dollar amount to provide all the services more a small- or medium-sized city or town. There are several ways to define and measure privatization. Here the reference to "more privatization" refers to using privatization to provide a portion of public services relative to portion where public employees are used.
18. See Appendices D and E for summaries of studies that have examined the effect of location.
19. See Miller, *City by Contract*.
20. See Appendix C for summaries of studies that have examined the effect of wealth and the use of privatization.
21. Independent cities are unique, but generally are found in large, rural areas. Montana is a good example because there are no large cities or metropolitan areas in the state. For example, Missoula is the fourth largest city in the state with a population of 60,000.
22. The studies included in Appendices D and E did not include enough independent cities to draw conclusions.
23. For a discussion about the findings on regional patterns of privatization, see Elaine Morley, "Patterns in the Use of Alternative Service Delivery Approaches," *Municipal Yearbook* (Washington, D.C.: International City/County Management Association, 1989), pp. 33–44. Largely due to the influence of Proposition 13, privatization is often associated with the West. Privatization is also associated with younger, postindustrial cities, which are mainly found in the West. However, no consistent regional patterns have emerged thus far. However, the mixed findings do not exclude the importance of region. The effect of political culture, for example, continues to make region a potential factor that cannot be overlooked.
24. See Appendices D and E.
25. The summaries included in Appendix D appear to confirm this. In these studies, cities with the lowest levels of privatization were compared to cities with the highest levels of privatization and no significant differences were found in their fiscal health.
26. The summaries provided in Appendices D and E provide some insight into the relationship among factors that may affect the use of privatization. The findings come from a conference paper prepared by the author for use in this book and from published articles. See, Jeffrey D. Greene, "Cities and Privatization: Re-Examining the Effect of Fiscal Stress, Location, and Wealth in American Cities." The paper was presented at the Annual Meeting of the Southern Political Science Association, November 6, 1999, in Savannah, Georgia. This study essentially replicated an older study using newer data, which was also conducted by the author. See Jeffrey D. Greene, "Cities and Privatization: Examining the Effect of Fiscal Stress, Wealth, and Location in Mid-Sized Cities," *Policy Studies Journal* 24 (spring 1996), pp. 135–144.

It is worth mentioning the methodology employed, which was nearly identical for all of the studies. The 1992 findings come from a study that used the 1,220 cities that responded to a 1992 International City/County Management Association (ICMA) survey on privatization. Cities from all ranges of population, location, and types (i.e., central, suburban, and independent) were included. The findings are compared to the results from a study of a 1988 ICMA survey on privatization conducted by the author. In that study, 188 cities were selected from the 1988 ICMA survey, but were limited to medium-sized cities (defined as cities with populations ranging from 45,000 to 150,000). All major regions were represented in both data sets. Although the use of privatization was higher in western cities, it should be stressed that the source of data were studies conducted by the ICMA. The differences in findings about region have more to do with the indicators used to gauge privatization. The ICMA did not find significant regional differences. It is not possible to conclude that privatization is higher in the West than in other regions based solely on this data. It is more significant to note that region was found not to be a significant factor in either of these inquiries, which is consistent with most other studies.

See the summaries provided in Appendix C. Some might argue that the term *privatization levels* excludes large cities by definition, while in fact, large cities use privatization on a scale that cannot be matched by smaller cities. While large cities expend tremendous sums of money on private contracting, municipal employees, through municipal departments, provide the majority of their services. Privatization is secondary in most large cities to the tasks performed by public employees through well-established municipal bureaucracies. Most of the studies included in Appendix C included many large cities and found that the breadth of privatization among services was much smaller. That is, the percentage of a service performed by private firms was much smaller in large cities.

27. Evidence suggests that fiscal stress and privatization tends to be negatively related. That is, as the use of privatization increases, the magnitude of fiscal stress decreases. The implication suggests that increasing the use of privatization might reduce fiscal stress. Although it is possible that privatization reduces fiscal pressure, it is also possible that the lack of fiscal stress may promote privatization. That is, cities that are successful at cutting costs may have a greater tendency to use privatization. Fiscally stressed cities may have too many difficulties coping with their existing situation to introduce a substantial policy change like privatization. However, cities with the lowest use of privatization appear to be no more fiscally stressed than cities with the highest levels of privatization. This suggests that cities may be well managed regardless of whether they use privatization. All of the studies included in Appendices C and D found that the most privatized and the least privatized cities were all fiscally healthy. This is a significant and interesting finding. It suggests that cities on both ends of the continuum (cities that use a lot of privatization versus those that use very little privatization) can be fiscally healthy, or perhaps well managed. For additional details, one should read the actual studies. For related studies that found that contracting saves money, see James Ferris, "The Decision to Contract Out," *Urban Affairs Quarterly* 22 (1988), pp. 289–311. Also see David Morgan, Michael Hirlinger, and Robert England, "The Decision to Contract Out: A Further Explanation," pp. 363–373.

28. Bowman and Pagano, "City Intervention: An Analysis of the Public Capital Mobilization Process," p. 359.

29. Ibid.

30. Charles Tiebout, "A Pure Theory of Public Expenditure," *Journal of Political Economy* 44 (1956), pp. 416–424.

31. This is the basis for the Census Bureau's classification of cities discussed earlier but more thoroughly developed in urban studies.

32. Ann Bowman, "Competition for Economic Development among Southeastern Cities," *Urban Affairs Quarterly* 25 (1988), pp. 511–527.
33. Tiebout was instrumental in developing the basic model about a market for local public goods and services. Tiebout developed a demand-side model. Paul Peterson added to Tiebout's model by introducing politics, such as the strategies developed and used by city officials. Peterson argued that the market for local goods and services is affected by the interests and motivations of city officials, which caused the focus of future research to be concerned with the supply-side of local markets. See Paul Peterson, *City Limits* (Chicago, IL: Chicago University Press, 1981); and Mark Schneider, *The Competitive City* (Pittsburgh, PA: University of Pittsburgh Press, 1989).
34. Tiebout believed the mobility of buyers (his concept of voting with one's feet) was the force that drives the market for local services. He saw intercity competition as a means of increasing efficiency and as an opportunity for buyers to shop for the "bundle of goods" that best satisfies their needs. See Charles Tiebout, "A Pure Theory of Public Expenditure."
35. Figure 3.1 is intended to illustrate the various systems that likely affect privatization. The model is conceptual and is not intended to demonstrate an empirical causal link. The systems are the same as those used by Ann Bowman and Michael Pagano, "City Intervention: An Analysis of the Public Capital Mobilization Process," p. 362.
36. It should be noted that Missoula, like many university towns, is considered to be an aberration from other cities and towns in the state. Generally, most college towns are more liberal than the rest of their state.
37. Michael Pagano and Ann Bowman, *Cityscapes and Capital* (Baltimore, MD: Johns Hopkins University Press, 1995). This book provides a convincing argument, supported by evidence, that politics matters. The evidence presented in the book demonstrates the critical role played by political leaders in molding a city's future and in forging political coalitions to ensure success. This includes how a city's capital and resources will be used.
38. Research has shown that city officials are very aware of the image of their cities and take action to enhance, maintain, or change the image. See Ann Bowman, *Tools and Targets: The Mechanics of City Economic Development* (Washington, D.C.: National League of Cities, 1987). Also see Pagano and Bowman, *Cityscapes and Capital*.
39. The orientations were developed by Bowman and Pagano, "City Intervention: An Analysis of the Public Capital Mobilization Process," *Urban Affairs Quarterly* 27 (1992), pp. 356–374.
40. Jeffrey D. Greene, "City Orientations and Privatization," *Southeastern Political Review* 25 (June 1997), pp. 339–352.
41. Although Bowman and Pagano developed the city-level orientations to study local economic development, they are useful here because they capture patterns of behavior that likely would affect the type of service delivery arrangement used by cities. The orientations reflect modes of behavior. For example, market cities are fiscally stressed and have a preference to use private markets. The presence of fiscal stress coupled with a discernible preference to use private markets provides reason to expect privatization levels to be high. Conversely, the incentive for expansionist cities to privatize is low because of their strong economies and the absence of fiscal stress. Similar cases can be made for each city-level orientation.

42. It should be noted that "a preference for using market forces" does not necessarily mean that market cities, by definition, prefer privatization. The Bowman and Pagano study identified market cities as cities that preferred letting market forces guide economic development. No evidence was revealed in the Bowman and Pagano study suggesting that market cities had a preference for a "hands off" approach to economic development carried over into the management of municipal services.

43. City-level orientations are not static. The context in which cities exist is constantly changing. Cities modify their behavior in response to environmental changes. For example, a city may seek to become a higher-order city (expansionist orientation) then seek to maintain its position (maintenance orientation). This study focuses on a "snapshot" in time. There is no way of knowing what the orientation of a city was in the past.

44. Privatization levels were calculated from city responses to an International City/County Management Association (ICMA) survey on alternative service delivery arrangements conducted in 1988. The survey recorded the incidence of privatization in 71 municipal activities across five broad functional areas that were used in this study. The five broad categories included in the ICMA survey were public works, public safety, utilities, parks and recreation, and support functions (general government). The specific types of privatization included were contracting with private, for-profit firms, contracting with nonprofit firms, self-help, franchising, and vouchers. Contracting with other governments was also included in the ICMA survey, but was excluded in the privatization scores. Privatization levels were based on the number of ICMA-surveyed activities in which cities used private delivery arrangements (0 = no privatization; 71 = 100 percent privatization level). Analysis of the variance (ANOVA) was used to determine if significant differences existed in the amount of privatization used by the four city-level orientations. The privatization score is reflected as the percent of the activities included in the ICMA survey that a city used one of the forms of privatization described above. Services that were not applicable for cities were excluded (such as snowplowing for a city in south Florida). The score is intended to gauge the breadth of privatization in cities among the surveyed activities. Privatization scores are not intended to be linked with a monetary value. It is recognized that there are other ways to operationalize the concept of privatization.

45. Morley, "Local Government Use of Alternative Service Delivery Approaches," pp. 34–44.

46. Examining these questions has revealed some different findings. Elaine Morley analyzed several of the ICMA surveys on alternative service delivery approaches. Her conclusions have been that the use of contracting, the most common form of privatization used by local governments, has remained relatively stable since 1982. However, it should be noted that the methodology used by the ICMA involved sending surveys to all local governments with populations above a specified number, usually 25,000, and sending surveys to a certain percentage of local governments below a specified population (below 10,000 for earlier surveys and below 25,000 for the more recent surveys). The response rate was relatively low, as one would suspect, to most of the ICMA surveys. One might ask, how has the use of privatization changed among cities that responded to each survey? This method would allow one to compare the same cities across time.

See Jeffrey D. Greene, "How Much Privatization? Examining the Use of Privatization by Cities in 1982 and 1992," *Policy Studies Journal* 24 (winter 1996), pp. 632–640.

47. There are many ways to measure privatization. One method is to simply count the incidences (cases) that one can find. Another way is to look at the percentage of a municipal budget that is spent for private contracts for services. Another way is to examine the level of privatization used by a city. That is, considering all of the services provided, how many services have been privatized in full or in part? Yet another method involves examining how many different types of privatization are used within each service area. See Note 44 for the method used to determine privatization levels and privatization diversity for the Tables 3.6, 3.7, and 3.8. It should be recognized that all of these methods have their limitations.

48. The data and methods for this study are as follows. The 596 cities used in this inquiry responded to two International City/County Management Association (ICMA) surveys on alternative service delivery approaches conducted in 1982 and 1992. The ICMA surveys included more than 59 services. Only services that were included in both surveys were used for comparison. The ICMA surveys included responses in five broad functional categories: public works, public safety, public utilities, parks and recreation, and support services. The types of alternative service arrangements included in the surveys were: contracting with private, profit-oriented organizations, contracting with private, nonprofit organizations, contracting with other governments, volunteers, self-help, franchising, and voucher systems. Contracting with other governments was excluded from the privatization calculations. Although the two surveys were not identical, both contained similar information. It was possible to merge the information into a comparable format to enable comparison. The five forms of privatization included in the modified versions were contracting with private, for-profit or nonprofit organizations, franchising, voucher systems, self-help, and volunteers. Only cities that responded to both surveys were examined to enable privatization to be compared in the same cities at two different periods of time. Two indicators of privatization were calculated using the ICMA data: privatization levels and privatization diversity.

Privatization levels represent the breadth of privatization among services. The ICMA surveys recorded the incidence of privatization in 59 municipal services across five broad functional areas. The surveys included most popular forms of privatization. Privatization levels were based on the number of activities in which cities used private delivery arrangements (i.e., 0 = no privatization; 59 = 100 percent privatization level).

Privatization diversity levels represent the amount of privatization a city uses within services. The diversity scores were based on the numbers of different types of privatization cities use to provide a specific service. For example, a city may use four different methods of privatization to collect garbage. Since there were five types of privatization included in the modified surveys, a city's diversity score for garbage collection would be 4 (or 80 percent). Summing the functions included in the surveys enabled a total diversity score to be calculated (i.e., 0 = no privatization; 295 = 100 percent privatization diversity). Dependent t-tests were used to determine if privatization levels and diversity levels significantly increased between 1982 and 1992. Dependent t-tests were also used to make regional comparisons.

The populations of the 596 cities ranged between 18,000 and 350,000 (average = 81,000). The composition included cities from 41 states (90 northern cities, 187 southern cities, 164 midwestern cities, and 155 western cities). All three of the Census Bureau's metropolitan location classifications were included (197 central cities, 381 suburban cities, and 18 independent cities).

49. It should be noted that the dependent-t tests used to determine significance were at the 99 percent confidence level, meaning that the likelihood of error is extremely slim.

50. See Appendix E for specific services. Examining the services by categories is revealing. With the exception of two utility services, the use of privatization increased for 57 of the 59 services. The percentage of the increase for many services was very large. Some of the increases were astronomical. For example, the largest increase in the use of privatization was in the area of support functions with an average increase of 508 percent. The second largest increase occurred in public safety functions (355 percent), the third largest increase was in public works (296 percent), and the smallest increase was in parks and recreation (218 percent).

51. For a compilation of numerous case studies, see John Hilke, *Cost Savings from Privatization: A Compilation of Study Findings* (Los Angeles, CA: Reason Foundation, March 1993).

52. Several qualifications should be noted. This study was limited to 596 cities that responded to the ICMA surveys. Although it's clear that the cities included in the study used more privatization in 1992 than in 1982, one must be careful drawing inferences to the larger universe of cities. However, examining all ICMA-surveyed cities (1,433 cities in 1982 and 1,220 cities in 1992) also revealed an increase in the use of privatization. This finding is not consistent with other analyses of the ICMA surveys, but privatization was not measured in the same manner in those analyses (most analyses were frequency-based measures, whereas an index was used in this study to capture the breadth of privatization). It must be stressed that one cannot conclude from this data that the use of privatization has increased by this magnitude for all cities because of methodological limitations. It is fair to conclude that privatization increased dramatically for the 596 cities that responded to both ICMA surveys over the ten-year period but one cannot conclude that privatization increased to this magnitude for all cities. It should be stressed that regional patterns cannot be determined from the findings of this study, although privatization was more prevalent in the West.

53. Jeffrey D. Greene, "Privatization Popular among Local Governments," *Montana Business Quarterly* 37 (winter 1999), pp. 17–20.

54. See Bob Anez, "Baker Talks Up U-System, Inc.," *Missoulian*, 17 January 1995, B-1; Kathleen McLaughlin "Magellan Quits before Being Fired," *Missoulian*, 3 March 1999, A-1; and Kathleen McLaughlin, "What the Market Will Bare," *Missoulian*, 9 November 1997, A-1.

55. The difference between Montana cities and ICMA-surveyed cities was 16 percent, which is a statistically significant difference (t = 2.8 at .00). The difference between Montana's counties and ICMA-surveyed counties was larger (36 percent). The difference was also statistically significant (t = 3.2 at .00).

56. T-tests are two-tailed tests at the 95 percent confidence level. Privatization levels are based on responses from two surveys. The International City/County Management Association conducted the national survey in 1992, and the author

conducted the Montana survey. The scores are shown as means (averages). Scores are based on the percentage of surveyed functions in which a city used private service delivery arrangements. The scores reflect the breadth of privatization among services. Because studies similar to the Montana survey are rare, comparable data is simply not readily available. Thus, one can only use the national surveys for comparison that often include only a few cities from many states.

PRIVATIZATION IN THE REAL WORLD: SUCCESSES, FAILURES, AND PERSISTENT ISSUES

In the everyday world, privatization is more than an ideological debate among academics. Privatization is a real phenomenon and it is commonly used to provide city services. The streetlights have to burn, garbage must be collected, and traffic signals have to work. City officials deal with real fiscal problems, such as tax-service imbalances, resistance to higher taxation from residents, and demands to correct problems ranging from potholes in city streets to crime. City services often appear to be mundane, but imagine what our lives would be like if the garbage were not collected, the water and sewage systems failed to work, fire and building codes did not exist, or sanitation inspections were not made in restaurants. Most of us take these and other services for granted, but they are part of the routine operation of cities. Cities' services are not free and some vendor, public or private, must deliver these services and be paid.

There is a long history in America of using private companies to provide public services, especially at the municipal level. This history is filled with successes and failures. The success stories range from cities saving millions of dollars by using private companies to provide services, such as Newark, New Jersey, which saved around $1 million by privatizing part of its garbage collection.[1] The failures usually involve corruption, payoffs, price-fixing, and excessive costs as city officials often pad their own pockets with money as they make shady deals with contractors and even organized crime.[2] These are evidenced by cases like Jersey City, New Jersey, where the city attempted to break a $20 million garbage collection contract with an alleged mob-controlled company. The case involved two former mayors who held a financial interest in the company. This action resulted in a civil suit that was eventually settled out of court for $500,000 with the city getting control of the landfill.[3] Cases like Albany,

New York, where political-machine-backed mayors once provided jobs and contracts for the party faithful to deliver city services, do little to help the reputation of private contracting.[4] They only serve to remind us of the pitfalls that can be associated with contracting out for city services. Despite these problems, contracting out for city services has always been, and continues to be, common in most cities. What are the results of privatization in the real world? They are evidenced not so much by the inquiries of academics, but by real stories and examples from the real world of municipal government.

In the real world of city management, there is a *politics of privatization*. Students will recall from introductory American government classes that one of the classic descriptions of politics is *who gets what, when, and how?*[5]

Who gets what? With privatization someone is getting something. What are they getting? Contractors get money because services are not free, regardless of who provides them. Contractors must be paid and they make money by providing public services for cities. Contracting can involve large sums of money. For example, the five-year contract for vehicle maintenance for Los Angeles County, signed in 1990, was worth $10 million for the first year. The value of the contract over the five-year period was approximately $60 million.[6] And the money to pay contractors generally comes from taxes, which are paid by ordinary citizens. Moreover, others may benefit from contracts aside from the contractors, such as public officials who may get illegal kickbacks or political contributions.[7] Privatization can also involve large, legitimate cash payments to cities that provide much needed revenue. For example, when public hospitals are sold, the payments made to cities usually involve millions of dollars.

When do they get their money? Assuming the lack of corruption, this is an easy question to answer and should only involve when contractors are paid. Contract payments vary greatly. Some contracts are paid in monthly or quarterly payments. Other contracts may involve consulting, which is often paid in two payments—once up front to begin the project, and the rest after the project is completed. Incentives can be written into contracts. For example, it is common to pay additional money to speed up completion of a project, such as rebuilding a bridge or completing a street project before winter. Contracts and leases often involve large up-front cash payments made to the city, so the politics of privatization can also mean large sums of money for cities.

How do they get their money? Most cities use various forms of bidding. The most popular are "sealed bids" in which contractors bid in a competitive process to provide a specified service. For years, cities tended to take the lowest bid because it was required by law (or by city policy), but most cities now provide themselves with some escape mechanism in the event that a firm places a bid and the city feels they cannot deliver the service. An example might be that a firm has a reputation of being unreliable, which would be a legitimate reason for a city to reject the bid. How a contractor or other beneficiaries of contracts get whatever they are getting is often controversial. This carries us into the shady deals that can occur because of cozy relationships between those awarding the contracts and the contractors. This, of course, is illegal in most cities, but it still occurs. Although most cities have processes for securing contracts that contain some types of checks and balances, there often are individuals who will take advantage of the system. Newspapers frequently report on questionable deals that raise suspicions that something went awry with the open bidding process.[8] Thus, there is a real *politics of privatization* that involves tangible goods and services for contractors, city officials, public employees, and citizens. Ideally, a truly competitive bidding process should benefit everyone (cities and their citizens) by saving tax dollars and getting high-quality services. Contractors benefit by making money by providing services.

But the politics of privatization can get messy. For example, when Westminster, California, sought to privatize its fire protection services, four of the five council members that favored privatization had to face recall elections that were led by the city's former firefighters. The recalls failed, but the service was not actually privatized; the municipal fire department was replaced with an intergovernmental contract that was awarded to the Orange County Fire Authority.[9] Fire protection in Rye Brook, New York, was returned to a municipal department after the private Rural Metro withdrew its service. The city and the Rural Metro had numerous problems with neighboring fire departments and firefighters' unions who opposed the very presence of a private fire fighting firm. Neighboring fire departments refused to respond to any calls in Rye Brook to back up the Rural Metro. After a $1 million house burned to the ground and the owner threatened to sue the city for failing to save the house, Rye Brook gave up on private fire protection.[10]

The politics of privatization often involves bitter disputes with public employee unions. Private contractors generally face strong opposition in cases where public employees may lose their jobs, particularly in heavily unionized areas. It is likely that politics weighs heavily in the decision to privatize services, particularly in municipal service areas like fire protection that have long traditions of public provision and unionization.

Collecting Garbage: Is There Gold in Cities' Trash?

No city service involving privatization has received more attention than collecting garbage. Collecting and disposing the nation's trash is an essential service. America produces billions of tons of garbage each year. Waste disposal is more complex than is commonly believed. Residential trash includes all that "stuff" that we produce in our homes ranging from newspapers, broken televisions sets and furniture, soft drink cans, and the like. Collecting and disposing of all of our trash raises many public health and environmental concerns. Collecting trash now involves recycling to try to lessen some of the environmental concerns about filling up the nation's landfills, polluting the air, streams and rivers, or even groundwater.[11] In the 1970s, evidence suggested that the nation's landfills were filling up with disposable products, such as diapers. Recycling items from paper products, glass bottles, or scrap metal from old cars or appliances has received a great deal of attention over the past twenty years and most cities have adopted recycling programs.[12] Burning various types of waste in high-heat incinerators raises issues about air pollution. In addition to household wastes, there are many other types of waste and garbage. Hospitals and medical facilities generate certain types of hazardous waste. Industries, such as metal plating shops, produce an abundance of hazardous waste, such as chemicals and dangerous sludge. Some types of industry produce highly dangerous waste byproducts, such as nuclear rods from nuclear power plants or nuclear waste from weapons facilities. Moreover, disposing of municipal waste is a significant policy concern for cities. In the early 1990s, 67 percent of municipal solid waste was disposed of in landfills, 17 percent was recycled, and 16 percent was destroyed through incineration.[13] Between 1988 and 1991, the number of landfills decreased from about 8,000 to 5,800 and continues to decrease.[14] Since 1980, roughly three-quarters of the nation's landfills have closed.[15]

Whether it is hazardous byproducts from pesticide factories or tons of household garbage, America generates a lot of it. Cities generate and collect more than 430 billion pounds of garbage each year and all of that trash must be collected and disposed of or recycled.[16] Although all levels of government are involved in various aspects of waste management,[17] collecting residential and industrial waste in our nation's cities is a *big business*. For example, Waste Industries, the nation's seventh-largest waste management corporation and based out of Raleigh, North Carolina, reported sales of $56.9 million during the first quarter of 2000.[18] Allied Waste, Inc. (based out of Scottsdale, Arizona), is the world's second-largest waste management corporation. As of December 31, 1999, the company operated 340 collection companies, 148 transfer stations, 151 landfills, and 95 recycling facilities in 42 states.[19] During the first quarter of 2000, Allied Waste's revenues were $1.4 billion.[20] Waste Management, Inc. (the largest waste management company operating in the world), reported revenues of $3.4 billion during the third quarter of 1999. Revenues of $3.4 billion and $1.4 billion for a single quarter by two corporations are, by any definition, big business.[21] Thus, it is fair to conclude that there is gold in a city's trash.[22]

Privatization's proponents have conducted numerous studies that suggest it is less costly to contract out to collect garbage, and they have cited an abundance of examples of success stories nationwide. Privatization's critics point toward numerous examples in which privatizing garbage collection produces less than desirable results. One journalist wrote that the companies that dominate garbage collection have a long history of price-fixing and scandalous behavior.[23] No municipal service has been more beset with scandal and corruption than collecting trash. How can privatization's proponents and critics use the same service to illustrate success and failure? How can they look at the phenomenon (collecting and disposing of garbage) and draw opposite conclusions? Actually, both sides have some valid claims. Virtually all studies on garbage collection have found private contracting to be the most economical means to collect trash in a city, yet examples of corruption and scandals in contractual arrangements abound and have consistently been a problem.

In theory, ethical procedures for awarding and monitoring contracts should minimize corruption. But the real world of politics is different from theories discussed in college classrooms. Payoffs are not supposed to occur. Laws prohibit such activities and public officials are supposed to uphold the law. Yet Browning-Ferris Industries, one of the world's largest garbage collection corporations at the time, revealed that between 1972 and 1976 it had paid public officials more than $110,000 to secure contracts in the Washington, D.C., area. Bear in mind that this was more than twenty years ago. In current dollars, this would be more than a quarter of a million dollars. Browning-Ferris's public confession came after the *Washington Post* had carried a series of stories about trash dumping in the District of Columbia area.[24] During this same period, Waste Management, Inc. (the second-largest garbage collection firm at the time), got caught in a scandal that involved a slush fund from a landfill in Florida. The slush fund was used for "political contributions."[25] In the early 1990s, Waste Management, Inc., and Browning-Ferris Industries handled about half of the nation's garbage collection and disposal business. Between the early 1970s and early 1990s, the two companies had paid more than $50 million dollars to settle charges of price-fixing, allocating customers, and bid-rigging.[26] Although formal charges were filed many times by the Securities and Exchange Commission (SEC), the companies denied the charges and usually settled out of court. The large waste management firms are not the only companies plagued with legal woes. A group of nine small garbage collection companies operating in the Hartford, Connecticut, area settled an antitrust suit for $1.1 million. The companies were accused of conspiring to rig bids and of allocating millions of dollars in business among themselves.[27]

The corruption and scandals involving garbage collection go further than the large corporations that operate nationwide. The influence of organized crime has also been well documented.[28] In one case involving Brooklyn, New York, the annual overcharges by mob-controlled companies to the city were estimated to average $20 million per year during the early 1970s.[29] In another case involving New York's Westchester County, investigations revealed that the mob controlled 90 percent of commercial garbage collection in the mid-1970s.[30] The influence of organized crime was illustrated in the 1990s when Browning-Ferris tried to collect garbage in New York City. This event even inspired a story on CBS's *60 Minutes*.

Price-fixing, kickback schemes, and the presence of organized crime have been common in the history of garbage collection in America's cities. Scandals have been frequent in cities like New York, Chicago, and San Francisco.[31]

Not all of the privatization stories involve corruption or even disappointments. In fact, most of the results of privatization appear to have been positive. Over the past thirty years, disappointments are the exception rather than the norm. Increases in fuel costs and landfill tipping fees have caused many cities to examine alternatives that may be cheaper than collecting garbage with publicly operated departments. Although most of the cost difference between public and private garbage collection is in labor costs, many cities have had positive experiences with private collection.[32] For example, Phoenix, Arizona, began competitive bidding for contracts for its collection districts in 1978.[33] The Phoenix public department lost the contracts for several years, but slowly won back many of the districts as the department became more efficient. City officials estimate that their competitive bidding process (referred to as managed competition) has led to increased efficiency of its own public works department and has saved the city millions of dollars since the late 1970s.[34] The public works director of Phoenix said that before the competitive bidding process was initiated, his department did not have a gauge for comparison. He believes that having to compete with private companies was healthy for his department, which can now collect garbage for less money per household than many of the private vendors in the Phoenix area. In fact, one of the public works department's bids was the lowest of all bids, $3.96 per month per household, versus $4.23 from the next closest bid in the mid-1980s. This is impressive considering the higher wages typically paid by cities.[35] Moreover, an audit by the city found that the public works department had fewer complaints and damage to property than the private companies that collected Phoenix's garbage in other districts. However, all conclude that it is the presence of competition for the contracts that led to the enhanced efficiency of Phoenix's public works department. The use of multiple vendors, public and private, to collect garbage in Lansing, Michigan, has also resulted in savings for the city.[36]

In Indianapolis, private contracting for garbage collection has consistently been around 25 percent less expensive than when public crews collected the city's trash.[37] In 1993, the city put out bids to privatize its garbage collection. The scope of the service included curbside collection of household waste and yard waste, and recycling. The city was divided into eleven districts as a result of previous contracting of commercial solid waste. One district was reserved for the city's own public works department, which was allowed to bid on the remaining ten districts. Motivated by competition, the city's own department beat its first-year bid target of $3 million in savings by more than $2 million (a total of $5 million in savings). The contract provided for incentive pay rewards. As a result, not only did Indianapolis save millions of dollars, but also, each of the 117 haulers and 26 members of the administrative staff received a $1,750 bonus check.

Competitive bidding for solid waste collection was also successful in Manhattan Beach, California. The savings for the city has been more than $1 million annually.[38] Conway, South Carolina, turned its garbage collection over to a private company and saved about $100,000 per year.[39] A feasibility study prepared for Mount Vernon, New York, compared Mount Vernon's public garbage collection to private contracted collection in East Orange, New Jersey, and found that the cost per household was $10 less in East Orange.[40] The study also found that in Mount Vernon four crew members per truck collected roughly one-third the quantity of garbage that two crew members per truck collected per day in East Orange. It costs the City of Pittsburgh around $15 million per year to collect and dispose of the city's trash with its public works department. This amounts to roughly $100 per ton. Waste Management, Inc., of Pittsburgh collects and disposes of garbage at a cost of around $50 per ton. A study that focused on the Pittsburgh, Pennsylvania, area revealed that the City of Pittsburgh could save as much as $9 million per year by privatizing its garbage collection and using competitive contracting processes.[41] About half the nation's cities contract out garbage collection and report savings ranging between 30 and 60 percent.[42] The *Wall Street Journal* reported that contracting out for refuse collection increased from 30 percent in 1987 to 50 percent in 1995.[43] Notwithstanding some disappointments, which often involve corruption, cities appear to have had positive experiences with privatizing garbage collection, particularly with the use of multiple vendors to collect garbage.

Collecting garbage also has the disposal dimension. The trash has to be dumped, recycled, or incinerated. In this area, cities have also found it less costly to use private companies. As noted earlier, the nation's landfills are being exhausted quickly. One solution, aside from recycling, has been to install large incinerators, which can reduce trash volume by 90 percent and can greatly expand the life of landfills. Incinerators are expensive and can cost $250,000 or more. In the New England area, some twenty towns located north of Boston use an incinerator owned and operated by Signal Environmental Systems, which was the first company of its kind in the nation. The cost reduction of incinerating trash versus dumping it in the area's landfills were dramatic: $22 per ton versus $100 per ton—a savings of $88 per ton. Signal burns the trash to boil water to make steam, which generates power that is sold to a local electricity utility.[44] Ash from the incinerator still must be dumped into landfills, but there is a lot less of it and the ash is less likely to contaminate the groundwater than raw trash. Signal operates a similar refuse-to-energy plant in Westchester County, New York, and is under a 20-year contract with the county.[45] The large waste-management corporations, like Waste Management, Inc., also operate incinerators throughout the nation. Thus, by privatizing services, many localities get environmentally sound operations that collect and dispose of trash in a manner consistent with regulations imposed by the Environmental Protection Agency and without any capital outlays for landfills or incinerators. Between incineration and recycling, the nation's landfills should remain open much longer. The privatization of landfills has many examples of success, including Indianapolis, which uses a private refuse-to-energy system for its landfill and a recycling center that brings in $20 million per year for the city. The recycling center is a public-private partnership.[46] Other cities that have enjoyed success by privatizing landfills include Simi Valley,

California (which has the lowest average trash fees in the nation); Fort Worth, Texas; Chandler, Arizona; and San Diego, California.[47] As of 1996, 35 percent of all cities were considering privatizing their recycling operations.[48] Of the 338 materials-recovery facilities (recycling centers related to solid waste collection) operating in the United States in 1996, two-thirds were privately owned, 29 percent were publicly owned, and 3 percent were public-private partnerships.[49] In 1996, 27 percent of cities were planning to privatize their landfill operations and 22 percent were planning to privatize their transfer stations.[50] Clearly, privatization of collecting and disposing of garbage appears popular in the new century.

COMPETITIVE BIDDING AND MANAGED COMPETITION

Many of the examples of successful privatization involve managed competition. Managed competition refers to a city allowing its own department to continue to provide a service (and to bid to provide the service in other areas of the city), but also awarding private firms contracts to provide the same service. Although not applicable to all services, this system forces public departments to compete directly with private firms in the bidding process.[51] Two cities stand out in their efforts to nurture managed competition, Phoenix and Indianapolis. Both cities have had remarkable success with this practice, which has served as a model that many other cities across the nation have emulated. For example, audits in Indianapolis suggest that the city is saving taxpayers more than $30 million per year by bidding out services formerly handled in-house. The projection of savings over a thirteen-year period, which includes planned increases in costs, amounts to $200 million. Indianapolis has been one of the most aggressive leaders with managed competition and privatization. As a result, city tax revenues have been relatively stable for a decade. The city has privatized its wastewater treatment plant, garbage collection, city pools, street repair, and its golf course. Aside from all of the other services, privatizing the city-owned wastewater treatment plant saved the city $68 million. The city also privatized its airport, which is expected to save taxpayers more than $100 million over the ten-year period of the contract. Renaming the Hoosier Dome brings the city $1 million annually from RCA for ten years. Privatizing its wastewater treatment plant reduced personnel from 328 to 174 (which amounted to a 44 percent reduction in personnel costs). And the managed competition and privatization continues in Indianapolis. In 1995, city workers won the $16 million contract for vehicle maintenance.[52] Such savings, without doubt, are impressive. Cleveland, Ohio, began bidding out some of its services in 1994, which now saves the city more than $2 million per year. However, in Cincinnati, Ohio, the city council rejected the idea of managed competition for parking lot management that would have saved the city 45 percent over the current costs of operations.[53]

Few cities have enjoyed more success in managed competition and privatization than Phoenix, Arizona. The first service that Phoenix privatized was custodial services in 1978. The city's Custodial Services section was the resting ground for civil service employees that were not able to carry out other jobs due to injuries or other reasons. The cost of in-house services was clearly more expensive than in the private sector. The Custodial Services section also had a negative effect on the productivity of other city workers. Contracting out this service saved the city an estimated $250,000 per year.[54] Currently, the city has more than 1,800 contracts with private companies for services ranging from aircraft maintenance to veterinary services. The value of these contracts exceeds $600 million per year, which is roughly 38 percent of the total city budget. Managed competition is used in many of the city's services including landscape maintenance, garbage collection, ambulance services, landfill operations, street sweeping and repair, and data entry services. The city has saved more than $30 million and provides high-quality services by using managed competition.[55]

Scottsdale is a city that uses the privately owned Rural Metro as its fire department. The city has contracted out for major services since 1951 and has a policy of no layoffs due to contracting. An aggressive contracting policy enabled the city to shrink its workforce from 10 to 8.5 employees per 1,000 residents. In 1999 the city contracted for more than $52 million in services (which excludes capital improvements) with private for-profit and nonprofit organizations. The city continues to use public employees to provide portions of many of its basic services, but contracts out for portions of most services. Tempe, Arizona, has more than $66 million in private contracts, which is about 25 percent of the total city budget. Even Chicago, a city with a rich history of machine politics and corruption, has saved millions of dollars through privatization and managed competition. By 1994, Mayor Richard Daley (the son of the mayor who controlled the city for decades) had privatized forty separate services and saved taxpayers more than $20 million. The services included custodial services, tire collection, traffic signal design, and drug and alcohol treatment centers. Privatizing towing abandon cars alone saves the city more than $3 million annually.[56]

All of the cities mentioned here use managed competition successfully, and to date, have generally been pleased with the results.[57] There appear to be few exceptions where managed competition has failed and most examples are not actually about failure, but about the desire of contractors to get a larger percent of the service. One example involves Lansing, Michigan, where a number of contractors and the city collect garbage. A vice president of one of Lansing's private garbage companies, which handles 20 percent of the city's collection, believed that if his company could serve all of the residents, the price would be lower.[58] Of course, this is exactly what managed competition is supposed to stop—monopolies. The goal of most businesses is to have all of the business in an area, but it is competition that keeps prices down and keeps monopolies from emerging. In the absence of competition, monopolies can form and the behavior of private monopolies is no different than that of public monopolies.

Most cities have a variety of services that fall into the area of parks and recreation, such as tennis courts, lakes, and public parks. Since the 1970s, there has been a trend toward privatizing these areas. In 1998, a private group officially assumed management of New York City's famous Central Park. No other city in the United States has such an arrangement with a private group to manage a major municipal park. The nonprofit organization is called *The Central Park Conservancy*. The group receives $1 million per year from the city, and can receive as much as $4 million based on the amount of money it is able to generate. The group has been raising more than $5 million per year for the park. By 1999, the group had raised more than $233 million.[59] Although the city remains in control of larger decisions about the park, such as the scheduling of concerts and events, the nonprofit group assumed control over daily operations, such as concessions, tree planting and other landscaping, and educational programs. The group had already played a significant role in restoring the park since the late 1980s. Three-quarters of Central Park's employees are now employed by the conservancy (which did annoy New York City's public employee union). Foundations, corporations, and wealthy residents who live near the park fund The Central Park Conservancy. Mayor Giuliani said that he would like to have a similar deal for other parks in the city.[60] On a smaller scale, the citizens of Indianapolis also saved one of their parks. Holiday Park, located near an upper-middle-class neighborhood in Indianapolis, was described as an "urban nightmare." Drug dealers and prostitutes had set up shop and local residents were fearful of going anywhere near the park after dark. In 1990 a private group raised $300,000 in private donations for security guards, new equipment, and better maintenance. The citizens group received permission from the city to literally take back the park. As a result, the park is now safe, well managed, and no longer drug-infested.[61]

One of the most famous cases involving parks and recreation also involved New York City. The Wollman Memorial Park's skating rink was the largest outdoor rink in the nation for 30 years. In 1980 the city closed the rink for repairs, estimating that the job would take two years and cost about $5 million. Six years passed, the city had spent $12.9 million and the work was still not complete. The *Washington Post* referred to it as one of the most embarrassing fiascoes in municipal construction history. City officials said that the renovation would take two more years and $3 million to complete. Donald Trump, a 40-year-old billionaire developer at the time, made a challenge to then Mayor Ed Koch. Trump claimed that the renovation amounted to nothing more than pouring a slab of concrete and he could complete it in four months. The mayor took the challenge and offered Trump $2.8 million to rebuild the rink. Two weeks under the four-month deadline and $750,000 under budget, Trump finished the rink. He even added features not included in the deal, such as teak railings, a brick changing room with padded benches, a 200-seat restaurant, and many other amenities. How could Trump complete (and repair the damage done by other contractors) in four months what the city had failed to complete in eight years at a cost that exceeded $12 million? Mayor Koch called a meeting to try to find out why the city construction costs were so much higher than Trump's. In short, many laws on the books (known as New York State's Wicks Law) forced the city to hire separate contractors for virtually every function. Only by declaring the need for an emergency contract could the city hire Trump to complete the whole project. But the most important difference was that Trump had flexibility that was lacking in city government. Trump could tell his contractors to complete the job under budget or he would never use them again. Trump also took over management of the Wollman Park and made an unexpected profit of $500,000 the first year, which he donated to a variety of charities.[62] This example has been used many times to illustrate the inefficiency of municipal construction versus private construction. New York City got Wollman Park back in four months. The park was nicer than ever, local charities received the profits, including Partnerships for the Homeless, and New Yorkers could once again skate in their famous rink.[63]

In the early 1990s, budget shortfalls forced Rancho Palos Verdes, California, to eliminate its recreation programs. Before the city got out of the recreation business, it found that cities in the surrounding area were using private for-profit and nonprofit firms to provide most of the recreation services the city was operating. After hearing that the city was planning to shut down its recreation services, many of the employees went to the city and offered to continue to provide the programs if the city would let them rent the facilities. As a result, most of the services are still being offered, at no cost to the city, and the city now collects rent for the facilities. What was once a losing venture now actually makes money for the city.

The primary responsibility of operating parks, golf courses, and other recreational facilities is shifting from the public to the private sector, largely due to budgetary constraints. Parks and recreation departments continue to shift to user fees. In Prince William County, Virginia, most recreational services now require user fees. In the past, such services generated little revenue to pay for maintenance and personnel. User fees place the burden of paying on those who use the facilities—"pay-to-play" as the saying goes. Most citizens do not use the golf courses, so why should everyone be taxed to subsidize a small minority of citizens who use municipal golf courses? By implementing user fees, cities can offer a full range of recreational services and facilities that are self-funding and generate money to provide for free services, such as public parks.[64]

Municipal golf courses have long been a drain on city budgets. One journalist commented that in cities from Los Angeles to New York, officials are increasingly considering contracting out the most nonessential of all nonessential public services—golf courses.[65] Between 1987 and 1995, the number of cities contracting for golf course services increased by 67 percent.[66] Nearly a quarter of all cities in the United States contract out for municipal golf operations.[67] In Los Angeles there are 16 public golf courses that are privately operated. In New York City, 13 public golf courses have been contracted out to private firms. Most cities lack the expertise to profitably operate golf courses. The National Golf Foundation views the nation's 2,500 municipally owned golf courses as a potential $2 billion per year market.[68] The Taquitz Municipal Golf Course in Palm Springs, California, serves as an excellent example of what can be done with municipal golf facilities. Since 1995, when Arnold Palmer took over operations, the course has exceeded expectations in every aspect of operations. Between 1995 and 1997, revenues increased 270 percent, rounds have increased 40 percent, and the facility now generates income of more than $370,000 per year. The golf course once showed a $400,000 per year loss on the city's books but now generates net revenue.[69] In the early 1980s, Miami, Florida, privatized its golf courses and saved $600,000 during the first year.[70]

Los Angeles County contracts out for 16 of its 19 golf courses. Of these 16 courses, 9 are leased to small firms or groups (usually local golf pros) and the other 7 to large management corporations. The county began contracting as a way to generate revenue and has been very satisfied with the results. One example of the county's success is the Mountain Meadow Course. Before the course was privatized in 1989, it produced revenues of $570,000. After the course was privatized, the revenues increased to $708,000. By 1996, the course was generating annual revenues of $1.4 million.[71]

Before contracting out 13 of its golf courses, New York City was losing $2 million each year. Since contracting out these courses, the city has gone from losing $2 million per year to generating net profits of more than $2 million per year from its golf courses. The American Golf Corporation now operates seven of the courses. City officials point out the poor condition of the courses prior to contracting and the numerous problems that existed with the facilities. The courses were littered with abandoned cars and trash, employees wasted more time than they spent working, and golfers were even mugged. American Golf Corporation quickly invested more than $4.5 million to improve the courses, which included overhauling the clubhouses, repairing the irrigation systems and grounds, purchasing new golf carts, and enhancing safety and security. Before American Golf Corporation took over the seven courses, the city was losing $1 million every year operating these seven courses. In 1997, the city was receiving $1.7 million per year in rent for the seven golf courses.[72] Similar successful experiences in privatizing golf courses can be found in other cities, such as Chicago and San Francisco. It is noteworthy to mention that Arnold Palmer Golf Corporation manages the Presidio Golf

Course in San Francisco, which brings in revenue in excess of $5 million each year.[73] These examples illustrate how a historically losing venture (e.g., operating municipal golf courses) can become a revenue-generating operation.

FACILITY AND CONVENTION CENTER MANAGEMENT

Most cities have a convention center, civic center, or some type of sports stadium. Stadiums and civic centers are not always profitable for cities. In the case of Asheville, North Carolina, the publicly owned and operated Asheville Civic Center has never enjoyed much success.[74] Although the civic center may not lose money every year, it has by no means been a cash cow for the city. This is true for many cities, particularly those located in secondary markets or in smaller cities. As the cases cited in this section will illustrate, the goal of cities is often not to make money but to minimize losses. The typical contract with private firms to manage these facilities is for three years. Publicly contracted private management of stadiums, arenas, convention centers, and similar facilities began nearly a quarter of a century ago when the Louisiana Super Dome was privatized in 1975. Nearly 45 stadiums and arenas (large and small) were under construction during the 1990s. Nearly four-fifths of the money to build these facilities came from public sources. Most of the 49 existing major-league football and baseball stadiums were built with public funds. Only five were privately funded.

The solution for some cities has been privatization. For example, Kansas's State Expo Center broke the $1 million mark for annual income after being taken over by private management in 1995. This was the center's best financial performance since opening in 1987. The increased efficiency of private management cut the $1.4 million annual subsidy by $600,000 per year. In its first year under private management, the West Palm Beach Auditorium (in Florida) reduced its annual operating deficit by more than $500,000. In the three years prior to being taken over by a private firm, the annual deficits averaged nearly $800,000. By 1995, the deficit was cut to around $200,000. In Coral Springs, Florida, the city's Center for Performing Arts cut its losses by contracting with a private company. After the first year under privatization, the center's attendance was up by 28 percent, revenue was increased by 19 percent, and the city's operating subsidy was reduced by 33 percent. Riverside, California, privatized its convention center in 1991 and saved $400,000 in the first year.[75]

As evidenced by these cases, cities still often subsidize these facilities. Even some of the most successful examples still involve "reducing" the amount of the subsidy rather than generating net revenues. For example, in Memphis, Tennessee, the city contracted out management of the Memphis Cook Convention Center in 1992. The city was paying around $1.8 million per year to subsidize the center. During the first two years of the contract, the firm reduced the subsidy from $1.8 million per year to $1.25 million per year, a savings of around

$500,000 each year. Much of the savings was attributed to changes in the food and beverage policies. The city had left concessions open to everyone, while the company contracted concessions via competitive bidding to an exclusive provider. This saved the center $250,000 per year. This transition had little effect on public employees since the private firm offered jobs to most of the center's full-time employees.[76] In Denver, Colorado, the Colorado Convention Center saved $500,000 by using a host of management improvements.[77]

Major sports facilities are also beginning to use privatization, in the form of private management, ownership, or public-private partnerships. The first major-league baseball park to be built with private financing since Dodger Stadium opened in 1962 is the new home of the San Francisco Giants. Chase Securities provided $140 million of the construction cost of Pacific Bell Park, named after the telephone company that put up $50 million to have its name on the park for twenty-four years. The remaining $225 million in construction costs are to be paid from other sources, such as concession rights, charter-seat sales, other forms of sponsorship, and future earnings from ticket sales from Giants' games. Similarly, in Denver, the NBA's Nuggets and the NHL's Avalanche are building a private arena, the Pepsi Center, which is also being financed privately. Naming centers after a sponsor, usually to raise revenue for cities, is becoming increasingly popular. For example, the RCA Center in Indianapolis, the Delta Center in Salt Lake City, Qualcomm Stadium in San Diego, and the United Center in Chicago are only a few of the major stadiums and centers that have corporate sponsorship in the name of the facility.[78] Sometimes cities refuse to make renovations or assist in developing new stadiums. This was the case in Miami, Florida, when the city refused to make renovations to the aging Orange Bowl, which was the home of the NFL's Miami Dolphins. The late Joe Robbie, who owned the Dolphins at the time, raised more than $100 million and built the stadium in 1987. Taxpayers had rejected bonds three times to help build the stadium and the city had refused to use tax dollars for either renovations or to help build a new stadium.[79] Also in Miami, a $53 million privatized multi-sports center to be built on city land helped the city win a National Basketball Association expansion franchise, the Miami Heat, in 1988.[80] However, the plan was abandoned in favor of a super-sized American Airlines Arena. Privatization appears to be increasingly popular for managing sports facilities and convention centers in many of the nation's cities and these examples show how corporate interests are becoming interwoven into urban affairs.

FLEET MANAGEMENT AND MAINTENANCE OF MUNICIPAL VEHICLES

Municipalities own a lot of cars and trucks. These range from police cruisers to dump trucks, and even include fire trucks. All of these vehicles must be maintained, fueled, and washed. Between 1982 and 1992, the use of private contractors for fleet management and vehicle maintenance increased 27 percent.[81] Fleet maintenance is one of the key areas that is being privatized by local governments.[82] One of the largest local government contracts ever awarded was for vehicle maintenance in Los Angeles County. The value of the contract exceeded $60 million.[83] Positive experiences in cities like Phoenix, Des Moines, and the County of Los Angeles illustrate that privatizing this service can result in considerable savings of as much as 38 percent below in-house municipal costs.[84] Similar results occurred in Des Moines, Iowa. In 1983, the city contracted out its fleet maintenance and saved $390,000 during the first year of the contract over what the cost had been handling the service in-house.[85]

San Mateo, California, contracted out its fleet maintenance in 1993 and thus far, the city has been very satisfied with the contractor's performance. Privatizing the service reduced costs by 20 percent. In 1994, San Mateo's city budget was $80 million. The 20 percent savings may appear small but as one city official noted, the 20 percent reduction in fleet maintenance amounts to the salaries of four police officers in terms of value to the city.[86] Coral Springs, Florida, also privatized its fleet maintenance in 1993. The public employees entered into head-to-head competition with private contractors and won the bid to maintain the city's vehicle fleet. Taxpayers also won, as the department was able to cut its expenses by 25 percent. This is another example of how managed competition can save a city and its citizens tax dollars. A similar situation occurred in Indianapolis, where the city garage had done ten years of total quality management studies. It was one of the most efficient departments in the city, but the mayor put it up for bid anyway. The department won the bid to keep the garage by cutting $2.5 million out of their overhead costs and further increasing their productivity per mechanic by 22 percent. The total cost of the savings for the city was $4.6 million during the life of the contract.[87]

Not all of the contracts awarded for vehicle maintenance have had successful results. For example, shortly after winning a three-year contract to maintain school buses in Fairfax County, Virginia, the contractor was fired by the county for poor service. The problem involved a backlog of buses waiting to be serviced. The problem was so bad that the county had to borrow buses from other counties to pick up schoolchildren. It took four months for the Fairfax County Board of Supervisors to terminate the contract and return the service to a public operation. The company that had been awarded the contract was a large firm with sales in excess of $6 billion. According to a member of the Board of Supervisors, the firm never seemed to take the $11 million contract seriously. In Albany, New York, the entire vehicle maintenance operation was contracted out in 1992. The premise was to replace salaried city workers with hourly paid workers at private garages. The city expected to pay only for the time spent on vehicles, which was to save the city between $100,000 to $200,000. In 1995 an audit revealed that the city had reduced its costs by 18 percent but the comptroller's office attributed the savings to aggressive supervision of the contractor's billing. Contractors were notorious for overbilling the city, which actually raised administrative costs.[88] These cases illustrate that privatization can fail to produce the anticipated results, and in some cases, services may be returned to public management.[89]

WATER AND WASTEWATER SYSTEMS

As discussed in Chapter 2, little difference in efficiency appears to exist between public or private provision of water.[90] However, examples abound where privatizing water systems has resulted in considerable savings for cities. For example, Jersey City, New Jersey, turned over its water system to private management (the company is United Water) in 1996. All of the bids that were submitted offered to run the water system at a lower cost than that at which the city had been able to operate the system. Jersey City expected to save more than $68 million over the five-year period of the contract. When the city operated the system, users were paying for only 66 percent of the water produced. The contract provided financial incentives for the contractor to improve this percentage. If the percentage improved 70 to 75 percent, the contractor would get to keep 5 percent of the money as a bonus. If the percentage increased further, to more than 80 percent, the contractor would get to keep 25 percent of the increased collections. The contractor took over all aspects of the city's water system, from pipes to payment collections. The company computerized the accounting system (the city had kept water records on three-by-five-inch index cards), and invested in infrastructure improvements to stop leaks in the system. Water rates were not affected and all 138 of the city's employees were hired by the contractor and guaranteed jobs for one year. During the second year of the contract, the workforce was to be reduced to 80 employees.[91]

Hawthorne, California (one of the Lakewood Cities), signed a long-term lease for its water system in 1996 to Southern California Water Service Company (Cal Water). The company paid $6.5 million up front and pays an annual lease of $100,000 for fifteen years. The agreement made the company responsible for all aspects of water service, including all capital improvements. The contract also required Cal Water to hire all of the city's waterworks employees at their same rate of pay. Cal Water was able to create an economy of scale by merging with its operations in adjacent Hermosa-Redondo Beach. Water rates were set the same as those in Hermosa-Redondo Beach. Hawthorne became the first city in the nation (in modern times) to enter into a long-term lease for an existing municipal water system with a private company.[92]

North Brunswick, New Jersey, also signed a long lease for its water system, a 20-year franchise for its water and wastewater systems to U.S. Water LLC. The company paid the township $30 million up front—$24 million of this was used to retire existing debt. The lease is bringing in a considerable amount of money to the town. The company paid a concession fee of $1 million the first year and is paying $600,000 per year for the next nine years, $1.5 million per year for the next five years, and $2 million per year for the last five years of the contract. The township saves about $45,000 per year over its old expenses with the water system, and the concessions provide much needed capital for other items the city needs to purchase.[93]

Chandler, Arizona, privatized its wastewater treatment system in 1983. It was the first privately financed, owned, and operated municipal wastewater plant in the nation. Chandler, located in the fast-growing Phoenix area, was growing rapidly and needed to expand this service. The city was low on the federal government's list of priorities for wastewater treatment facilities, so it contracted with the Parsons Corporation of California. The 25-year contract is expected to save the city more than $1 million per year and user fees have dropped significantly to $8.85 per month from the $18.50 that residents were being charged.[94]

Although most cities do not have privatized water and wastewater systems, many cities are now experimenting with turning these systems over to private firms. Thus far, the experiences have been positive in cities that have privatized their water systems. However, the pattern for providing water and sewerage in cities remains under the public sector's domain. Most cities have opted not to privatize this service. This is largely due to politics. For example, after conducting a feasibility study, New Orleans opted not to privatize its water system despite the potential savings. The decision was largely based on internal pressures from public employees and political concerns.[95] Political pressure from those who stand to lose when privatization is under consideration is likely a significant force in the decision to privatize.

TREE TRIMMING, LANDSCAPING, STREET REPAIR, AND OTHER MUNICIPAL SERVICES

Services such as tree trimming, landscaping, and street repair have been popular services for contracting. More than a third of all cities contract out for tree trimming. Cost savings from "outsourcing" (the new name often used for contracting) for tree trimming and landscaping range from 16 percent to 35 percent. During the 1990s tree trimming became a highly competitive business, which has actually lowered the cost of the service. Successful examples abound in these areas. For example, Newport Beach, California, takes its trees very seriously. So seriously that it has a Citizen's Street Tree Committee that advises city council on tree-related matters. The city hired a consulting firm in the early 1990s to examine its tree maintenance program and found that Newport Beach's cost to trim a tree with its own employees was $81. After examining the market rates for trimming trees, the consulting firm recommended that the city contract out for tree trimming and maintenance, which would save the city more than $200,000 per year. The differences were linked to the compensation and productivity of city crews. In 1993 the city contracted out for tree trimming and maintenance. The contractor agreed to hire the displaced city workers. By 1997 the city had saved more than $600,000.[96]

Is monitoring this type of contract difficult? Indianapolis has a grass-cutting contract in which the contractor keeps the grass at four inches high and is paid by the acre. Monitoring the contract is rather easy. At random times, someone literally goes out with a ruler and measures the grass in the areas under contract. Prior to this contract, the city paid to have the grass cut every six weeks in the city's forty-five neighborhood parks. Complaints were high because grass needs to be cut more often than once every six weeks. The cost of the new contract is roughly the same and the new contract did not affect city workers who concentrate on the larger parks. Success stories with tree trimming and landscaping are common throughout the nation. For example, cities throughout southern California, including most of the famous seventy-five Lakewood Cities, contract out for these services.

Using private firms to repair streets is also a commonly contracted service. For example, Laguna Niguel, California, began contracting out for street repair in the early 1990s and saves around $360,000 annually. The savings are largely due to the billing method, which is for unit-of-work rather than time-and-materials. Even the public works director has been pleased with the contractor's performance. In addition to the savings, there are 44 percent fewer complaints about the streets.[97]

Of course, there are examples of failures in these areas, particularly when larger infrastructure projects are involved. Usually these cases involve some form of corruption or at least charges of corruption. For example, New York City awarded a $9.7 million contract to Yonkers Contracting Company to overhaul the Manhattan Bridge. The city awarded the contract even though the company failed to disclose a history of questionable business practices and falsified its application for the contract. The firm also failed to disclose a pending civil suit brought by the New York State Attorney General's Office and twenty-five municipalities. The lawsuit claimed that the company, among other things, had worked with other companies and "carved up" Westchester County into territories and decided which companies would get the contract for resurfacing or repairing a particular road. The suit also charged that the companies overcharged jurisdictions $6 million for asphalt repair.[98] Although examples of potential corruption remain a reality for cities, recall from Chapter 2 that private asphalt paving is typically 95 percent less expensive than when the paving is performed by publicly operated departments.[99] This, of course, assumes the absence of corruption.

Even in services that appear easy for the private sector to handle, failure still can occur. For example, the Salt Lake City (Utah) School District contracted out to bus about one-quarter of the district's students. On the first day of school, more than one hundred children were left standing at bus stops or arrived late at school due to poor planning by the company. The company then asked for an additional $16,000 because it had underestimated the true costs of providing bus services for the district. The school board denied the request and worked out an agreement to repurchase the buses from the contractor and resume the services in-house. The school district resumed the services three months before the contract actually expired.[100] A similar case occurred in Charleston, South Carolina. Although the school district did not take back the service, it withheld $238,000 from one of the payments to the contractor and refused to pay the amount until the problems were resolved.[101] In Ohio, Lebanon's one-year experience with private bus service resulted in costs rising $684,000 more than the previous year when the service was handled in-house.[102] An examination of school busing costs for all of Ohio's school districts revealed that costs of private busing were higher than handling busing in-house for most districts.[103] Clearly, privatization can produce some disappointing results. However, proponents of privatization will argue that yes, there are bad contractors, too, but at least they can be fired when they fail to deliver the services. This is more difficult to do with civil-service-protected employees.

Some services, such as emergency medical services (EMS), appear to universally favor the private sector. For example, when Santa Barbara, California, studied the cost of providing its own ambulance service, it discovered that hiring a private company could save the city $730,000 per year. Thus, paramedical services were contracted. The firm is entirely self-supporting and does not require any subsidy from the city. Newton, Massachusetts, had the same experience when it privatized its ambulance service, which saved the city more than $500,000 each year.[104]

URBAN TRANSPORTATION AND AIRPORTS

Urban transportation has many dimensions, including bus systems, rail systems (such as subways), and highways. Transportation systems involve infrastructure such as bridges, tunnels, and roads, and all involve enormous sums of capital to build and maintain. Highways are heavily subsidized because drivers only pay part of the costs through taxes.[105]

Most urban transportation systems lose money. Buses carry only a handful of passengers, rail systems run half empty, but the freeways and streets are jammed with automobiles and trucks. Cities across the nation have tried to encourage mass transportation to reduce pollution and traffic congestion. Freeways now have special lanes for carpooling. Some cities have "drive-and-ride" programs, in which people drive to a designated area then ride a bus into the city, often for free. Even small cities, like Missoula, Montana, have a bus system that allows many to ride free (such as faculty and staff members who work at the University of Montana). Although the Mountain Line (Missoula's municipal bus system, which is publicly operated) is more successful than bus systems in many cities of similar size, the buses are not usually packed with people.[106] In Missoula, like most areas of the country, most people prefer to drive rather than use the city's bus service. In Columbia, South Carolina, the University of South Carolina tried to operate a bus system in the university district to reduce traffic congestion but the idea was quickly abandoned because most students, faculty, and staff would not ride the buses.

Public transportation has been a municipal loser for decades in the United States.[107] When Miami's Metrorail opened, the daily ridership stayed around 24,000, which was one-eighth of what planners had predicted. Miami voters rejected all attempts by the city to get taxpayer dollars to help the losing Metrorail. One federal official estimated that it would have been cheaper for the federal government to buy everybody that uses the Metrorail a new car every five years than to build and maintain the 20-mile rail system.[108] Subways and other rail systems, whether in Chicago, New York City, or Atlanta, are usually bottomless holes for city budgets. Why do cities continue to dump billions of dollars into these systems? For years the federal government provided much of the money for these systems through the Urban Mass Transportation Administration (UMTA).[109] In 1985, Senator William Proxmire gave his famous "Golden Fleece" award to the UMTA for giving local transit systems $50 billion during a twenty-year period. During the Reagan years some of the funding was cut, but cities continue to build and operate all types of public transportation. These systems, which include buses and various forms of rail transportation, cost taxpayers billions of dollars.

Where did the urban transportation dilemma originate? Mass transit has its origins in the United States with the nineteenth-century electric streetcars that are still used in some cities like parts of New Orleans. During that era most streetcar systems were operated under franchises, which were private (and often corrupt) monopolies. Mass transit began to decline rapidly during the 1950s as the use of the automobile increased and suburban life expanded. At the same time, the federal government and the states invested heavily in highways to handle the increased traffic, including the interstate highway system. Mass transit ridership fell dramatically from 17 billion riders per year in 1950 to 9 billion in the early 1960s. To survive, bus companies and rail systems needed to raise prices and drop unprofitable routes, but instead they got more regulations from government (including price controls). When mass transit companies asked for increases in fares, most cities denied their requests and as a result nearly two hundred bus companies went out of business between the mid-1950s and 1963. In 1964 Congress passed the Urban Mass Transportation Act, which allowed local governments to purchase their local transit companies. Private monopolies quickly became public ones and within fifteen years, local governments owned more than 90 percent of all bus and municipal rail systems in the nation. Ridership on local transit systems continued to decline as deficits continued to mount. By 1985, the nation's local transit deficit was $6 billion.[110] Thus, mass transportation was destroyed by the combination of changing technology (the automobile), changes in lifestyle preferences (the preference for the automobile and the desire to live in suburbia) and government regulation. Cities bought mass transportation systems (better described as urban dinosaurs at the time for most cities) just as Americans were buying cars and moving to the suburbs. It is certainly true that transportation problems have changed since the 1950s and 1960s when cities were buying up bus and rail systems. The justification for operating mass transit systems are to help the poor who cannot afford other methods of transportation, or more recently, to help reduce traffic congestion (which is a problem for most metropolitan areas), and to reduce pollution. But do cities need to be in the bus or rail business? Why not turn these systems into public-private partnerships or privatize them to reduce the enormous cost of operations? There are examples of private firms owning and managing light-rail systems in Europe, but most American systems remain entirely under the control of government.

Metropolitan transit authorities make arguments to justify their existence. Proponents of mass transportation argue that commuter rail systems represent the future. Commuters must be transported from the suburbs to downtowns and other areas of cities and mass-transit systems (buses and rail systems) are viewed as the only viable solution.[111] The American Public Transportation Association (APTA), which is the professional trade organization for the nation's transit systems, claims that ridership increased nearly 5 percent in the first quarter of 2000 over the previous year for all public transit systems. In 1999, the APTA reported that ridership was up 4.5 percent for the year. Ridership on public buses rose in cities such as Ft. Meyers, Florida, by 20 percent, in Phoenix, Arizona, by 10 percent, and in Salt Lake City, Utah, by 21 percent. The Altamont Commuter Express in San Jose, California, showed a 50 percent increase in ridership. According to the APTA, rail systems are also booming, with ridership up in Los Angeles's Red Line subway by more than 62 percent and in San Francisco by 16 percent.[112] But most public transit systems, despite the rise in ridership, lose money, including most of the ones cited here.[113] Grants from the federal government are the reason that most mass transit systems can continue to operate. Most cities could not afford to operate their bus and rail systems without these large subsidies from the federal government, and ridership would drop greatly in most cities if tickets reflected the true cost.

Why are these systems necessary? Proponents claim that mass transit is necessitated by the realities of urban living. Life in a large city is very different from life in rural Wyoming. Many of the smaller metropolitan areas have larger populations than the entire state of Wyoming. Highways are everywhere and in many cases cannot handle the loads at peak times despite the fact that many freeways contain ten or more lanes.[114] But mass transit does not always solve this problem. The primary purpose of most municipal rail systems is to move people from the suburbs to downtowns, yet downtown areas are the slowest-growing job markets in America. Metropolitan areas with more than 1 million people have fewer than 10 percent of the areas' jobs located in the downtown areas.[115] In fact, only four cities have more than 250,000 jobs located in downtown areas. Chicago's Metra (the city's suburban light-rail system)[116] is often cited as a successful mass-transit rail system.[117] The Metra is one of the few rail systems that has a relatively high ridership; nearly 61 percent of Chicago's downtown workers use the Metra.[118] The annual capital investment to maintain these systems is astronomical. For example, based on data from the *1998 Fact Book* of the Chicago area's Regional Transit Authority, the capital asset value of the Metra was $7.2 billion. This equates to a capital cost of $710 million annually. Most municipal rail systems lose money, even if their ridership is strong. For example, the subsidy to operate the Metra, including capital costs per boarding in 1997 was approximately $12 (or $24 per person for a round trip). More than 72 million passengers boarded the Metra in 1997, all being subsidized $12 each time they boarded.[119] Clearly, this creates an enormous burden on taxpayers.[120] Similar stories can be found with many of the nation's rail systems, including San Diego's Trolley (which has not seen a decline in ridership, but only a small portion of the system is profitable).[121] The St. Louis MetroLink has seen its ridership drop significantly, from 84 million riders in 1980 to 51 million riders in 1995.[122] Part of the reason for low ridership is that the rail systems in many cities do not go where people want to go.[123] Most were designed to take people from the suburbs to downtown. For example, when Miami's Metrorail has constructed, it did not go to the beach, the Orange Bowl, or the airport.[124] Thus, the highways remained congested with traffic.

Municipal rail systems remain dominated by public management in the United States. Transportation policy will remain a significant issue in the new century, but precisely what needs to be done is unclear. Does the nation invest in rail systems, bus systems, or build more highways? In large cities like New York City, Chicago, and Detroit, subway systems and other mass transportation have long been a way of life and have long been a necessity (although the cost of operations and the subsidies are enormous). In the case of New York's physically deteriorating subway, the system still does an outstanding job of distributing people throughout the city and it is crowded most of the day and during the evenings. The only slow times are usually after midnight. Although the city controls the subway system, it is noteworthy to mention that the subway was originally a public-private partnership.[125] It is not clear that operating municipal rail systems can generate a profit at this point, but it is possible that rail systems could reduce the amount of subsidy needed for operations.[126] Considering the dilemmas caused by traffic congestion, pollution, and other environmental issues, it is possible that light- and heavy-rail systems may be a viable form of transportation in the new century for metropolitan areas aside from the nation's larger cities, but management of these systems will have to improve and new options for ownership will have to be explored.[127] Urban mass-transit rail systems represent a classic case of public ownership and management, and another area where government monopolies produce inefficiency and waste. This has been one of the persistent issues in urban government for many years.[128]

Although virtually all rail systems remain publicly owned and operated in the United States, there are examples of successfully privatizing municipal bus systems. Studies have shown that privatizing municipal bus systems can lower costs by as much as 50 percent.[129] Table 4.1 illustrates the savings that were realized by privatizing municipal buses in selected American cities (see Appendix A, Bus Service, for summaries of additional studies).

In 1988, bus service in Los Angeles County's Foothill Transit Zone was privatized. The Foothill Transit Zone came about when Proposition A mandated that funding be stopped for the Southern California Rapid Transit District, which had served this area of twenty communities northeast of downtown Los Angeles. As a result, the money that had subsidized fares was shifted to other rail projects and debt service. The county's transportation commission created the Foothill Transit Zone so public transportation would continue for residents, although establishing the new privatized bus service was challenged by a variety of lawsuits and legal obstacles from public employee unions. In 1991, after its first year of operation, an audit of the Foothill Transit Zone found that the operation had managed to achieve a 43 percent reduction over the projected costs.[130] The case illustrates the potential of competitive contracting for transit services in cities. The success of the Foothill Transit Zone project also illustrates that contracting can hold down costs while providing quality services. Urban bus systems cannot be eliminated in most cities, but they can be better managed.

TABLE 4.1   PRIVATIZING MUNICIPAL BUS SERVICES IN SELECTED CITIES[131]

CITY	SAVINGS REALIZED BY CONTRACTING
Denver	33%
Houston	37
Indianapolis	22
Las Vegas	33
Los Angeles (1988)	38
Los Angeles (1989)	48
Miami	29
New Orleans	50
San Diego	44

Source: Adapted from E. S. Savas, *Privatization and Public-Private Partnerships* (New York: Seven Bridges Press, 2000), p. 152.

One other area of modern transportation deserves to be mentioned: airports. Many cities and counties have responsibility for operating airports. These range from relatively small regional airports, such as the Asheville Regional Airport, in Asheville, North Carolina, to large international airports in Atlanta, Chicago, and New York City. Privatization is relatively new to this area in the United States, but internationally, many cities have privatized their airports. For example, the most famous sale of airport operations occurred in Great Britain in 1987 with the sale of the British Airport Authority that operated Heathrow, Gatwick, and Stansted airports in London, and other airports in Scotland. All of the British Airport Authority was offered to investors in the form of shares. At the time, investors valued the company at $2.5 billion, but after five years of successful management, the market value grew to $4 billion. All of the operations became more efficient, generated more revenue, and more investment. Moreover, capital spending increased for improvements that included hotels and the construction of a rail system that runs from Heathrow to downtown London. Similar cases can be found in cities outside of the United States, such as the Toronto, Vienna, and Copenhagen. Privatized airports are operated as businesses and usually make a profit. This is not to suggest that government airport authorities fail at management; there are many well-managed airports in the United States and abroad. But privatized airports go a step further, largely due to the flexibility of private firms. They generate profits because they can more effectively satisfy travelers' needs. Between 1985 and 1993, nearly $400 billion in airport assets were divested. Most privatized airports have received high marks for their performance. Privatizing airports includes a variety of models, which range from total divestiture (like the case with the British Airport Authority), to management leases or contracts by specialized companies that operate airports. In the United States, the largest airport management firms include Johnson Controls World Services and Lockheed Air Terminal. Johnson Controls World Services manages several U.S. airports including Republic, New York; White Plains-Westchester, New York; and Atlantic City, New Jersey. Lockheed Air Terminal manages a number of airports including Burbank, California and Albany, New York. Airports are increasingly viewed as enterprises rather than public services. Airports can be moneymakers, even for cities. Between 1982 and 1992, the use of private contractors for airport operations increased by 16 percent. In 1995, Indianapolis privatized its airport and Riverside County, California, contracted out for its airport operations in 1997. Cost savings at contracting for airport management range between 15 and 40 percent over publicly managed airports. In the United States, it is more common for a city to either form a special authority to operate its airport, or lease its airport to an existing special authority. One example involves the lease by New York and Newark of Kennedy, LaGuardia, and Newark airports to the Port Authority of New York and New Jersey.[132] In 1989, Albany County, New York, attempted to sell its airport but the Federal Aviation Administration blocked the sale.[133] Albany settled on a management contract to operate the airport, with the management firm Lockheed Air Terminal. Thus far, Albany has been satisfied with its contracted airport's performance.[134]

In 1998, the State of New York selected a British firm to lease Stewart Airport for 99 years. Stewart became the first airport in the United States to be fully privatized and the first participant in the Federal Aviation Administration's privatization pilot program. The firm offered $35 million in cash up front and a percentage of airport revenues. The firm, National Express Group, is itself a privatized company. It is the former British government intercity bus operator and was privatized under the Thatcher administration in 1988. Since then, the firm has been successful at operating bus and rail systems in Europe. It also owns and operates regional airports in England and manages Subic Bay Airport in the Philippines. By most indicators, the performance of the firm has been excellent at all of the airports it manages or owns.[135]

Westchester, New York, contracted the White Plains-Westchester Airport in the late 1970s. The 800-acre airport, which is located near affluent suburbs and office parks, has an interesting history. The federal government gave the airport to Westchester County after World War II. For thirty years, the airport's fuel supplier operated the facility. In 1977, the county began five-year contracts with airport management firms due to large annual operating losses. Pan Am World Services initially operated the airport, which later was taken over by Johnson Controls World Services, which continues to manage the airport. Since being contracted, the airport has become financially stable and profitable. The airport now generates net income of around $3 million each year.[136] Most major airports are publicly operated, but feasibility studies have been conducted for many of the nation's large airports. It is likely that we will see more private management of the nation's airports in the new century.

HUMAN SERVICES: SOCIAL SERVICES AND HEALTH CARE

Considering all of the examples above, one might conclude that privatization appears to work in most cases. Aside from the possibility of corruption, most cases seem to endorse the use of private contractors to provide public services. However, there are some areas in which privatization has been "less" successful.[137] Most of the examples used thus far have been what are referred to as *hard services*. That is, garbage collection, street repair, fleet maintenance, construction, and so forth. *Soft services* usually refer to human services, such as health care, social services, or welfare-related services. Soft services are different. They are less mechanical, more unique in many ways, and perhaps more delicate. They often involve clients or patients with special needs rather than pouring concrete or replacing streetlights. Managing a hospital is very different from managing a sports arena. Paving a street is very different from handling patients who need mental health care. Although there are many success stories with privatizing soft services, there are also some notable failures. Relative to the overwhelming success at privatizing hard services, there are many reasons for finding less success using for-profit firms to privatize soft services. Soft services such as welfare are less profitable for private firms than many hard services and are often privatized using nonprofit organizations rather than for-profit firms.

Yet much of society's social services, even some of the most delicate of services, are provided by the private sector. Around 90 percent of America's homeless shelters are operated by religious or private voluntary organizations. Most emergency food distribution is performed by the private sector. In some cases, organizations that were once nonprofit have become profit oriented to use the profits to provide free care. One example is Hospice Care of Miami, which provides services for the terminally ill. The company founder realized that to expand the organization it needed capital and so decided to get the needed capital by becoming a profit-driven organization. The company tripled its admissions by using Medicare reimbursements and expanded its operations into Dallas and New York. The firm continues to provide care to the indigent without reimbursement.

Covering the costs of health care is considered to be one of the most pressing policy issues in the new century. Health care costs have risen to astronomical levels and this has led to many changes that affect all Americans. Health benefits have decreased in all sectors of society and insurance companies have taken aggressive efforts to control their costs. Today, health care benefits are not as robust as in the past. Insurance companies pay an increasingly smaller portion of medical bills that were once covered by most policies. Group health benefits are likely to continue to erode as medical and health care costs continue to skyrocket. Moreover, many Americans do not have insurance, or have inadequate health coverage. This will likely shift the burden toward government until some compromise is reached. During the early 1990s, President Clinton tried to nationalize health care, but his efforts failed. Experts do not predict nationalized health care in the near future, but it is likely that large corporations (and government) will resist paying the higher insurance premiums for their workers. In the United States, we essentially have a very privatized health care system, which has government support for the elderly and the poor. The United States has the best health care in the world, but it is built on a principle that those with the ability to pay will have the best access.

Providing health care is a significant concern for cities and local governments; they must deal with health care problems on a daily basis. Privatization has become increasingly common in the area of health care (see Appendix A, Hospitals, for summaries of studies on managing hospitals). For example, private contracting for management of hospitals has increased significantly since the early 1980s. Over the past two decades, hundreds of public hospitals have been sold to private companies or nonprofit organizations. The number of public hospitals has been shrinking for years, largely due to the escalating costs of operations. In 1975 there were nearly 1,800 state and local public hospitals. By 1995, the number dropped to around 1,300. Public hospitals account for 22 percent of the more than 6,200 hospitals in the United States. About 30 percent of public hospitals are in inner cities and the remaining are located in suburban or rural areas. The federal government also operates hospitals, which account for 17 percent of all hospitals. Many hospitals, including many public hospitals, are now managed or owned by large, professional hospital management corporations. However, many corporations, which operate, own, or manage hundreds of hospitals, have been under fire in recent years. The pursuit of profit coupled with rising expenses, has caused some firms to base treatment entirely on economics and allowing hospital policies, rather than the physicians, to determine treatment for patients. Many of these charges have been refuted and corrected, but the bad publicity has caused large hospital corporations (and HMOs) a lot of problems. These same corporations often take over or buy America's aging public and community hospitals.

Leasing or selling public hospitals can bring in significant revenues. The revenues can take the form of up-front payments from the sales of a facility, a percentage of revenues, annual rent from leases, or taxes. By leasing its public hospital, Austin, Texas, now receives $2.3 million annually. The city also removed many operational headaches, payroll expenses, and other liabilities by privatizing its hospital. Navarro County Memorial Hospital in Corsicana, Texas, was in abysmal shape and faced loss of accreditation because of numerous violations. Hospital Corporation of America agreed to build a new $27 million hospital on land adjacent to the old facility, with a repurchase agreement for the county included in the agreement. The company bought much of the hospital's equipment and hired all of the existing employees. A few years later, the hospital was providing high-quality health care to the rural community and paying $300,000 per year in county taxes. The old hospital required a county subsidy of around $50,000 each year.[138]

Amarillo, Texas, sold its public hospital and received a number of immediate benefits. The sale created a $200 million trust, paid off $13 million of debt, eliminated a an *ad valorem* tax burden of $8.5 million for Amarillo's residents, brought in $3 million in annual property taxes, and paid for ongoing, hospital-related costs to indigents at the hospital. Local officials were pleased with the deal and felt that the community had better health care than in the past and lower taxes.[139] Conroe, Texas, also sold its public hospital to Columbia-HCA, one of the world's largest hospital-management corporations. The final sale price was $104 million, which was $20 million above the estimated fair market value. Conroe realized a net gain of $30 million after $58 million in bond debt was paid off. Moreover, the taxes paid by the hospital allowed the city to reduce its tax rate by 42 percent.[140] Similar cases can be found throughout the nation but there are some examples of disappointments when public hospitals are turned over to the private sector.[141] For example, an examination of

California's public hospitals found little difference in the quality of care or general operations of management-contracted hospitals and those operated by local governments or the state.[142] Some cities have opted not to sell their public hospitals, but to form special hospital authorities to run them. This is how some larger cities, like Denver, Colorado, handle their community hospitals. This is also the case with New York City's eleven public hospitals.[143] Selling hospitals to private companies eliminates governance problems, but it breaks the ties to the public sector accountability.[144] Selling the local public hospital can be controversial in some communities. After a long controversy over selling the community hospital in Cookeville, Tennessee, citizens overwhelming voted in favor of keeping the hospital a city-owned, public hospital.[145]

One very interesting health care case occurred in Montana. Although it involved the state, it ranks as one of the largest privatization failures to date at the state and local level. The case involved Montana privatizing its mental health care in 1997 to save money and improve efficiency. The innovative endeavor quickly turned into a disaster. The contractor, Magellan Health Service, was not paying claims on time, was not reimbursing some providers at all, and was losing $1 million a month. Moreover, Magellan was planning drastic cutbacks in patient eligibility to recoup losses. Liberal Democrats in the state legislature had complained from the very beginning that privatization of this service was not a good idea. Oddly enough, it was a very conservative Republican that joined with the Democrats to cast the deciding vote that cancelled the $400 million contract with Magellan. The failed experiment ended in 1999 and the state formed an advisory council to examine what to do next. The state does not plan to return to full-scale managed care. The contract, which involved $400 million over a five-year period, was the single largest mental health privatization contract in U.S. history, but it failed. The contract covered 70,000 insured Montanans and 5,000 uninsured Montanans. During the first year of operations, Magellan managed to lose nearly $16 million. As of this writing, the state is still examining its options. The legislature will ultimately determine how the state will handle mental health care in the future.[146] Some states, such as New York, have had better luck privatizing mental health care. New York, Missouri, and New Hampshire have reported annual savings of at least 30 percent.[147] However, a national survey found that most states that had privatized mental health care realized savings of less than 5 percent.[148]

As noted earlier, welfare is a marginally profitable business. However, it is big business for government—more than a $200-billion-per-year business for all levels of government. There are numerous problems with welfare policy in the United States, but one of the significant issues is that only a small portion of the funding gets into the hands of recipients.[149] Most of the money is used up in administrative costs. Thus, welfare creates a lot of administrative jobs. Additionally, the success of welfare programs has always been marginal at best. There are many bold efforts on the part of states to manage welfare. Although states play a larger role, municipal governments are involved in the welfare system and often contract with nonprofit firms to help provide services.[150] Welfare is a significant problem and involves large sums of money for cities such as New York, Chicago, and Los Angeles. It is beyond the scope of this book to address the complexities of welfare policy, but examples of privatization of certain welfare-related services at the local level are plentiful. For example, welfare recipients in San Francisco without small children are required to attend an employment and training program that is administered by a private company. The dropout rate has remained around 17 percent, which is much better than when the city administered the program. Moreover, the company places 40 to 60 people who complete the program in jobs each month.[151] Newport, New Hampshire, closed down its welfare department in 1996. The small town of only around 6,000 contracted with a nonprofit organization to handle welfare-related matters. The contract saves Newport 50 percent over what it cost the town to handle welfare services with its own employees.[152]

In the 1960s, the federal government greatly increased the number of government-financed social and health programs. This trend continued until the changes in Washington led to the devolution of many social- and health-related responsibilities back to the states and their local governments, a process that began with President Nixon and continues currently. Many state and local governments have relied on privatization to deliver social and health services to the poor and disabled. A national survey found that 25 percent of all government social services were purchased from the private sector in 1971. By 1979, 55 percent of government social services were being purchased from the private sector (mostly from nonprofit organizations).[153] This trend continues at the state and local level.[154]

SUMMARY

The purpose of this chapter was to present a variety of examples from the real world of municipal government to illustrate what occurs when privatization is actually used. Few of the examples involved academic studies. They were taken from the everyday world of large cities like Atlanta and Chicago, and smaller cities like Asheville, North Carolina and Rye Brook, New York. What do we make of these examples? We can see that privatization has some impressive results when implemented by local governments. But there are also some disappointing results, such as the health care case with Magellan in Montana or in the cases that involved corruption on the part of contractors and city officials.[155] By and large, privatization appears to work across a broad range of services. From collecting garbage to managing hospitals and airports, private firms seem to perform better than their public sector counterparts. Private firms can provide quality services at a lower cost than government.

They can either make money or reduce the subsidies needed to provide essential services. And, in some cases, it is clear that cities may not even need to be in certain service areas, such as operating golf courses or hospitals. Selling or leasing facilities such as golf courses or hospitals can bring in a considerable amount of revenue for cities, and get cities out of losing ventures that drain their budgets every year. In some persistent service areas for cities, such as mass-rail transportation, we have not seen how well (or how poorly) private companies in the United States perform. In other areas, particularly in hard services like collecting and disposing of garbage, the private sector seems to greatly outperform publicly managed organizations. These examples from the real world of city government lead one to suspect that privatization can save cities and taxpayers money.

Like most policy areas, many questions arise with regard to privatization. For example, are there costs that are not revealed? What are the consequences of privatization? Who wins and who loses with privatization? Should cities begin privatizing on a wholesale basis? Should cities emulate the famous Lakewood City Plan, where most services are contracted? In the 1980s, Lakewood, California (from which the name *Lakewood City Plan* is derived), had less than 10 full-time employees, yet offered a full range of services for residents.[156] Can larger cities operate in this manner? Finally, what about political accountability and concerns about equity? What impact does privatization have on the political structure and institutions in our cities? Is privatization a viable solution for providing public services in the new century? Does privatization serve the public interest? These and many other important questions are the subject matter of the final chapter.

NOTES

1. International City/County Management Association, *Service Delivery in the 90s: Alternative Approaches for Local Governments* (Washington, D.C.: author, 1989), p. 4. The original source of the Newark case is *New Jersey Municipalities* (November 1987), p. 6. For a more in-depth discussion of Newark's experience, see Randall Fitzgerald, *When Government Goes Private: Successful Alternatives to Public Services* (New York: Universe Books, 1988), pp. 64–65.
2. John Hanrahan, *Government for Sale* (Washington, D.C.: American Federation of State, County, and Municipal Employees, 1986). Also, see John Hanrahan, *Passing the Bucks: The Contracting Out of Public Services* (Washington, D.C.: American Federation of State, County, and Municipal Employees, 1983). Both books are filled with examples of where contracting failed. Many of the examples involve corruption. Additionally, see John Miller and Christopher Tufts, "Privatization Is a Means to More with Less," in *Annual Editions: State and Local Government*, 5th ed., ed. Bruce Stinebrickner (Guilford, CT: Dushkin Publishing, 1991), pp. 216–219. This article provides a number of examples in which privatization was implemented, but the city had to take back the services. The services include garbage collection, police protection, and parking meter service.

3. John Hanrahan's, *Government for Sale: Contracting Out, the New Patronage* (Washington, D.C.: American Federation of State, County, and Municipal Employees, 1977), Chapter 2, contains many examples of the influence of organized crime in the New York City and New Jersey areas.

4. Ibid. Chapter 1 of Hanrahan's, *Government for Sale: Contracting Out, the New Patronage* is devoted entirely to the history of Albany and the corruption associated with contracting.

5. This classic definition comes from Harold Lasswell, *Politics: Who Gets What, When, How* (New York: Meridian Press, 1972).

6. Stephen Moore, "Los Angeles County's Pioneering Fleet Maintenance Contract," *Partnership Focus: The Magazine for Public-Private Partnerships* (October 1990), pp. 14–17.

7. One example involved Chicago and a multi-million-dollar kickback scheme to public officials to haul sludge for the Chicago Metropolitan Sanitary Department during the 1970s. The scheme resulted in eight public officials and businessmen being indicted by a federal grand jury. In another scandal, a Dane County, Wisconsin, jury convicted a trash collection company of bid-rigging its contracts to haul garbage. Both of these case studies are included in John Hanrahan's, *Government for Sale: Contracting Out, the New Patronage*, Chapter 2.

8. John Hanrahan's, *Government for Sale: Contracting Out, the New Patronage* contains numerous examples of cases where the open-bidding process produced questionable results. One example involved a New Jersey town where many of the town's contracts were awarded to companies owned by the mayor.

9. This case is part of the Reason Foundation's privatization database at <http://www.privatization.com> under *fire protection*.

10. William Glaberson, "Experiment in Private Fire Protection Fails for a Westchester Village," *New York Times*, 13 March 1998, B-1.

11. Recycling programs vary across the nation. See Deb Stark and Dianna Gordon, "Reducing the Rubbish Heap," in *Annual Editions: State and Local Government*, 8th ed., ed. Bruce Stinebrickner (Guildford, CT: Dushkin/McGraw Hill, 1997), pp. 271–272. Also, see Ann Bowman and Richard Kearney, *State and Local Government*, 4th ed. (Boston, MA: Houghton Mifflin, 1999), pp. 495–497.

12. The companies that collect garbage often handle recycling at their landfills. For example, in Asheville, North Carolina, the majority of the city's residential garbage is hauled to neighboring South Carolina, where Waste Management, Inc., owns a landfill. This deal was controversial because it cost the city more than $1.1 million in tipping fees at the city's landfill. See Jason Sandford, "Trash Disposal Deal Struck: Buncombe, Henderson Garbage to Go to S.C. Landfill," *Asheville Citizen-Times*, 5 March 1993, A-1.

13. Jim Glen, "The State of Garbage," *BioCycle* (April 1992), p. 46. The *Mobro 4000*, a garbage barge that spent four and a half months and traveled six thousand miles seeking a port where it could unload its commercial trash, symbolized the problem of disposing of the nation's garbage.

14. Ibid, p. 47. For an excellent discussion created by trying to recycle municipal solid waste, see Tom Arrandale, "Making Recycling Work," *Governing: Incorporating City and State* (May 1994), p. 62. Also, see Tom Arrandale, "Trash Management: The Changing Mix," *Governing: The Magazine for States and Localities* (August 1995), pp. 67–70, and Tom Arrandale, "Confessions of an Eco-Criminal," *Governing: The*

Magazine of States and Localities (May 1995), p. 80. In this commentary, Arrandale argues that recycling may be an "upper-class thing." That is, considering that recycling programs have not been very effective in most cities, because of the lack of a market, programs exist mainly because it is politically correct to attempt to recycle.

15. Keith Schneider, "Burning Trash for Energy: Is It an Endangered Industry?" *New York Times*, 11 October 1993, A-21. Also, see Bob Hall and Mary Lee Kerr, *1991–1992 Green Index* (Washington, D.C., Island Press, 1991), p. 3.

16. Ivan Amato, "Can We Make Garbage Disappear?" *Time*, vol. 19, 8 November 1999. This article is available on Time.com at <http://www.time.com/time/articles/0,3266,33436,00.html>.

17. Although most areas of solid waste disposal are regulated and controlled by the states, Congress has intervened in a variety of ways. For example, in 1965 Congress passed the Solid Waste and Disposal Act, which provided funds and technical assistance for states and local governments. The Resource Recovery Act of 1970 maintained a hands-off approach by the federal government and continued to provide funding for local governments. It was not until the Conservation and Recovery Act of 1976 that the federal government entered into solid waste management to any significant degree. Although this act was greatly concerned with hazardous waste, the federal government's role moved beyond providing only funding and technical support. The act required states to develop solid waste management plans. For a discussion about the environmental concerns involving solid waste, see Zachary Smith, *The Environmental Paradox* (Englewood Cliffs, NJ: Prentice Hall, 1995), pp. 166–170. Also, see Daniel Mullins, Alfred Tat-Kei Ho, and Chia-Ying Chou, "The Solid Waste Crisis: Is Recycling a Response?" *Municipal Yearbook 1997* (Washington, D.C.: International City/County Management Association), pp. 16–25.

18. Dudley Price, "Waste Industries Trashes Plan; Focus is Less on Buyout, More on Landfills," *The News & Observer* (Raleigh, NC), 5 May 2000.

19. The source of this information is the Allied Waste, Inc., Web site located at <http://www.awin.com>. It should be noted that Allied Waste also owns Browning-Ferris Industries (BFI), which was the largest waste management company in the United States for many years before being purchased by Allied Waste, Inc.

20. The source of this information is the first-quarter financial report for Allied Waste, Inc. This report is available on their Web site at <http://www.awin.com>.

21. Waste Management, Inc., is the largest company in North America that provides comprehensive waste management services. Based in Houston, the company operates an unequalled network of service facilities throughout the United States, Canada, Mexico, and Puerto Rico that serve more than 10 million residential customers and 1 million businesses. Waste Management is the largest company in its industry. Its service assets include more than 300 state-of-the-art land disposal sites, 16 trash-to-energy plants, more than 300 transfer stations and over 1,400 collection facilities which provide recycling and waste-collection resources to thousands of communities large and small. In addition, the company is the largest collector of recyclable materials from businesses and households in the world and its 150 materials-recovery facilities (MRF) process more than five million tons of recyclable commodities each year. The company has 60,000 employees. The data is available on their Web site, <http://www.wastemanagement.com> and is included in their annual report.

22. It should be noted that the large corporations handle all forms of waste management (nonhazardous and hazardous waste, recycling, and all forms of disposal).
23. This comment was made by the late *Chicago Daily News* columnist, Mike Royko, and is cited in John Hanrahan's, *Government for Sale: Contracting Out, the New Patronage*, p. 37.
24. Allied Waste recently purchased Browning-Ferris Industries (BFI), which was the second-largest waste management corporation in the world.
25. Ibid, pp. 38–43. Both the Browning-Ferris and Waste Management, Inc., cases involved investigations by the Securities and Exchange Commission. Publicly held corporations that trade on the stock exchange must file reports with the Securities and Exchange Commission. One can view many of these reports on the Web sites of companies, such as that of Waste Management, Inc.
26. American Federation of State, County, and Municipal Employees, *Government for Sale: Solid Waste*. The on-line version of *Government for Sale* is available on the AFSCME Web site at <http://www.afscme.org>.
27. Ibid.
28. See Hanrahan, *Government for Sale: Contracting Out, the New Patronage*, Chapters 1 and 2.
29. The overcharges were based on estimates by the district attorney's office. See Hanrahan, *Government for Sale: Contracting Out, the New Patronage*, p. 47.
30. Ibid, pp. 48–49.
31. For a thorough description of these and other scandals, see Hanrahan, *Government for Sale: Contracting Out, the New Patronage*, Chapter 2.
32. Julie Bennett, "Privatization Cuts Hauling Costs, or Does It?" *City and State* (November 5, 1990), p. 12.
33. For a complete discussion about the successful experience with privatizing garbage collection in Phoenix, see Robert Franciosi, "Garbage In, Garbage Out: An Examination of Private/Public Competition," *Arizona Issue Analysis* 148. This study is available on the Goldwater Institute Web site in Adobe Acrobat format at <http://www.goldwaterinstitute.org>.
34. Robert Franciosi, "Privatization in Arizona's Largest Cities," The Goldwater Institute, *Privatization Report Number 01* (September 1998), p. 5. This report is available on the Goldwater Institute's Web site at <http://www.goldwater institute.org>.
35. International City/County Management Association, *Service Delivery in the 90s: Alternative Approaches for Local Governments* (Washington, D.C.: author, 1989), p. 124.
36. Bennett, "Privatization Cuts Hauling Costs, or Does It?" p. 12.
37. National Center for Policy Analysis, 727 15th Street N.W., Washington, D.C. 20005. The article can be viewed on their Web site at <http://www.ncpa.org/pd/private/privb3.html> (2000). The title of the article is "Privatization in Chicago," which also includes some findings from other cities, such as Indianapolis.
38. The Indianapolis and Manhattan Beach case studies (and several other similar case studies) are included in Reason Foundation's Public Policy Institute, Privatization Database, "Solid Waste/Recycling," p. 1. The article is available on the Reason Foundation's privatization database located at <http://www.privatization.com>.

39. Randall Fitzgerald, *When Government Goes Private* (New York: Universe Books, 1988), p. 66.
40. Barbara Stevens and E. S. Savas, "An Analysis of the Feasibility of Private Refuse Collection and Disposal in Mount Vernon, New York," a report prepared for the Mount Vernon Urban Renewal Agency (January 1977). Cited in E. S. Savas, *Privatization and Public-Private Partnerships* (New York: Seven Bridges Press, 2000), p. 159.
41. Paul Kengor and Jake Haulk, "The Case for Competitive Contracting of Residential Refuse Collection in the City of Pittsburgh" (Pittsburgh, PA: Allegheny Institute for Public Policy, 1999). The study is available from the Allegheny Institute, 835 Western Avenue, Suite 300, Pittsburgh, PA 15233. A summary of the study is available on-line at <http://www.alleghenyinstitute.org>.
42. Ibid.
43. Reason Foundation's Public Policy Institute, Privatization Database, "Solid Waste/Recycling," p. 1.
44. Fitzgerald, *When Government Goes Private*, p. 66.
45. Ibid, p. 67.
46. Geoffrey Segal and Adrian Moore, "Privatizing Landfills: Market Solutions for Solid Waste Disposal," *Policy Study Number 267* (Los Angeles, CA: Reason Foundation's Public Policy Institute, 2000), p. 23. This article can be viewed on-line at <http://www.rppi.org>. This report includes an excellent discussion about the positive and negative aspects of privatizing landfills and resources recovery centers. The report includes a number of case studies.
47. Ibid, pp. 23–26.
48. Bethany Barber, "Privatization: Not Just Garbage," *Recycling Times* (September 1, 1998).
49. Reason Foundation's Public Policy Institute, Privatization Database, "Solid Waste/Recycling," p. 1.
50. Ibid. The privatization survey was R. W. Beck's *National Privatization Survey* (1998). R. W. Beck is an Orlando, Florida-based consulting company.
51. Public employee unions usually oppose most efforts to privatize or contract out services. For example, citizens in Los Angeles County approved a referendum to amend the county's charter (by a margin of 65 percent to 35 percent) to allow for competitive bidding in 1978. Unions and the city's bureaucracy stalled implementation of the referendum for two years. It was not until sympathetic politicians were elected to the county's Board of Supervisors that the referendum was implemented. See Fitzgerald, *When Government Goes Private*, p. 63.
52. The source of these examples about Indianapolis is Anthony Jewell, "Indianapolis Ahead in Privatization Races," *Washington Times*, 7 November 1995. The summary can be viewed on-line on the National Center for Policy Analysis's Web site at <http://www.ncpa.org> under *Privatization Issues*.
53. The source of these examples is Jeff Williams, "The Do's and Don'ts of Competitive Contracting: Cleveland, Cincinnati, and Indianapolis," *Perspective* (October 1997), Buckeye Institute for Public Policy Solutions, 131 Ludlow Street, Suite 317, Dayton, OH 45402. This can be viewed on-line on the National Center for Policy Analysis's Web site, <http://www.ncpa.org> under *State & Local Issues*.
54. Contracting out for custodial services failed in the Hernando, Florida, school district. Soon after the school district contracted with ServiceMaster, Inc., to supervise the district's custodial and maintenance department, allegations of

questionable conduct on the part of school officials and ServiceMaster during the bidding process surfaced. This led to a grand jury investigation. The district's finance officer testified that she was instructed to use budget figures that were inflated over planned spending levels to show the savings that could be realized through contracting. In addition, the company provided the district with bid specifications that only ServiceMaster could meet. The following year a new superintendent requested a review of ServiceMaster's savings. The finance officer concluded that the costs of operating the departments had increased more than $600,000 during the first full year of the contract. Moreover, ending the contract would cost the district $500,000 because the district would have to repurchase the supplies and equipment that it no longer owned. The school board eventually brought the departments back in-house following expiration of the contract with ServiceMaster. This case can be viewed on the American Federation of State, County, and Municipal Employee Web site in the on-line version of *Government for Sale* at <http://www.afscme.org> under *Custodial Services*. Clearly, this is not a good example of managed competition.

55. Franciosi, "Privatization in Arizona's Largest Cities," pp. 5–6.
56. William Eggers, "Revitalizing Our Cities: Perspectives from America's New Breed of Mayors" (February 7, 1996). The article is available from the Washington Institute for Policy Studies, Post Office Box 24645, Seattle, WA 98124. The summary of this article can be viewed on-line on the National Center for Policy Analysis's Web site at <http://www.ncpa.org> under *Privatization Issues*. Also, see Charles Mahtesian, "The Privatizing Daley," *Governing: The Magazine of States and Localities* (April 1994), pp. 26–33.
57. Ibid, pp. 6–7.
58. Bennett, "Privatization Cuts Hauling Costs, or Does It?" p. 12.
59. Blaine Harden, "Neighbors Give Central Park a Wealthy Glow," *New York Times*, 22 November 1999. The article can be viewed on-line at <http://www.nytimes.com/99/11/22/news/national/regional/ny-park-conserve.html>.
60. Douglas Martin, "Management of Central Park is Going Private," *New York Times*, 12 February 1998.
61. Reason Foundation's Privatization Database, "Parks and Recreational Services," p. 1. This article can be viewed on-line at <http://www.privatization.com>.
62. "Trump Reports Large Profit from Wollman Rink," *New York Times*, 1 April 1987, B-3.
63. Fitzgerald, *When Government Goes Private*, pp. 68–69. Fitzgerald provides an excellent discussion about the Wollman Rink incident.
64. Paul Downing, "User Charges and Service Fees," in *Budget Finance*, ed. Jack Rubin, W. Bartley Hildreth, and Gerald Miller (Athens, GA: University of Georgia Press, 1981), pp. 73–82.
65. Charles Mahtesian, "Revenue in the Rough," *Governing: The Magazine of States and Localities* (October 1997), pp. 42–44. Also, see Lisa Snell, "Fairway Practices: Privatizing Golf Courses, Part I," *Cal-Tax Digest* (June 1998). Available on-line at <http://www.caltax.org/MEMBER/digest/Jun98/jun98-5.htm>.
66. Public interest and access to golf courses increased dramatically in the twentieth century. In 1931, there were 5,691 golf courses in the United States. Approximately 22 percent of these courses were open to the public. By 1998, there were 16,010 golf courses. Only 4,698 were private clubs (not open to the general public); 8,716

were privately owned courses that were open to the public, and 2,596 were government-owned. Source: National Golf Foundation, 1150 South U.S. Highway One, Suite 401, Jupiter, FL 33477. The National Golf Foundation's Web site is <http://www.ngf.org>.

Moreover, between 1986 and 1997, the number of golfers increased 24 percent (to a total of 27 million). At the end of 1997, there were approximately 932 courses under construction or beginning expansion, including 125 municipal golf courses. The construction of golf courses ranges from $3 to $10 million dollars. It is estimated that the cost to taxpayers could be $375 million for construction and renovation. The most recent trend for municipalities is to form public-private partnerships to build new golf courses or renovate old ones. Public-private partnerships put very little public money at risk. See Lisa Snell, "Getting Greens in the Black: Golf-Course Privatization Trends and Practices," *Policy Study Number 260* (Los Angeles, CA: Reason Foundation's Public Policy Institute, 2000), p. 5. This is an excellent study that includes a number of case studies, which includes Los Angeles, New York City, Detroit, Chicago, and San Francisco. This report is available on the Reason Foundation's Web site at <http://www.rppi.org>. The typical municipal golf course generates about $892,000 per year, which is well below the potential of most municipal golf courses, according to the National Golf Foundation.

67. *Contracting Public Services Survey, 1995 Update* (Atlanta, GA: Mercer Group).
68. Snell, "Getting Greens in the Black: Golf-Course Privatization Trends and Practices," p. 5.
69. Snell, "Getting Greens in the Black: Golf-Course Privatization Trends and Practices," p. 4.
70. Fitzgerald, *When Government Goes Private*, p. 69.
71. Snell, "Getting Greens in the Black: Golf-Course Privatization Trends and Practices," p. 15.
72. Ibid.
73. Ibid, p. 16.
74. Interview with Larry Fisher, City Finance Director, October 1985. It should be noted that the Asheville Civic Center has had mixed results over the years, which is often attributed to its location in the heart of downtown Asheville where parking is not plentiful.
75. Reason Foundation's Privatization Database, "Facility and Convention Management," p. 1. This article can be viewed on-line at <http://www.privatization.com> under *State and Local Privatization, Facility and Convention Management*. Also, see Charles Mahtesian, "Escalation in the Convention Center War," *Governing: Incorporating City and State* (July 1994), pp. 19–21.
76. Ibid, p. 2.
77. Ibid.
78. Ibid, pp. 2–4.
79. Fitzgerald, *When Government Goes Private*, pp. 70–72. Also, see "Dolphins Reel in Funds on Their Own," *Washington Post*, 23 March 1987, A-7.
80. Ibid, pp. 71–72.
81. Rowan Miranda and Karlyn Andersen, "Alternative Service Delivery in Local Government, 1982–1992," *Municipal Yearbook 1994* (Washington, D.C.: International City/County Management Association), pp. 26–35.

82. This survey was the *1990 National Privatization Survey* conducted by the Mercer Group, Atlanta, GA.

83. Moore, "Los Angeles County's Pioneering Fleet Maintenance Contract," pp. 14–17.

84. Reason Foundation's Privatization Database, "Fleet Management and Maintenance," p. 1. This article can be viewed on-line at <http://www.privatization. com> under *Fleet Management and Maintenance.*

85. Fitzgerald, *When Government Goes Private*, p. 66.

86. Ibid.

87. Ibid, p. 3.

88. Elliot Sclar, "The Privatization of Public Services: Lessons from Case Studies" (Washington, D.C.: Economic Policy Institute, 1997).

89. "School Bus Maintenance," *Government for Sale* (Washington, D.C.: American Federation of State, County, and Municipal Employees). This case study can be viewed on the AFSCME Web site in the on-line version of *Government for Sale*. The Web site is located at <http://www.afscme.org>.

90. There are a few exceptions that were not included in Chapter 2. For example, a 1996 study of water companies in California found that investor-owned water companies made a profit, even though they had to charge the same for their water as government-owned operations. This study was conducted by the Reason Foundation, which also notes that savings for contracting out for water range between 10 and 25 percent. The study is available on the Reason Foundation's Web site at <http://www.reason.org> under *Privatizing Water Utilities and Water Works*.

91. Reason Foundation's Privatization Database, "Water," p. 1. The article can be viewed on-line at <http://www.privatization.com> under *Water Treatment*.

92. Ibid, p. 4.

93. Ibid, pp. 4–5.

94. Fitzgerald, *When Government Goes Private*, pp. 176–177. For additional studies about privatizing water and wastewater systems, see Holly June Stiefel, "Municipal Wastewater Treatment: Privatization and Compliance," *Policy Study Number 175* (Los Angeles, CA: Reason Foundation's Public Policy Institute, 1994). Also, see Kathy Neal, Patrick Maloney, Jonas Marson, and Tamer Francis, "Restructuring America's Water Industry: Comparing Investor-Owned and Government Water Systems," *Policy Study Number 200* (Los Angeles, CA: Reason Foundation's Public Policy Institute, 1996). Also, see David Haarmeyer, "Privatizing Infrastructure: Options for Municipal Water-Supply Systems," *Policy Study Number 151* (Los Angeles, CA: Reason Foundation's Public Policy Institute, 1992). These studies are available on the Reason Foundation's Public Policy Institute's Web site at <http://www.rppi.org>.

95. This case is available on the American Federation of State, County, and Municipal Employees Web site located at <http://www.afscme.org>.

96. "Privatizing Tree Trimming and Landscaping Services," pp. 1–2. Reason Foundation's Public Policy Institute at <http://www.privatization.com/ Collection/SpecificServiceAreas/landscaping-local.html> (2000).

97. Donna Lee Braunstein, "Maintenance Contract Saves Cities Thousands of Dollars," *Privatization Watch*, no. 209 (Los Angeles, CA: Reason Foundation, 1994). This article is available on the Charles Abbott Associate, Inc., Web site at <http://www.caa-online.com>.

98. *Government for Sale: Infrastructure.* This article is available on-line on the American Federation of State, County, and Municipal Employee's Web site at <http://www.afscme.org> in the on-line version of *Government for Sale.*

99. Barbara Stevens, "Comparative Study of Municipal Service Delivery," a report prepared for the Office of Policy Development, Department of Housing and Urban Development (February 1984).

100. *Government for Sale: School Bus Service.* This article is available on-line on the American Federation of State, County, and Municipal Employee's Web site at <http://www.afscme.org> in the on-line version of *Government for Sale.*

101. American Federation of State, County, and Municipal Employees, "Schools for Sale: The Privatization of Non-Institutional School Services." This study can be viewed on the American Federation of State, County, and Municipal Employees Web site at <http://www.afscme.org>. The article provides many excellent examples of failures with services in the schools, including busing, food services, and custodial services.

102. Joanne Huist Smith, "Bus Service Switch Costs $684,000 More," reprinted from the *Dayton Daily News,* 8 June 2000. This report is included in *Privatization Update,* which is located on the American Federation of State, County, and Municipal Employee's Web site at <http://www.afscme.org>.

103. Mark Cassell, "An Assessment of the Privatization of School Transportation in Ohio's Public School Districts." This study is available on the American Federation of State, County, and Municipal Employee's Web site at <http://www.afscme.org>. The study examined Ohio's school districts over a five-year period.

104. These and many other public safety examples are included in Fitzgerald's, *When Government Goes Private,* p. 72.

105. For many years, economists have been advocating congestion-pricing and toll roads to help offset some (or potentially most) of the costs associated with pollution and traffic congestion. Under congestion-pricing, drivers would pay variable rates (tolls) for road use according to the time of day they were driving, the routes they used, and the amount of congestion. Technology now makes this option more feasible due to nonstop electronic toll collection equipment. Toll roads, public and private, are an option that is slowly becoming more common than in the past. Although toll roads and bridges have always been a part of the urban landscape in some areas, it is believed they will be even more common in the future. Many states are experimenting with private toll roads, including Virginia, Massachusetts, and California. However, toll roads have critics with legitimate complaints. For example, in California a toll road system is being constructed that would relieve traffic on the public freeways. Critics charge that we will develop a two-tier system with the rich able to drive unimpeded on the expensive private roads, while the poor and much of the middle class sit in traffic jams on public freeways that will still be congested.

106. The Mountain Line provides excellent access throughout the city of Missoula. It is a publicly operated system that functions from an independent tax district and is governed by a special authority, the Urban Transportation District Board. The bus system is funded by taxes and grants from the Federal Transportation Administration.

107. There are many reasons for low ridership on America's mass-transit systems that go beyond the scope of this book. One of the main reasons is the price of fuel. Gas prices at the pump in the United States are significantly lower than in most other

counties. Moreover, the nation spends billions of dollars in highway construction and maintenance. And, with the exception of the nation's larger cities (like New York and Chicago) parking is available and freeways (no matter how crowded) still carry commuters around the city. Also, most Americans live in the suburbs and have maintained a preference for using their cars. If gas prices rose significantly, parking became unavailable (or outrageously expensive), and highway systems became incapable of moving traffic, it is believed that ridership would increase. Although this may occur in the future, at the present time, with the exception of only the largest cities, the automobile remains the preferred mode of ground transportation for Americans. Although billions of dollars have been spent to improve municipal mass-transit systems, highways are still considered to be mainstream transportation policy at all levels of government. The need for mass-transit systems is real and likely to increase in the future.

108. David Stockman, director of the Office of Management and Budget during the first Reagan administration made this comment, which is cited in Fitzgerald, *When Government Goes Private*, p. 152.

109. The Urban Mass Transportation Administration still exists, but has been renamed the Federal Transportation Administration (FTA).

110. Much of the summary provided here comes from Randall Fitzgerald's excellent discussion about urban transportation in *When Government Goes Private*, pp. 151–163. A thorough presentation of the history of urban mass transit is also included in James Delong's, "Myths of Light-Rail Transit," *Policy Study Number 244*. This study is available on the Reason Foundation's Web site at <http://www.rppi.org/ps244.html>.

111. Paul Weyrich and William Lind, "Conservatives and Mass Transit: Is It Time for a New Look?" The article makes the case for saving mass transportation systems in the nation's cities. It is available on the American Public Transportation Association's (APTA) Web site at <http://www.apta.com/info/online> (2000). Also available on the APTA's Web site is Weyrich and Lind's newer article, "Does Transit Work? A Conservative Reappraisal" (2000). Both are interesting articles that make arguments for increasing mass transit systems and include case studies to illustrate their position.

112. "Public Transportation Ridership Continues to Soar," *Transit News* (Washington, D.C.: American Public Transportation Association, 2000). This article is available on the American Public Transportation Association's Web site at <http://www.apta.com>.

113. At the time this book was being written and published, the Reason Foundation was developing its Web page for transportation. By the time this book is released, the page will be available at <http://www.privatizaton.com> under the *Privatization Database, Transportation*. Theses pages include trends, surveys, case studies, and analysis.

114. For an interesting discussion about privatizing highways, see Howard Ullman, "McHighways," *The New Republic*, 4 September 1989, pp. 18–19,

115. For an excellent discussion of changes in urban areas, see Joel Garreau, *Edge City: Life on the New Frontier* (New York: Doubleday, 1991).

116. Chicago's subway system is called the "L," which is a separate system. Both systems operate in the downtown area and in the suburbs and are publicly managed operations.

117. It should be noted that there are two types of commuter rail systems, heavy-rail

and light-rail. Heavy-rail are the large subways like the New York City Subway or the Chicago L. These are large and expensive systems that require enormous capital investment. Light-rail systems are found in San Diego's Trolley, St. Louis's MetroLink, and Miami's Metrorail. Light-rail systems are also expensive, but less expensive than the heavy-rail subways. They are also usually smaller systems.

118. In the case of Chicago, downtown workers represent around 8 percent of the cities' workforce.

119. The Chicago mass-transit system is a large organization. The Chicago Transit Authority (CTA) is an independent governmental agency created by state legislation. The CTA began operating on October 1, 1947, after it acquired the properties of the Chicago Rapid Transit Company and the Chicago Surface Lines. On October 1, 1952, CTA became the sole operator of Chicago transit when it purchased the Chicago Motor Coach system. The CTA operates the nation's second-largest public transportation system and covers the City of Chicago and thirty-eight surrounding suburbs. On an average weekday, 1.5 million rides are taken on the CTA. CTA has approximately 1,900 buses that operate over 129 routes and 1,932 route miles. Buses make about 1 million passenger trips a day and serve 12,000 posted bus stops. CTA's approximately 1,100 rapid transit cars operate over seven routes and 289 miles of track. CTA trains make about 1,434 trips each day and serve 141 stations. Chicago is one of the few cities in the world that provides rapid transit service to two major airports. From the downtown area, the CTA's Blue Line takes riders to O'Hare International Airport in about 40 minutes and the Orange Line to Midway Airport in about 30 minutes. The CTA generates revenue from fare box collections and also receives supplemental funding for operating expenses from the Regional Transportation Authority (RTA). The CTA budget for fiscal year 2000 was $841 million for its operating budget and $409 million for its capital budget. The CTA employs more than 11,000 employees. The Regional Transportation Authority (RTA) was established in 1974 to oversee local transportation operators in the six-county Chicago metropolitan area. Illinois state law requires the three RTA service boards—CTA, Metra (the suburban rail system), and Pace (the suburban bus system) to recover collectively at least 50 percent of operating costs from fare box and other system revenues. The RTA provides public funding for the agencies' remaining operating expenses. (This information comes from the CTA's Web site at <http://www.yourcta.com/welcome/overview.html>). This is an excellent Web site that also contains a history of Chicago's famous "L," the city's subway system.

120. The figures are included in Peter Gordon's, "Does Transit Really Work? Thoughts on the Weyrich and Lind Conservative Reappraisal," pp. 3–4. This article is available on the Reason Foundation's Public Policy Institute's Web site at <http://www.rppi.org/transportation/ftebrief101.html>.

121. In San Diego's case, 15 percent of the capital cost (known as the Blue Line) generates 77 percent of the ridership.

122. Ibid, p. 4.

123. There are other reasons, like the low cost of gasoline in the United States and America's preference for automobiles. In all fairness to the nation's public transportation bus and rail systems, highways are also heavily subsidized. The cost to the individual is small but the cost of maintaining highway systems is significant for governments.

124. Fitzgerald, *When Government Goes Private*, p. 151.
125. James Ramsey, "Selling the New York City Subway: Wild-eyed Radicalism or the Only Feasible Solution," in *Prospects for Privatization*, ed. Steve Hanke (New York: Academy of Political Science, 1987), pp. 94–95. This is an excellent article that presents a strong case for privatizing New York's subway system. For a good discussion of public-private partnerships, see William Colman, *State and Local Government and Public-Private Partnerships* (New York: Greenwood Press, 1989).
126. Ibid, pp. 92–103.
127. Private firms have options and flexibility that are not available to cities. For example, public employee unions are generally successful at demanding higher wages and benefits. In the private sector, firms usually respond to increases in labor costs by substituting capital and technology for labor. In the case of most rail systems, as labor costs increased, capital and technology were not substituted. If the nation's municipal rail systems were privatized, it is likely that this would occur. During difficult times, private firms will reduce output or sell non-profitable portions of the firm. These options, for political reasons, are not available to municipal transit authorities. Ownership arrangements will have to be explored, such as leases, investor-owned arrangements, contracts, or, potentially, divestiture of some municipal rail systems in the future.
128. For interesting commentary on the future of mass-rail systems in cities, see Charles Mahtesian, "The Snail's Pace of High Speed Rail," *Governing: The Magazine of States and Localities* (August 1994), pp. 25–29.
129. E. S. Savas, *Privatization and Public-Private Partnerships* (New York: Seven Bridges Press, 2000), pp. 152–153.
130. John O'Leary, "Comparing Public and Private Bus Transit Services: A Study of the Los Angeles Foothill Transit Zone," *Policy Study Number 163*. The study is available from the Reason Foundation's Public Policy Institute, 3415 South Sepulveda Blvd., Suite 400, Los Angeles, CA 90034, or on their Web site at <http://www.rppi.org/transportation/ps163.html>.
131. The original source of the data is, E. S. Savas, "A Comparative Study of Bus Operations in New York City," Report Number FTA NY-11-0040-92-1 (Washington, D.C.: Federal Transit Administration, U.S. Department of Transportation, 1992) and Wendell Cox et al., "Competitive Contracting for Public Transit: Review of the Experience," *1996 Public Transportation Assessment, Supplemental Report*, Legislative Transportation Committee, State of Washington, February 1, 1997. In Savas' book, *Privatization and Public-Private Partnerships*, the discussion and tables also include the results from cities in other countries.
132. Reason Foundation's Privatization Database, "Airports." This summary of trends and case studies is located at <http://www.privatization.com/Collections/SpecificServiceAreas/airports-local.htm> (2000).
133. The Federal Aviation Administration has since implemented a pilot program for privatizing airports.
134. There are several types of airports: air-carrier airports and general aviation airports. Most of us are more familiar with air-carrier airports, which is where the large airlines operate. General aviation airports are smaller, multi-purpose airfields. There are far more contracted general aviation airports than air-carrier airports in the United States at this time.

135. "Airports," p. 4.
136. Ibid, p. 5.
137. See Richard Tradewell, "Privatizing Public Hospitals: Strategic Options in an Era of Industry-wide Consolidation," *Policy Study Number 242* (Los Angeles, CA: Reason Foundation's Public Policy Institute, 1998). This study is available at <http://www.rppi.org/ps242.html> (2000). At the state level, Kansas is the only state that has totally outsourced child welfare. It was a bold four-year experiment at the time this book was published. Analysts have yet to conclude whether privatizing welfare in Kansas is a successful or a failed experiment. For an excellent assessment of this case, see Rob Gurwitt, "The Lonely Leap," *Governing: The Magazine of States and Localities* (July 2000), pp. 38–44.
138. Fitzgerald, *When Government Goes Private*, pp. 133–134.
139. "County Healthcare," pp. 2–3, Reason Foundation's Privatization Database, which can be accessed at <http://www.privatization.com>.
140. Ibid, pp. 3–4.
141. For other examples of disappointments, see Penelope Lemov, "Dumping the Public Hospital," *Governing: The Magazine of States and Localities* (September 1996), pp. 43–46. The cases included in the article include Cookeville, Tennessee, where selling the hospital was so controversial that it was to be placed before the voters. The citizens of Cookeville voted to keep the Cookeville Regional Medical Center a city-owned, public hospital.
142. Harry Hatry, "Privatization Presents Problems," in *Annual Editions: State & Local Government*, 5th ed., ed. Bruce Stinebrickner (Guilford, CT: Dushkin Press, 1989), pp. 220–221. This article also includes other examples of disappointing results when services were privatized.
143. Ibid.
144. Penelope Lemov, "Dumping the Public Hospital," p. 46.
145. Ibid.
146. Alan Ehrenhalt, "Mental Adjustment," *Governing: The Magazine of States and Localities* (March 2000), p. 84.
147. Linda Wagar, "The Tricky Path to Going Private," *State Government News* (February 1994), pp. 17–19.
148. Ibid. The national survey is *State Trends & Forecasts*, which is a fifty-state survey conducted by the Council of State Governments. This report is available from the Council of State Governments, 3560 Iron Works Pike, Lexington, KY 40578.
149. The amount of money that actually makes it into the hands of welfare recipients varies from year to year and from study to study. It is generally conceded that the federal government and the states use much of the appropriated funds for administrative costs. Welfare is a mega billion-dollar-per-year business and creates thousands of permanent jobs for bureaucrats. Milton Friedman has argued for direct payments to the poor for years. Ronald Reagan often commented that if all of the funds that are appropriated could go straight to those on the welfare roles, those on the welfare roles would fall into middle-class tax brackets. For further discussion of this issue, see Milton Friedman, *The Tyranny of the Status Quo* (New York: Basic Books, 1984) and Milton and Rose Friedman, *Free to Choose: A Personal Statement* (New York: Harcourt Brace Jovanovich, 1980). Also, see James Lester and Joseph Stewart, *Public Policy: An Evolutionary Approach* (New York: West Publishing, 1996), Chapter 11, for a good critique of welfare policy.

150. Texas and California are experimenting with privatized welfare. Texas operates more than thirty separate welfare programs and has more than 700,000 on its welfare roles. The cost to the state exceeds $550 million. Some states have been more successful than others with managing welfare. Wisconsin is considered to be among the leaders and has been extremely innovative with its policies. Utah has implemented programs that have achieved the best results for getting people off the welfare rolls. For an excellent overview of welfare policy in the state and local arena, see Bowman and Kearney, *State and Local Government*, Chapter 17.

151. "Welfare Administration/Welfare-to-Work Services," p. 2. Reason Foundation's Privatization Database located at <http://www.privatization.com>. This article contains trends, the results of studies, cost savings, and case studies. The direct link is <http://www.privatization.com/Collection/SpecificServiceAreas/welfare-local.html> (2000).

152. Ibid, p. 2.

153. William Eggers and Raymond Ng, "Social and Health Service Privatization: A Survey of County and State Governments," *Policy Study Number 168* (Los Angeles, CA: Reason Foundation's Public Policy Institute, 1993). The direct link to the Executive Summary of this study is <http://www.rppi.org/es168.html>. The complete study is available from the Reason Foundation, 3415 S. Sepulveda Blvd., Suite 400, Los Angeles, CA 90034, (310) 391-2245.

154. Surveys by the International City/County Management Association have found that one of the areas in which the use of private contracting has increased is the area of social services. Some of the increases are shown in Appendix B. See Elaine Morley, "Local Government Use of Alternative Service Delivery Approaches," *Municipal Yearbook 1999* (Washington, D.C.: International City/County Management Association), pp. 34–44.

155. It should be noted that this chapter includes selected cases. There are many, literally thousands, of cases from around the world of successful experiences with privatization. Of course, there are also many other cases about disappointing experiences with privatization, which often involve tales of corruption and scandal. Also, there are many service areas not included in the chapter in which examples of successes and failures can be found.

156. City of Lakewood, *The Lakewood Plan*, 3rd rev. (Lakewood, CA: author, 1961). It should be noted that the City of Lakewood engaged in extensive contracting, most of which was intergovernmental contracting rather than privatization. As mentioned in other parts of this book, intergovernmental contracting is often included in the privatization literature but is technically not a form of privatization. Many of the Lakewood Cities do use privatization and intergovernmental contacting to provide local services.

Conclusion: Prospects for Privatization in the Twenty-First Century

Although it is early in the new century and the privatization debate is now more than a quarter of a century old, privatization remains a prominent issue as a remedy for the financial woes of cities. The forces that drove privatization back in the 1980s have been coupled with new forces, such as efforts to reinvent government (which even got the endorsement of Democrat Vice President Al Gore and led to a national performance review during the Clinton Administration).[1] By the early 1990s, Democrats like President Clinton were extolling the virtues of reinventing government, implementing performance measures, and partly endorsing privatization. Even Chicago's Mayor Daley embraced privatization to resolve some of the city's financial problems, and Chicago was not considered to be a likely place to have a major privatization program implemented.[2] No level of government has escaped the "Great Privatization Debate," which remains an ideologically charged dialogue pitting the merits of a positive government against the virtues of capitalism and free markets. As illustrated in Chapter 1, the privatization debate is complex and involves attempting to balance the often-conflicting goals of efficiency, equity, and public accountability.[3]

Cities face many challenges in the new century. These challenges range from skyrocketing health-care costs for employees, increased resistance from citizens to higher taxation, urban sprawl, and a plethora of transportation problems. Cities do not operate in a vacuum. They are affected by the condition of the national economy and national political agendas and policies. Among the greatest problem for cities is how to pay for services and privatization offers an alternative to traditional, in-house provision. This final chapter examines many of the questions that arise about privatization, including the politics of privatization, and looks at the prospects for using privatization in the new century.

RECURRING ISSUES AND QUESTIONS ABOUT PRIVATIZATION

The policy and financial challenges faced by cities are numerous, and privatization offers an opportunity for cities to maintain or even increase service levels while reducing the tax burden placed on citizens and industry. Thus, privatization remains an important issue for municipal governments. At the end of Chapter 4, a series of questions were posed that deserve some attention. The questions are commonly included in the privatization debate and deal directly with concerns raised by critics. These questions also include concerns that have carried over into the new century.

Are there costs that are not revealed in past studies about privatization? There are hidden costs regardless of which method of service delivery is used by cities. Government provision has a long history of waste and inefficiency. There is an old joke about the number of public employees needed to collect residential garbage: one to drive, one to ride, one to pick up and empty the cans, and one to watch. There is some truth to this joke. Many private firms use only two employees per crew and collect more trash per hour than most municipal departments. Why? Public employee unions have historically done an excellent job protecting the positions of their members. Research has found that municipal departments often collect garbage more often than private, contracted companies. In some cities, residents may prefer to have their garbage collected more often than once a week, but for most cities, once-per-week collection is one way to lower the costs of operations. Bear in mind that cities set the quality standards, such as once-per-week or twice-per-week collection. Public employee unions and city officials can influence service levels.[4] Privatization is not a cure-all and does have some risks and hidden costs. For example, there are costs associated with monitoring contracts. There have been cases in which cities sold off their equipment after contracting out a service and the contractor went broke. In cases of purer types of privatization, such as selling off the public hospital, there are greater risks because the services have been devolved to the market. In the marketplace, public accountability comes in the form of government regulation, and with government regulation come costs to government, taxpayers, and businesses.

What are the consequences of privatization for cities? There are many consequences associated with privatizing services, some positive and some negative. Positive consequences include saving tax dollars that can be better spent on other projects and services. In some cases, privatization has led to expansionary city government. That is, services increased because cities had more money to spend because of privatization. There are other cases in which privatization led to significantly lower taxes for communities. Considering the evidence on efficiency, privatization should save money in most city services. There are a few exceptions in which efficiency does not appear to be significantly different in some service areas, such as pumping water into the nation's cities or data processing.

Perhaps the most severe negative consequence involves the possibility of corruption. Urban America has a long history of scandals involving private contracting, which often involved corrupt city officials. Cozy relationships can develop between those granting the contracts and contractors. Of course, there are examples of corruption among city officials in which neither contracting nor any form of privatization was involved. Corruption is always a potential problem, but proper oversight in competitive bidding procedures can help reduce this problem. Privatization is not a panacea capable of curing the possibility of corruption in city management, but operating public departments at significantly higher costs than would be incurred if contracting were used has not proven to be the answer. Corruption, waste, and inefficiency have occurred in public departments where formal accountability to city officials was in place. Moreover, problems involving equity have occurred in the absence of privatization, such as snow being removed from wealthy neighborhoods before being removed from poorer districts.[5]

Who wins and who loses with privatization? Privatization does not come without costs, and there are potentially winners and losers. Ideally, everyone should win if privatization is properly implemented. Cities save money that can be spent elsewhere, perhaps on more critical projects. Taxpayers save money and, in many cases, either see lower taxation or slower increases in taxes. Citizens also win by having quality services delivered at a lower cost. Contractors win because they are paid to deliver services for cities. However, contracts can cause public employees to be laid off, although most cities have implemented policies to eliminate or reduce this problem (these are referred to as no-lay-off policies). And everyone can end up losing if privatization is not properly implemented and monitored, such as in cases involving corruption. In these cases, the only winners are those getting city checks or kickbacks from the contractors. Again, protections must be in place to ensure that corruption is minimized.

Should cities begin privatizing services on a wholesale basis? Or, should cities try to emulate the famous Lakewood City Plan,[6] in which most public services are contracted? Realistically, the answer to both of these questions is no. For a variety of reasons, all cities cannot be managed under the Lakewood City Plan. First of all, much of the contracting used in the Lakewood City Plan is intergovernmental. What enables the Lakewood Cities to contract is the presence of larger cities, like Los Angeles, and large counties, like Los Angeles County. Of course, there is a great deal of private contracting in these communities, but the presence of central cities (which was discussed in Chapter 3) is critical. Can large, central cities privatize many of their services? Yes, and they have privatized many services over the years. However, privatization contains several dimensions: economic and political. If the political culture of a city prefers privatization, like the market-oriented cities discussed in Chapter 3, the city may demonstrate a propensity to use privatization. If the political culture prefers to have the city oversee and provide a full range of services, and if there is a lack of fiscal stress, the city may opt not to privatize. Resistance to privatization is even greater in cities where large, powerful public-employee unions exist. Fiscal conditions, particularly severe fiscal stress, likely serve as a significant impetus to privatize. The lack of money may cause any city to at least consider some form of privatization.

But there is also a political dimension to privatization that cannot be ignored. The demands of citizens, coupled with political leaders attempting to maintain their power, affects privatization. If citizens demand that services be provided, resist higher taxation, and threaten to vote out political leaders if some community problem is not resolved, political leaders may be forced to follow the will of the people. Although local controversies makes interesting news for journalists and newspapers, most cities operate in a routine fashion and deal with problems as they arise. Controversies that cause changes on the scale of California's Proposition 13 are rare.[7]

Cities are public organizations that simply administer a broad range of services, such as police and fire protection, water and sewerage, transportation systems, and the like, within the jurisdictional boundaries of their municipality. Some cities, like Chicago and Los Angeles, have government operations that are larger than some states. The scope and magnitude of municipalities like New York City make it impossible to operate their municipal systems like those of small towns, but privatization has been widely used for years in most large cities. The Lakewood Cities are small- to medium-sized, suburban cities. For all cities, regardless of size or location, privatization should be handled on a case-by-case basis. There are too many factors and too many political and economic dynamics unique to each city to make a universal claim that all cities should try to privatize as many services as possible. New developments have occurred recently that may make privatization more palatable to more cities; for example, particularly the practice of competitive bidding, which leaves public departments intact, but brings in private contractors to handle the same services in other areas of a city. The results of this technique have been impressive thus far. This method provides middle ground for politicians, public workers, and contractors and may deliver the best quality services possible.

What about political accountability and concerns about equity? No areas have raised more concerns from critics than accountability and equity. The concern over public accountability is legitimate. What happens if a city privatizes its fire department, sells off its equipment, and the company goes bankrupt? Hopefully, there would be a thorough discussion in the political arena to avoid this type of situation, but such fiascoes have happened. Who is responsible when this type of situation occurs? Citizens would likely blame their municipal officials, particularly if no public input were allowed. Over the years, such incidents have been rare because replacing a public monopoly with a private monopoly, with no backup in the event of an emergency, is too risky for most cities. Even the most adamant proponents of privatization warn against privatizing an essential service without some type of backup. Recall that the key to lower costs is found in some form of competition rather than private ownership. The absence of competition is what makes government inefficient. The lack of competition makes private firms equally inefficient. In other words, a private monopoly is no better than a public monopoly. The behavior of both is similar in the absence of competition.

One must also keep in mind that there are many forms of privatization. Most of this book has concentrated on various forms of private contracting. In the case of contracting, neither accountability nor equity should be an issue. If the city properly administers and monitors the contract, and if appropriate competition exists (meaning that more than one company is providing the service for the city), accountability and equity should not be a concern. The city is still responsible for financing and providing the service; they merely contract out for production and delivery of the service. The same applies to equity. As mentioned earlier, there are some types of privatization in which public accountability and equity can be lost. For example, if a city devolves a service entirely to the market, only those who can afford to pay for the service are served. Notwithstanding some statutory protection for the poor imposed by government, a vendor will only serve those with the ability to pay.

What impact does privatization have on the political structure and institutions in our cities? In the case of contracting, privatization has no real effect on political structure. Government structure and the institutions of city government remain intact. In reality, privatization does not seek to dismantle formal political structures or institutions. This is a myth that often surfaces in the debates regarding privatization. Some critics view privatizing services as dismantling the state, when, in fact, contracting has always been common at all levels of government, particularly at the state and local level. There is an impact to municipal institutions (but not to the structures created to govern) if a department is dissolved and entirely replaced with private firms. In reality, this rarely occurs. Currently, the approach has been to utilize competitive bidding that guarantees the public department a zone in the city to continue operating and allows the public department to bid for other zones against private firms. This practice has been very successful in cities like Phoenix and Indianapolis. Numerous examples of successful competitive bidding were provided in Chapter 4. When a department is downsized or eliminated, the evidence suggests that most cities reassign employees, utilize early retirement packages, or arrange for public employees to be hired by the contractors. However, political structures and political institutions designed for governing are not changed. The effect of privatization is no greater than the influence of reinventing government methods, which seek to improve the performance of public management and government operations.

Does privatization serve the public interest? This question often emerges in discussions about privatization. Critics of privatization are quick to argue that privatization cannot be in the public interest, but is in the self-serving interests of contractors or others who stand to gain financially from privatizing municipal functions.[8] Privatization's proponents argue that privatizing services is in the public interest because it saves cities money and lowers taxes.[9] This is a complex question. Politicians, journalists, and academics commonly make references to the "public interest." But what is the public interest? Scholars have debated the meaning of the public interest for centuries and no clear consensus has ever been established. There are only categories of definitions. The concept of the public interest has different meanings to different people. The public interest can be synonymous with majoritarian politics (whatever the majority of people want is viewed as the public interest). It can take on a utilitarian definition, meaning whatever brings the most good to the most people. The public interest can refer to whatever is in the *best interest* of the people or the state. That is, decisions and actions sometimes have to be taken that are in the *best interest* of citizens, even if citizens do not agree with the decision at the time. Examples include public health and safety matters that people and groups may oppose because they do not understand the dangers of certain types of pollution or because the actions of government will harm their vested interests in some type of industry. Or, it can refer to the many interests that exist in society being combined together to form the "public interest." In this view, there exists an amalgamation of interests that are often conflicting. At some point among these many interests, there is a compromising area, or "middle ground," that might represent the "public interest."

Some argue that the public interest is a vacuous concept that has no real meaning whatsoever. In this vein of thought, the concept of a public interest is merely political dogma used by politicians. It can also refer to an *ideal*, meaning the greatest good that can be achieved for society through politics. That is, something that is not achievable, but which serves as an aspiration or goal to try to improve the quality of life in society. And to many, the concept simply means taking some action that serves some public good (meaning something that brings about something desirable for the community). The public interest is a "slippery" concept that goes well beyond the scope of this book and each of the definitions offered here (and there are others) have unique problems.[10] For our purposes here, the public interest refers to action that serves some greater or public good.

Clearly, determining whether privatization serves some greater good for society is highly ideological in nature. Sitting on either side of the ideological table, liberal or conservative, will provide a different answer. If privatization is viewed as a way to free up funds that can be used more wisely by reducing waste and inefficiency, then privatization serves a greater public good. If on the other hand, privatization is seen as an attempt to dismantle government (which is an extremist view), then privatization is not in the public interest. In reality, privatization is just another tool available to cities for providing services, and one that usually saves money. So long as appropriate checks and balances remain, such as monitoring contracts or being cautious when privatizing services, privatization seems to have far more advantages than disadvantages.[11]

Is privatization a viable solution for providing public services in the new century? Notwithstanding some exceptions, such as privatizing prisons[12] (which have produced inconsistent results), privatization is likely here to stay. It has always been a part of the municipal landscape and privatization is more than a passing fad. But choosing between government production and delivery of services versus privatization is a choice between imperfect alternatives.[13] There are numerous problems with either mode of service delivery. When government produces, finances, and delivers a service, one runs the risk of all of the problems associated with nonmarket failures. That is, bloated, inefficient, wasteful municipal bureaucracies that are monopolies with few incentives to improve performance and with ineffective and insufficient oversight.

When one opts to privatize by devolving something to the market, the risks associated with market failure described in Chapter 1 become a real possibility. Markets are imperfect. However, simple contracting does not include all of the pitfalls associated with truly open, competitive markets. With contracting, the best of both worlds can be realized with few risks. Competition is introduced. Government remains responsible for the provision and financing of services, but contracts out for production and delivery of the specific services with private firms. These firms are monitored and must be held to quality and performance standards. This is usually easier than trying to improve the performance of in-house departments in the absence of competition. However, if a city contracts out for a service and no competition exists (with only one vendor), a public monopoly is simply being replaced with a private monopoly. Over time, the behavior of private monopolies resembles that of government monopolies. Thus, nothing will be gained and many potential problems will likely arise. Guidelines about contracting generally make this point clear. Privatization is an appropriate way to provide services in the new century, but privatizing services must be carefully and correctly implemented.[14]

The principal promise of privatization is increased efficiency. Proponents of privatization believe that increased efficiency can be achieved by altering the incentive structures of the nonmarket service-delivery arrangements typically found in municipal settings. This position is predicated on the assumption that the positive attributes associated with competitive markets can be transferred or simulated by contracting out for services. Proponents contend that government organizations operating under monopoly conditions will have little incentive to innovate or reduce costs. Proponents also contend that the behavior of individuals in nonmarket organizations produces bloated, unresponsive, and inefficient operations. This theoretical position helps explain why government organizations do not perform better. The evidence presented in Chapter 2 and in Appendix A suggests that private firms outperform government operations in most services. Although privatization is commonly used by cities, the evidence also clearly suggests that public employees provide most public services. This is somewhat surprising considering all of the attention that privatization has received over the years. It is natural to ask, why? Potential explanations include the possibility that the use of privatization may have been overstated. That is, although privatization has received widespread attention, the rate of its adoption may not be as great as commonly believed. Other explanations include various forms of political pressure that serve as a disincentive for city officials to consider privatizing services, such as pressure from public-employee unions.[15]

Few studies on privatization capture the human element. People operate all organizations, whether the organization is a private business or an agency of government. Individuals provide the dynamic element for all organizations. It is unlikely that private business has attracted all of the good managers, leaving the less qualified for public organizations. Good management can be found in both the private and public sectors. The influence of a good manager in a private business can determine whether a firm succeeds or fails. A good manager can take over a poorly performing firm and make it perform better. Conversely, a poor manager can take over a successful firm and the firm can function poorly. Managers do make a difference. However, monopolies are monopolies and this fact can overshadow the work of good managers. But the threat of privatization coupled with good management can help public departments perform better. One of the consistent findings of efficiency studies is that competition is the key element, not private ownership. Even some of the most adamant critics of privatization view the threat of privatization as beneficial.[16]

There are a variety of factors that influence the use of privatization and help explain why public employees continue to provide most public services. Privatization researchers often ignore the unique characteristics of the market for local services. Because public managers must juggle efficiency, effectiveness, accountability, and equity in a political environment, it is generally conceded that efficiency cannot be the cardinal virtue of public service. Public choice theorists[17] contend that the political system is inadequate for providing the necessary incentives to promote efficiency, which is largely attributed to the fact that most municipal organizations are monopolies. These theorists believe that the competitive marketplace contains adequate incentives to force managerial efficiency, even for the modern corporation where management and ownership are separated. It is generally acknowledged that control of the modern corporation has shifted to management. Stockholders have little ability to monitor management's performance. A variety of mechanisms have been developed to provide an incentive for management to remain efficient, such as profit sharing and stock options. Such mechanisms, however imperfect, help overcome some of the problems related to the dilution of stockholder control. Some have suggested that it is possible that something similar exists in public organizations, but has been overlooked by researchers because our understanding of public-sector control mechanisms is less understood. It would be odd if individuals in their role as stockholders were capable of recognizing property rights conflicts and devising methods of overcoming them, but were naïve and helpless in similar conflicts in their roles as citizens.[18] It is not inconceivable that the public can demand efficiency and devise methods to ensure that it is attained through the political system. It is possible that the political system may be capable of demanding efficiency through the budgetary system, but this has not been demonstrated in the literature at this writing. Proposition 13, the California initiative that significantly reduced local property taxes in the late 1970s, always serves as a reminder that citizens can rise and force demands on their government.

Another factor is internal organizational politics. Public employees and public managers are not likely to give up their political power easily. Most public services are still provided by public employees because of politics and a resistance to change the status quo. Inertia is common in public and private organizations and it is difficult to implement change in most organizational settings. It is unlikely that privatization will ever be adopted on a wholesale basis in most cities. The more likely scenario involves "middle ground" solutions like the competitive bidding programs discussed earlier. The middle ground approach is more likely because people do not easily give up their positions, power, or security. A political force exists that is difficult to break down. It is likely that most public services will continue to be provided by public employees in the new century, but the use of privatization will likely continue to increase due to fiscal stress.

THE POLITICS AND ECONOMICS OF PRIVATIZATION

The politics of privatization has not received a great deal of attention in the literature or popular press. Efficiency has dominated most discussions about privatization at the local level while ideological debate over the size and scope of the public sector has dominated discussions among ideologues (those with strong ideological commitments on one side or the other of the privatization debate). As summarized at the beginning of Chapter 4, there is a politics of privatization. In the real world of municipal government, there are winners and losers in political struggles that involve privatization. Politicians must get elected. Most politicians resist change and prefer not raising taxes, which is usually very unpopular during election years. To stay in power, politicians must lead the city and maintain some sense of stability. Moreover, politicians do not live in a vacuum. They usually are members of the community and have a keen sense of what people want, the course of action needed to satisfy the wants, desires, and expectations of citizens and members of the business community, and the level of taxation citizens are willing to pay.

The political systems of cities are not much different from the larger political systems of states, just smaller and more localized. There are many interest groups in cities making demands that can cause fiscal pressures. One alternative to reduce operating expenses for cities is to privatize some of its services. This inevitably leads to political conflict in some cities, mainly from public-employee unions or other groups with a vested interest in protecting their jobs. This is normal and predictable behavior. Moreover, as mentioned earlier, the dynamics of cities vary (*dynamics* refers to the unique political, social, demographic, and economic characteristics of a city). Some cities are politically liberal while other cities are politically conservative.

Trying to predict the use of privatization based solely on politics can produce some odd findings. For example, Missoula, Montana, is considered to be a progressive, liberal, university town while most of the Lakewood Cities in California are more conservative. The Lakewood Cities use a lot of privatization, but so does Missoula. Recall from Chapter 3 that the Lakewood Cities were created due to political conflicts between the wealthy and the poor, and were not some quest to enhance the efficiency of their communities. Wealthy residents attempted to minimize city services to avoid redistributive benefits to the poor. Missoula has a liberal political climate (and is a political aberration from all other cities in Montana). It has implemented every imaginable program to reduce environmental pollution and traffic congestion, such as cheap or free public transportation, bicycle lanes on all major streets, bike racks, park-and-ride programs, and the like. Missoula also passed a large bond issue to buy up open space around the city (and there is a lot of it around the town) to preserve the natural look of the city and control economic development.[19] For many years, the dominant leadership in the mayor's office and on the city council has been liberal Democrats who support these types of policies. Oddly enough, privatization is fairly common in Missoula. There are several reasons, including lack of appropriate finances, less financial aid from the state, and a relatively weak tax base.[20]

Other cities, such as conservative Asheville, North Carolina, seek to maintain the status quo of the community (that is, the city generally resists major social and economic changes to the community). Asheville is a politically conservative, retirement-resort city located in the mountains of western North Carolina. Privatization is not widely used in Asheville. The city is fiscally healthy with a strong tax base. Coupled with its moralistic political culture, Asheville resembles the full-service city model described in Chapter 1. Public departments provide most public services for two reasons: The culture *expects* the city to provide most services in a traditional manner and the city can *afford* to provide services in a traditional manner. The political dynamics of Asheville and Missoula produce interesting outcomes regarding privatization. The liberal city uses privatization while the conservative city uses very little privatization. This exemplifies an important point. Every city in the nation has its own unique political characteristics and these political, social, economic, and cultural characteristics likely affect the use of privatization.[21] When determining whether to privatize services, politics is likely a critical factor, but it is coupled with economic conditions.

We live in an interesting time for urban studies and privatization; an era characterized by the ideals of a movement known as "reinventing government." This has created an interesting environment for cities and represents a change in the way that we manage our cities. Cities face many policy problems that involve privatization. Urban life is changing and privatization, which includes public-private partnerships, is becoming increasingly common. The Republican National Convention to nominate George W. Bush as the Republican nominee for president was held in Philadelphia at the First Union Center.[22] It serves as a reminder of how cities have changed. Imagine a major political convention being held in one of America's largest and politically historic cities in a state-of-the-art convention complex named after a bank, not after the historic city of Philadelphia. As discussed in Chapter 4, convention centers, stadiums, and sports arenas across America are being renamed to generate money for cities, which can often be millions of dollars in revenue. Cities face the ever-increasing demand for services and the dilemma of how to pay for them. And, they are getting more creative than ever in finding new sources of revenue. Fiscal dilemmas have many causes, but one of the most important reasons is the public's general resistance to higher taxation, which is a component of the politics and economics of privatization.

What will be the driving determinant of privatization in the future? The determinants will most likely be a combination of economics and politics. In all of the research that has been conducted, politics has been largely ignored. Aside from clashes from public employee unions who have a vested interest to oppose privatization, the efficiency issue has overshadowed politics. In other words, economists have dominated the literature and the debate. Economists have a tendency to examine a phenomenon, like privatization, make recommendations, and leave the final decision to be made in the political arena. This is where the decision should be made. But discussions in the political arena have also been dominated by efficiency. Many cities have remained skeptical about adopting privatization. They are probably wise to do so. In the real world of municipal government, other issues aside from efficiency are present. Political pressures from interest groups, public-employee unions, the dynamics of the local political culture, the aspirations of municipal officials, and fiscal realities are all factors. Politics is probably as important as economics in the decision to privatize, although this has not been demonstrated in the literature on privatization. The politics of privatization is illustrated in the struggle to determine how services will be provided for cities in the future. Will contractors hired by cities provide public services? Or, will publicly operated departments continue to handle most basic municipal services in-house? The politics of privatization is also represented in the struggle between public-employee unions and city management. One can view part of the struggle on the Web pages of various organizations. The American Federation of State, County, and Municipal Employees (AFSCME) provides training and materials to help their members resist privatization. The Reason

Foundation, one of the leading advocates of privatization, provides guidelines and materials that help city officials privatize municipal services. America is a society prone to conflict, and the struggle between city management and labor will likely carry on in the new century.[23]

SUMMARY

Privatization raises larger questions about the size and scope of the public sector and has broken a trend in the United States that lasted nearly three-quarters of a century.[24] This trend was toward the centralization of power with the federal government and government provision and financing of an ever-increasing amount of services. By the 1960s, government had become dominated with concerns regarding process, public accountability, and equity. The basis of the process model holds that how government accomplishes something is as important as what it accomplishes.[25] This position assumes that the "right" process would produce the "right" results. Concerns over equity and public accountability were paramount and overshadowed concerns for efficiency, which had dominated urban management earlier in the twentieth century. The process-orientation brought attention to some serious problems in society, but government seemed unable to turn ideas into reality. Although the intentions were noble, most problems were not resolved and government seemed more wasteful and inefficient than ever.[26] By the 1980s, during the Reagan administrations, the focus was changing to the results-oriented principles that were later made popular by David Osborne and Ted Gaebler in *Reinventing Government.*[27] America's political dynamics had grown more conservative and privatization, which is actually older than the nation itself, emerged as a controversial *new* way to provide public services. But privatization was not a new idea. In the 1960s, Peter Drucker included a chapter in the *Age of Discontinuity*[28] titled, "The Sickness of Government." Drucker eloquently described what he believed was wrong with government: Government is well suited for governing but poorly equipped to produce services. Drucker referred to increasing the role of the private sector in the production and delivery of public services as *reprivatization* because throughout the history of the United States the private sector had often been used to provide public services for all levels of government, particularly in cities. A debate ensued that continues to this day.

The public sector has grown tremendously since the 1930s and has assumed more and more social and economic responsibilities. Government employs more than 17 million workers and many public workers view privatization as a sure way of losing their jobs. Thus, public-employee unions and liberal academics who sought to expand the role of the public sector became the leading critics of this so-called *new* idea. Proponents of privatization, like E. S. Savas, began publishing studies during the 1970s that illustrated how much less expensively public services could be produced by private firms.[29] Over the years, these studies have been amassed into a large body of literature that in virtually all service areas favors private production. Study after study seemed to confirm that the private sector produces goods and services more efficiently than the public sector. Why would there be such a controversy over collecting garbage or managing hospitals? As we have already seen, throughout much of the nation's history the private sector provided many public services, including subways and utilities. But the era of modern liberalism envisioned a positive, more active role for government, especially at the federal level. Government was believed to be capable of correcting many of society's problems. Government provision seemed to be a viable alternative because many of the privatized public services in urban America's past were filled with corruption and scandals. But replacing privately run public-service monopolies (that were often political footballs for the political machines that ran cities) with government-operated monopolies did not turn out to be a panacea. In *Markets or Government*, economist Charles Wolf argued that choosing between government and private provision of services is a choice between imperfect alternatives.[30] It is my belief that he is correct. Selecting government or private provision of services is not a black-and-white decision; like most social choices, the decision comes in shades of gray. When one selects government provision, one must contend with all of the problems and shortcomings of government monopolies with the hope that the political process can maintain public accountability. When one selects privatization, one runs the risk of the problems associated with market failure. With the exception of contracting, public accountability can be severed with other forms of privatization. Recall the example of Cookeville, Tennessee's public hospital. The people of Cookeville voted overwhelmingly in favor to keep their community hospital public, and one of the primary reasons had to do with accountability. It is clear that most privatization at the municipal level involves contracting, which minimizes most of the problems that are associated with other forms of privatization. Clearly, if a city wants to save money, privatization (in the form of contracting) is a viable alternative to public provision. But the decision, as we have seen, also involves politics. It is possible that politics may be the most critical element of all. People with political power (and political entities like cities) do not like to give up power. Political forces may have found middle ground between the ideals of reinventing government, which suggests that government can be improved, and the pragmatism of private contracting, where government still maintains control over the quality and financing of public services that are devolved to the private sector.

After nearly 30 years, the privatization debate continues in the new century. The debate over the proper size and scope of the public and private sectors will not be resolved in the near future. Privatization coupled with the results-oriented ideals of the reinventing government movement will likely continue to apply pressure for public sector organizations to improve their performance.[31] Privatization offers promise in the new century as a way to maintain or even expand public services, but it is not a panacea capable of solving all of the financial dilemmas of cities. Interest in privatization is not likely to fade as long as fiscal pressures persist for cities in the new century.

NOTES

1. It should be noted that performance evaluation of the federal government is not new but the focus on shifting power from the public sector to the private sector is relatively new. Prior to 1932 and the New Deal Era, the private sector was very involved in service provision at all levels of government. Between the 1930s and 1980s, the tendency for government was to become more centralized at the federal level with federal control in most dimensions of the national agenda. Control over many policy matters was shifting more and more to Washington and the states and their local governments were viewed as a conduit through which to pump federally mandated programs. Liberals sought more federal control in the name of accountability and equity. Coupled with the civil rights era, Washington created nearly five hundred new federal programs between 1960 and 1978, which usually were mandated back to the states and local governments to achieve national goals. The shifting of responsibility from the states to the federal level began slowly reversing under the Nixon administration during the 1970s and accelerated in the 1980s. The 1980s are generally referred to as the Decade of Devolution because so much power and responsibility was returned to the states. President Reagan also looked internally within the federal bureaucracy for more efficient ways to do business and cut costs. For example, bonuses were implemented for employees who could find ways to save the government money (the practice was stopped in the 1990s because many felt that as civil servants, one should not be getting large bonuses for doing one's job). It was also during the Reagan administration that the famous Grace Commission Report found several thousand ways to cut the federal deficit (which was escalating at the time) and made numerous recommendations to enhance the efficiency of the federal government. The Reagan administration embraced the idea of privatization and numerous studies and reports were published by federal agencies. It was also during the 1980s and early 1990s that most privatization studies were conducted by academics. By the early 1990s, the reinventing government movement was under way and continues in the new century. For an excellent discussion about changes in federalism, see E. Blaine Liner, ed., *A Decade of Devolution* (Washington, D.C.: The Urban Institute, 1989). Also, see "The Gore Report on Reinventing Government, National Performance Review," *From Red Tape to Results: Creating a Government that Works Better and Costs Less* (Washington, D.C.: U.S. Government Printing Office, 1993).
2. Mayor Daley is the son of Richard Daley, who led one of the most powerful and legendary Democratic machines in the nation in Chicago for many years. Generally, Democrats (especially those who are liberal) have been less favorable toward privatization than Republicans (who tend to be more conservative) in the United States. See "The Privatizing Daley," *Governing: Incorporating City and State* (April 1993), pp. 26–33.

3. Nancy Hayward, "The Productivity Challenge," *Public Administration Review* 36 (September/October, 1976), pp. 544–550. Also, see Frederick Hayes, *Productivity in Local Government* (Lexington, MA: Lexington Books, 1977).

4. This example is what public choice theorists refer to as *overproduction*. That is, producing more services than needed. It is true that some communities may demand higher levels of service and be willing to pay for them through taxes. Public choice theory suggests that officials and public employees, who have a vested interest in empire building and budget maximization, will overproduce services.

5. Ron Moe, "Exploring the Limits of Privatization," *Public Administration Review* 47 (November/December 1987), pp. 453–460. Also, see J. F. Leiber, *Private Means—Public Ends* (New York: Praeger Press, 1982).

6. City of Lakewood, *The Lakewood Plan*, 3rd rev. (Lakewood, CA: author, 1961). It should be noted the City of Lakewood engaged in extensive contracting, most of which was intergovernmental contracting rather than privatization. As mentioned in other parts of this book, intergovernmental contracting is often included in the privatization literature, but is technically not a form of privatization. Many of the Lakewood Cities do use privatization and intergovernmental contracting to provide local services.

7. Local controversies over every issue imaginable are common. The point being made here is that controversies and scandals commonly occur, but rarely alter the politics of cities. It is common for citizens to become aroused over policies and issues, but usually the problems are either resolved or forgotten by the time of the next election. This position may sound cynical, but one need only examine voter turnout in local elections for evidence of apathy.

8. Richard Stillman, "Ostrom and the Federalists Revisited," *Public Administration Review* 49 (January/February, 1987), pp. 82–84.

9. Robert Poole, *Cutting Back City Hall* (New York: Universe Books, 1981).

10. It should be noted that discussions of the public interest go well beyond the purpose of this book. Each of the definitions used have their own set of inherent problems. For example, the idea that whatever the majority wants is the public interest (which comes from Rousseau) does nothing to protect minority rights. The idea that the public interest refers to whatever is in the best interest of the people or society clashes with democratic principles. Who is to determine what is in the people's best interest? Politicians or experts in the bureaucracy? Most of the writings on the public interest come from political theory.

11. It is recognized that some will disagree with this statement. It is also recognized that examples can be found where privatization did not serve the public interest, regardless of which definition one uses for the public interest. However, it must be stressed that the decision to privatize services is ultimately determined in the political arena.

12. Privatizing prisons was not discussed in this book, mainly because it affects the federal and state governments more than cities. Privatizing prisons did offer promise in the past but the results have been very mixed. Despite the inconsistent results, states continue to experiment with privatized prisons. It is conceded that private firms can handle inmates more cheaply than the state can, but other problems have emerged, such as constitutional matters and health-care treatment concerns, that continue to make private prisons controversial. For a good discussion about privatizing prisons, see Charles Mahtesian, "Dungeons for Dollars," *Florida Trend*

(October 1, 1996), p. 80. Also see "State Liable in Suits by Cons in Private Prisons," *Associated Press*, 13 October 1999. Cheryl W. Thompson, "D.C. Sues Private Prison Firm in Contract Dispute; CCA Failed to Protect and Defend the City in Two Lawsuits, Complaint Contends," *Washington Post*, 19 December 1998, B-7. Another unpopular area of privatization involves private toll roads, which have been used by some states for many years. Private toll roads are unpopular with most citizens and have produced marginal benefits. In the 1980s, expanding the construction of private toll roads was considered to be the wave of the future to reduce congestion on public highways, but some states quietly abandoned the idea. There are many reasons, such as legal problems acquiring land on which to construct roads, equity issues and political issues. An example of political issues involves state highway departments, which provide lucrative contracts for construction firms to build and maintains public highways. Contrary to theory, private toll roads are often even more poorly maintained than public roads. For some interesting commentary on expanding private toll roads, see Howard Ullman, "McHighways," *The New Republic*, 4 September 1989, 18–19.

13. See Charles Wolf, *Markets or Governments: The Choosing between Imperfect Alternatives* (Cambridge, MA: MIT Press, 1988). The theme of this book is about the choice between imperfect alternatives.

14. The idea of carefully and correctly implementing contracting has been well thought through by many organizations. For example, the International City/County Management Association (ICMA) has written extensive guidelines to help cities make the transition from in-house provision to contracting or other forms of privatization. The detail of many of their guidelines is impressive. These materials are available from the ICMA via their Web site at <http://www.icma.org>.

15. It should be noted that many other explanations exist that are not covered here.

16. Harry Hatry, "Privatization Presents Problems," in *Annual Editions: State and Local Government*, 5th ed., ed. Bruce Stinebrickner (Guilford, CT: Dushkin Publishing, 1991), p. 220.

17. Public choice theory was discussed in Chapter 1.

18. George Downs and Patrick Larkey, *The Search for Government Efficiency: From Hubris to Helplessness* (Philadelphia, PA: Temple University Press, 1986), p. 39.

19. There are many examples that illustrate the liberal political environment in Missoula. For example, the "living wage" nearly passed. The "living wage" policy is an attempt to force contractors and anyone doing business with a city to pay its workers a wage that is reflective of the cost of living in the area, which is usually higher than the federal minimum hourly wage. If this policy had passed, Missoula would have been one of only a few cities in the nation that adopted the "living wage" ordinance. The reason it failed had less to do with city leaders not wanting to implement it, but more to do with finances. Missoula is not a poor community, but is not a wealthy community. Of course, there were political forces mounted against the "living wage" ordinance from the business community. Such a policy would not even be considered by city councils in most cities, but it was seriously debated in Missoula.

20. Recall from the example included in Chapter 3 about Montana's local governments that privatization is widely used throughout the state. The political culture in Montana is not adamantly opposed to privatization, which likely affects Missoula.

21. Asheville and Missoula were selected because of the convenience of first-hand, personal knowledge about each community. It should be stressed that Missoula is an *independent* city (as defined in Chapter 3) and Asheville is a *central* city. This likely changes the use of privatization since central cities must provide broader ranges of services. Recall from Chapter 3 that central cities tend to use less privatization than suburban cities. Although Asheville does resemble the full-service city model, it should be stressed that no city handles everything in-house. Like most cities, Asheville must contract out for certain services like repairing or building major bridges, but public departments provide most essential city services. The populations of Missoula and Asheville are comparable, although Asheville is a much larger metropolitan area and has more suburban development. But the political climates of the two cities are vastly different. Missoula is a very liberal community while Asheville is a southern retirement-resort community with very traditional values. Both cities are located in beautiful mountainous areas and provide a high quality of life for their residents.

22. The name of the complex in Philadelphia is the Pennsylvania Convention Center. It is a state-of-the-art convention facility built in 1994. In Chapter 4, a number of examples were provided in which cities were renaming their convention centers and sports facilities after businesses that pay millions of dollars to have their name displayed. Naming arenas and civic centers after companies or prominent citizens is not new, but the magnitude of changing the names of public facilities to generate revenue for cities is new and has increased significantly in recent years.

23. America is noted to be a society prone to conflict, which is part of the nation's heritage. This is reflected in labor versus management and business versus government. Both the AFSCME and the Reason Foundation provide extensive materials for either resisting or making smooth transitions with privatization. These Web sites have been cited numerous times in the notes of this book and are located in Appendix F, Privatization Resources on the Internet. The Web site for the AFSCME is located at <www.afscme.org> and the Reason Foundation's site is located at <www.reason.org>.

24. Jude Wanniski, *The Way the World Works* (New York: Simon & Schuster, 1983). Wanniski provides an excellent discussion about the expanding scope of government.

25. It should be noted that removing the process orientation and replacing it with the results-oriented ideals of reinventing government might come at a price. The process orientation deliberately moves slowly and is more accountable than a faster-moving, results orientation. This is because to achieve results quickly, more latitude and discretion has to be granted to managers. This, of course, can cause problems with accountability.

26. For the counterargument, see John Kenneth Galbraith, *The Age of Uncertainty* (Boston, MA: Houghton Mifflin, 1977).

27. David Osborne and Ted Gaebler, *Reinventing Government* (New York: Addison Wesley, 1992).

28. Peter Drucker, *The Age of Discontinuity* (New York: Harper & Row, 1969).

29. E. S. Savas, *Privatization: The Key to Better Government* (Chatham, NJ: Chatham House Press, 1987).

30. Wolf, *Markets or Governments: The Choosing between Imperfect Alternatives*.

31. For several different positions about the future of public organizations, see Barry Bozeman, *Bureaucracy and Red Tape* (Englewood Cliffs, NJ: Prentice Hall, 2000); and

Barry Bozeman, *All Organizations are Public* (San Francisco, CA: Jossey-Bass, 1987). Also see Charles Goodsell, *The Case for Bureaucracy: A Public Administration Polemic*, 3rd ed. (Chatham, NJ: Chatham House, 1994) for an argument in favor of maintaining public bureaucracies. For the reinventing ideals, see David Osborne and Peter Plastrik, *The Reinventor's Fieldbook: Tools for Transforming Your Government* (San Francisco, CA: Jossey-Bass, 2000); and David Osborne and Peter Plastrik, *Banishing Bureaucracy: The Five Strategies for Reinventing Government* (New York: Addison-Wesley, 1997). For the public choice arguments, see Elinor Ostrom, *Governing the Commons: The Evolution of Institutions for Collective Action* (New York: Cambridge University Press, 1990); and Vincent Ostrom, "Some Developments in the Study of Market Choice, Public Choice, and Institutional Choice," in *Handbook of Public Administration*, ed. Jack Rabin, W. B. Hildreth, and Gerald Miller (New York: Marcel Dekker, 1989), pp. 861–882. For the classic arguments about bureaucratic inefficiency and empire building, see William Niskanen, *Bureaucracy and Representative Government* (Chicago, IL: Aldine Atherton, 1971). The equivalent book to David Osborne and Ted Gaebler's *Reinventing Government* for the private sector is Thomas Peters and Robert Waterman, *In Search of Excellence: Lessons from America's Best-Run Companies* (New York: Warner Books, 1988). Although *In Search of Excellence* dealt with private businesses, it had a great deal of impact on public administration and management in the public sector. Both *Reinventing Government* and *In Search of Excellence* provide excellent discussions about the results orientation of management that has been discussed in this book.

Summaries of Major Efficiency Studies
for Selected Municipal Services

Activity/Author	Inquiry Subject	Findings
1. Bus Service		
Oelert (1978)	Selected West German Cities, municipal v. private firms.	Cost per km of public services was 160 percent higher than the private companies.
Morlok and Moseley (1986)	Survey of 31 bus systems.	Average savings of private, contracted bus systems was 29 percent.
Perry and Babitsky (1986)	Private v. cost-plus private, contract v. public.	Private operators are significantly more efficient in all indicators of efficiency.
Teal and others (1987)	Study of 864 bus systems.	For large bus systems, private costs are 44 percent less than public cost. Contracting should save 36–50 percent for systems of more than 25 buses.
Sherlock and Cox (1987)	Study of 567 bus systems.	During a 13-year period, the cost per mile for private buses decreased by 3 percent while costs increased by 52 percent.The average savings for private contracting for bus service was 32 percent lower than the cost of public bus systems.

Activity/Author	Inquiry Subject	Findings
1. Bus Service (cont.)		
Walters (1987)	Study of bus service in five large cities.	Private operators were 50 to 65 percent less expensive than municipal bus systems. Weak evidence found for private sector superiority.
Feldman (1987)	68 U.S. bus organizations, public and private comparison.	Private operations were significantly more efficient.
Hensher (1989)	16 bus operations in Australia.	No significant differences found in efficiency or quality of service.
Musgrove (1988)	Busing in 88 school districts in Missouri.	Contracting lowered transportation costs.
Bails (1979)	School transportation costs in six U.S. states.	Contracting lowered transportation costs.
2. Cleaning Services		
Buderechnungshot (1972)	West German post offices, public v. private contracting.	Cost of public production was 40 to 50 percent higher.
Hambuger Senat (1971) and Fisher-Menshausen (1975)	West German public buildings, public v. private contracting.	Cost of public production was 50 percent higher in both studies.
Domberger, Hall, and Li (1997)	61 cleaning contracts in Sydney, Australia.	Cost savings from contracting out were 34 percent.
3. Electric Power		
Wallace and Junk (1970)	Public v. private operations, by regions in U.S.	Operating costs 40 to 75 percent higher in public firms. Investment per kwh 40 percent more in public operations.
Moore (1970)	Sample of U.S. utilities, 27 municipal v. 49 private utilities.	Total operating costs of public firms significantly higher.
Meyer (1975)	Sample of 60 to 90 U.S. Utilities, public v. private.	Weak indication of higher cost of private production.
Spann (1977)	Four major U.S. cities, public v. private firms.	No significant difference with respect to operating costs and investment per 1,000 kwh.
Yunker (1975)	Public v. private operations.	No significant differences.
Neuberg (1977)	Public v. private operations.	Public more efficient.
Pescatrice and Trapani (1985)	Public v. private operations.	Public more efficient.

Activity/Author	Inquiry Subject	Findings

3. Electric Power (cont.)

Fare, Grosskopt, and Logan (1986)	Public v. private operations.	No significant differences.
Atkinson and Halvorsen (1986)	Public v. private operations.	No significant differences.

4. Fire Protection

Ahlbrandt (1973)	Selected U.S. areas, Scottsdale, AZ v. Seattle, WA area (municipal).	Cost per capita 39 to 88 percent higher for municipal ✓ departments.

5. Hospitals

Clarkson (1972)	Sample of U.S. hospital, public nonprofit v. private for-profit.	Variations in input ratios greater in nonprofit hospitals. Higher cost found in nonprofit output indicators.
Lindsay (1976)	Sample of U.S. hospitals v. Veterans Administration (VA).	Cost per patient day less in VA hospitals.
Wilson and Jadlow (1978)	1,200 U.S. hospitals producing nuclear medicine, government v. private units.	Deviation of private hospitals from a perfect efficiency index was less than public hospital's deviation. ✓
Domberger, Meadowcroft, and Thompson (1987)	Domestic service costs for 1,500 hospitals in Great Britain, public v. private contracting.	Contracting reduces operating ✓ costs.
Wheeler, Zuckerman, and Aderholdt (1982)	10 hospitals under management contracts in 7 U.S. states.	Improved profitability occurred ✓ under private management.
Mennenmeyer and Olinger (1989)	Medical care for Medicare patients in 267 California hospitals in the 1980s.	Contracting lowered costs ✓ between 11 to 23 percent.

6. Multiple Services and Other City Services

Ferris (1988)	Multiple municipal services in 500 U.S. cities.	City expenditures decrease ✓ with the increased use of contracting.
Carver (1989)	Property tax assessment in 100 Massachusetts communities.	Public provision was found to be less costly than contracting.
Pack (1992)	Computer networking reliability for 55 public clients.	Contracting with private firms resulted in a 30 percent ✓ increase in quality and reliability.

ACTIVITY/AUTHOR	INQUIRY SUBJECT	FINDINGS
7. REFUSE COLLECTION		
Hirsch (1965)	24 cities in the St. Louis County area, public v. private collection.	No significant differences.
Collins and Downes (1977)	53 cities in the St. Louis County area, public v. private contracting.	No significant differences.
Stevens and Savas (1976), Edwards and Stevens (1976), Savas (1977), Stevens (1978), Savas (1980)	Various types of U.S. cities, public v. private collection. Includes various types of service arrangements.	Cost of public collection 40 to 60 percent higher than private contracting, but private monopolies were only 5 percent higher than private nonfranchise collection. These findings were fairly consistent in all of the studies. Private contracting was found to be the most efficient collection method.
Petrovic and Jaffee (1977)	83 cities in the Midwestern U.S., public v. private collection.	Cost of public collection 15 percent higher.
Kemper and Quigley (1976)	101 Connecticut cites, private monopoly contract v. private nonfranchise v. municipal organizations.	Municipal costs were 14 to 43 percent higher than contract costs, but private nonfranchise arrangements were 25 to 36 percent higher than the costs of city collection.
Kitchen (1976)	48 Canadian cities, private v. municipal collection.	Municipal collection significantly more costly.
Savas (1977)	Minneapolis, MN, 50 private v. 30 public organizations.	No significant cost differences.
Pier, Vernon, and Wicks (1976)	26 cities in Montana, public v. private collection.	Municipal collection more efficient.
Pommerehne and Frey (1976)	102 Swiss municipalities, public v. private collection.	Unit costs of municipal collection 15 percent higher.
Spann (1977)	Survey of U.S. cities, municipal v. private collection.	Cost of public collection 45 percent higher.
Bennett and Johnson (1979)	Fairfax County, VA, 29 private firms v. public collection authority.	Private firms in open competition significantly more efficient.
McDavid (1985)	126 Canadian cities, public v. private collection.	Public collection 41 percent more costly.
Domberger, Meadowcroft, and Thompson (1986)	610 cities in Great Britain, public v. private collection.	Municipal costs were 28 percent higher than competitive contracting.

ACTIVITY/AUTHOR	INQUIRY SUBJECT	FINDINGS
8. VEHICLE MAINTENANCE		
Campbell (1988)	Public v. private contracting for the service.	Contractors were 1 to 38 percent below in-house municipal costs.
9. WATER UTILITIES		
Crain and Zardkoohi (1978)	112 U.S. firms, municipal v. private.	Public firms 40 percent less productive with 65 percent higher capital-labor ratios than private equivalent firms.
Mann and Mikesell (1977)	U.S. firms, public v. private.	Cost of public firms was 20 percent higher.
Morgan (1977)	143 firms in six U.S. states, municipal v. private suppliers.	Cost of public firms was 15 percent higher.
Bruggink (1982)	Public v. private operations.	Public more efficient.
Feigenbaum, Temples, and Glyer (1986)	Public v. private operations.	No significant differences.
Byners, Grasskopt, and Hayes(1986)	Public v. private operations.	No significant differences.
Teeples and Glyer (1987)	Public v. private operations.	No significant differences.
Holcombe (1991)	Public v. private operations for wastewater treatment in U.S. cities.	Higher costs associated with private provision.

The Use of Private Contracting by Local Governments (Percentage)

Service	1982	1988	1992	1997
Public Works/Transportation				
Residential solid waste collection	34	36	38	49
Commercial solid waste collection	44	38	55	60
Solid waste disposal	30	25	33	41
Street repair	28	36	30	35
Street/parking lot cleaning	9	15	18	20
Snowplowing/sanding	14	15	10	14
Traffic sign/signal installation and maintenance	28	27	25	24
Parking meter maintenance and collection	7	7	6	10
Tree trimming/planting and maintenance	31	36	33	36
Maintenance/administration of cemeteries	19	11	17	22
Inspection/code enforcement	8	9	5	8
Operation of parking lots/garages	12	14	15	18
Operation/maintenance of bus systems	34	26	22	30
Operation/maintenance of paratransit systems	45	30	35	38
Operation of airports	28	30	19	20

SERVICE	1982	1988	1992	1997
PUBLIC UTILITIES				
Utility operation and management	—	—	—	—
Electricity	n/a	11	41	43
Gas	n/a	12	58	60
Water distribution	n/a	4	6	8
Water treatment	n/a	3	5	6
Sewerage collection/treatment	n/a	6	6	8
Disposal of sludge	n/a	19	19	28
Disposal of hazardous materials	n/a	44	38	39
Utility meter reading	10	7	20	18
Utility billing	14	32	29	13
Street light operation	41	46	n/a	n/a
PUBLIC SAFETY				
Crime prevention	10	4	2	1
Police/fire communications	4	1	2	1
Fire prevention/suppression	5	1	4	3
Emergency medical services	25	18	22	23
Ambulance services	36	24	37	37
Traffic control/parking enforcement	2	1	2	2
Vehicle towing and storage	80	80	86	82
HEALTH AND HUMAN SERVICES				
Sanitary inspection	1	3	2	4
Insect/rodent control	19	15	15	21
Animal control	15	11	14	17
Operation of animal shelters	32	17	34	34
Operation of daycare facilities	72	34	88	79
Child welfare programs	31	17	17	27
Programs for the elderly	37	19	30	34
Operation/management of hospitals	30	24	61	71
Public health programs	37	19	13	30
Drug and alcohol treatment programs	51	34	54	56
Operation of mental health programs and facilities	50	35	44	45

Service	1982	1988	1992	1997
Health and Human Services (cont.)				
Prison/jails	n/a	1	1	3
Parole programs	n/a	3	n/a	n/a
Operation of homeless shelters	n/a	43	59	66
Food programs for the homeless	n/a	26	n/a	n/a
Parks and Recreation				
Operation/maintenance of recreation facilities	20	12	8	15
Park landscaping/maintenance	12	13	12	20
Operation of convention centers and auditoriums	12	11	14	23
Recreational services	22	8	n/a	n/a
Cultural and Arts Programs				
Operation of cultural and arts programs	n/a	23	48	42
Operation of libraries	n/a	1	5	6
Operation of museums	n/a	8	39	45
Support Functions				
Buildings and grounds maintenance	21	27	22	28
Building security	9	13	13	20
Fleet/vehicle maintenance	—	—	—	—
Heavy equipment	32	41	29	35
Emergency vehicles	31	41	30	37
All other vehicles	29	38	27	34
Payroll	10	7	5	6
Title records/plat map maintenance	n/a	14	9	8
Tax billing	17	9	6	n/a
Tax assessment	11	10	7	7
Data processing	23	17	9	15
Collection of delinquent taxes	13	14	9	15
Legal services	51	55	50	53
Secretarial services	4	7	5	7

SERVICE	1982	1988	1992	1997
SUPPORT FUNCTIONS (CONT.)				
Personnel services	6	8	4	7
Public relations/public information	9	10	7	9
Labor relations	24	33	n/a	n/a

Note: The use of private contracting is shown as the percentage of local governments (cities and counties) re-porting that private contracting was used in the specified services. All of the data comes from surveys con-ducted by the International City/County Management Association. The number of local governments varied with each survey and the number of local governments reporting varies with each service. Variations also existed in the format of the surveys. Some services were not included in all of the surveys. These ser-vices are indicated as n/a in the table. Utility services, such as operation of electricity and gas facilities were included in a 1982 survey conducted by the International City/County Management Association, but were not reported in their analyses, thus they are excluded here.

Source: International City/County Management Association surveys (original data sets for the 1982, 1988, 1992, and 1997 surveys on alternative service delivery approaches). These data sets can be purchased from the International City/County Management Association, <http://www.icma.org>. It should be noted that minor variations exist in some of the data sets purchased from the International City/County Management Association (ICMA). Thus, the findings reported here may vary from some of the ICMA publications.

The International City/County Management Association has publications that have analyzed each of the surveys. See Carl Valente and Lydia Manchester, *Rethinking Local Services: Examining Alternative Delivery Approaches* (Washington, DC: International City/County Management Association, 1984); Elaine Morley, "Pat-terns in the Use of Alternative Service Delivery Approaches," *Municipal Yearbook 1989* (Washington, DC: International City/County Management Association); International City/County Management Association, *Service Delivery in the 1990s: Alternative Approaches for Local Governments* (Washington, DC: author, 1989); Rowan Miranda and Karlyn Andersen, "Alternative Service Delivery Approaches, 1982–1992," *Municipal Yearbook 1994* (Washington, DC: International City/County Management Association); and Elaine Morley, "Local Government Use of Alternative Service Delivery Approaches," *Municipal Yearbook 1999* (Washington, DC: International City/County Management Association).

EXPLAINING VARIATIONS IN MUNICIPAL PRIVATIZATION

COMPARISON	MAJOR FINDINGS (1988)	MAJOR FINDINGS (1992)
Profiles of cities. The profiles are based on fiscal stress, location, population change, wealth, and region.	Privatization levels higher in western cities and lowest in northeastern cities. Fiscal stress worse in north-eastern cities and lowest in Mid-western cities. Population change greater in the South and West. (Sample size = 188)	Identical findings, except fiscal stress lowest in western cities. (Sample size = 1220)
Regression analysis used to predict privatization levels for five variables for all cities.	Population change, location, fiscal stress, and wealth were all significant predictors. Region did not seem to matter. Privatization levels were negatively related to fiscal stress. (Sample size = 188)	Identical findings. (Sample size = 1220)
Regression analysis used to predict privatization levels for five variables for western cities.	Location, fiscal stress, and wealth were all significant predictors. Population change was a poor predictor, but all western cities had experienced population growth. Privatization levels were negatively related to fiscal stress. (Sample size = 51)	Identical findings. (Sample size = 292)

COMPARISON	MAJOR FINDINGS (1988)	MAJOR FINDINGS (1992)
Central and suburban cities were compared using analysis of the variance (ANOVA).	Suburban cities had significantly higher levels of privatization than central cities. Population change was significantly different. Central cities tended to experience less population growth than suburban cities. Fiscal stress was significantly different in 1982 between central and suburban cities. Central cities tended to be fiscally stressed while suburban cities were not. Wealth was significantly different between central and suburban cities. Suburban cities tended to have wealthier residents. (Sample size = 57)	Identical findings, except fiscal stress was not significantly different. (Sample size = 131)
Cities with the highest levels of privatization were compared to cities with the lowest levels of privatization using analysis of the variance (ANOVA).	Population change was significantly different, suburban cities tended to gain more population. The cities with the lowest privatization levels tended to be central cities while the cities with the highest levels of privatization tended to be suburban cities. The cities with the highest levels of privatization tended to have wealthier residents than cities with lower levels of privatization. Fiscal stress was not significantly different. (Sample size = 201)	Identical findings. (Sample size = 713)
Conclusions.	Fiscally healthy, wealthy, suburban cities had the highest levels of privatization.	Same conclusion.

Sources: Jeffrey D. Greene, "Cities and Privatization: Examining the Effect of Fiscal Stress, Wealth, and Location in Mid-Sized Cities," *Policy Studies Journal* 24, no. 1 (spring 1996), pp. 135–144; and Jeffrey D. Greene, "Cities and Privatization: Re-examining the Effect of Fiscal Stress, Location, and Wealth in American Cities: A Research Note," a conference paper presented at the Annual Meeting of the Southern Political Science Association in Savannah, Georgia (November 1999).

Municipal Fiscal Health
and Privatization

Comparison	Major Findings (1988)	Major Findings (1992)
Profiles of cities. The profiles are based on fiscal stress, tax burden, location, population, population change, bond ratings, debt/revenue ratio, level of state aid, and region.	Privatization levels higher in western cities. Fiscal stress worse in northeastern cities and lowest in western cities. Population change greater in the South and West. Level of state aid highest in the North and lowest in the South. Tax burden highest in the northeast cities, lowest in the midwestern cities. Debt/revenue ratios highest in the North and West, lowest in the South. (Sample size = 102)	Identical findings, except fiscal stress lowest in western cities. (Sample size = 1220)
Regression analysis used to predict privatization levels for eight variables for all cities.	Population change, location, bond rating, and tax burden were all significant predictors. Level of state aid did not seem to matter. Privatization levels were negatively related to fiscal stress, which was not a significant predictor. (Sample size = 102)	Identical findings, except fiscal stress was a significant predictor and bond rating was not a significant predictor. (Sample size = 1220)
Cities with the highest levels of privatization were compared to cities with the lowest levels of privatization using analysis of the variance (ANOVA) to examine a variety of factors.	Location was significantly different. The cities with the lowest privatization levels tended to be central cities while the cities with the highest levels of privatization tended to be suburban cities. Population change was significantly different, cities with high levels of privatization gained more population (and tended to be	Identical findings, except bond ratings were not significantly different. (Sample size = 227)

COMPARISON	MAJOR FINDINGS (1988)	MAJOR FINDINGS (1992)
	suburban cities located in the South and West). Region was significantly different. The cities with the highest privatization levels tended to be located in the West. Fiscal stress, bond ratings, debt/revenue ratios, tax burden, and level of state aid were not significantly different between cities with high levels and low levels of privatization. The low-level privatization group experienced significantly more expenditure growth, utilized more annexation, and had significantly larger work-forces. Both groups tended to have budget surpluses. (Sample size = 24)	
Major conclusions.	Demographic factors coupled with fiscal stress appear to be better predictors of the use of privatization than most fiscal attributes of cities. Cities located in suburban areas that were experiencing population gains used the most privatization. Relationship between privatization and fiscal stress was negative, meaning that higher privatization levels were associated with lower levels of fiscal stress. Fiscal stress was comparable between cities with the highest and lowest levels of privatization whereas most cities included in the study were fiscally stressed. Very little difference in cities with low and high levels of privatization for any of the fiscal factors.	Similar conclusions.

Sources: When cities with the highest and lowest levels of privatization were removed from the sample, fiscally healthy cities tended to use more privatization. The findings shown for 1988 and 1992 in Appendix D come from three studies, Jeffrey D. Greene, "Municipal Fiscal Health and Privatization," *Southeastern Political Review* 23 (1995), pp. 49–66; Jeffrey D. Greene, "Municipal Finances, Demographics, and Privatization," a conference paper presented at the Annual Meeting of the Western Political Science Association (March 1998) in Los Angeles, California; and Jeffrey D. Greene, "Fiscal Health, Spending Patterns, and Privatization," a conference paper presented at the Annual Meeting of the Southern Political Science Association (November 1995) in Tampa, Florida. It is noteworthy to mention that the findings of a fourth study revealed nearly identical findings. Jeffrey D. Greene, "Examining the Use of Privatization and Fiscal Conditions in American Cities," (working paper). This analysis used data from the 1997 International City/County Management Association's survey on alternative service delivery approaches. This survey included 62 municipal services to gauge the use of privatization in 1,221 cities. The findings were essentially identical to the findings of earlier studies that used ICMA data sets from 1988 and 1992. Namely, that suburban cities use more privatization than central cities and that very little difference existed between the fiscal indicators of cities that make extensive use of privatization and cities with very low levels of privatization. These findings are significant because they are consistent across three separate surveys.

PRIVATIZATION DIVERSITY LEVELS COMPARED BY SERVICE

SERVICE	1982 MEAN & RATING	1992 MEAN & RATING	PERCENT CHANGE
PUBLIC WORKS			
1. Residential solid waste	.49 H	.73 H	48
2. Commercial solid waste	.54 H	.56 H	4
3. Solid waste disposal	.38 H	.66 H	73
4. Street repair	.32 H	.97 H	203
5. Street parking/cleaning	.11 M	.90 H	718
6. Snowplowing	.11 M	.70 H	536
7. Traffic signals/signs	.37 M	.93 H	151
8. Parking meters	.15 M	.34 H	126
9. Tree trimming	.36 H	.93 H	158
10. Cemeteries	.12 M	.43 H	258
11. Inspection code enforcement	.11 M	.97 H	781
12. Parking lots and garages	.11 M	.47 H	327
13. Bus transit systems	.29 H	.37 H	28
14. Paratransit systems	.29 H	.33 H	14
15. Airports	.16 M	.39 H	143
PUBLIC UTILITIES			
16. Water systems	.11 M	.84 H	664
17. Sewerage systems	.11 M	.84 H	664

SERVICE	1982 MEAN & RATING	1992 MEAN & RATING	PERCENT CHANGE
PUBLIC UTILITIES (CONT.)			
18. Disposal of sludge	.15 M	.76 H	406
19. Electricity	.35 H	.33 H	−6
20. Gas	.39 H	.28 H	−39
21. Utility meter reading	.19 M	.64 H	236
22. Utility billing	.21 M	.49 H	133
23. Other utilities	.11 L	.86 H	681
PUBLIC SAFETY			
24. Crime prevention/patrol	.17 M	.96 H	465
25. Police/fire communication	.11 M	.96 H	772
26. Fire prevention	.17 M	.94 H	452
27. Emergency medical (EMS)	.35 H	.86 H	145
28. Ambulance service	.43 H	.77 H	79
29. Traffic control	.04 L	.91 H	2,175
30. Vehicle towing/storage	.75 H	.77 H	3
HEALTH AND HUMAN SERVICES			
31. Sanitary inspection	.09 L	.68 H	655
32. Insect/rodent control	.15 M	.62 H	313
33. Animal control	.15 M	.86 H	473
34. Animal shelters	.29 H	.69 H	137
35. Daycare facilities	.22 M	.28 H	27
36. Child welfare programs	.12 L	.33 H	175
37. Programs for elderly	.45 H	.67 H	49
38. Hospitals	.14 M	.24 M	71
39. Public health programs	.21 M	.48 H	128
40. Drug/alcohol treatment	.23 M	.44 H	91
41. Mental health programs	.14 M	.38 H	171
PARKS AND RECREATION			
42. Operating rec. facilities	.39 H	.91 H	133
43. Landscaping and maintenance	.16 M	.91 H	468
44. Operation of auditoriums	.07 L	.34 H	385

SERVICE	1982 MEAN & RATING	1992 MEAN & RATING	PERCENT CHANGE
CULTURAL AND ARTS PROGRAMS			
45. Cultural programs	.48 H	.57 H	19
46. Operation of libraries	.23 M	.73 H	217
47. Operation of museums	.23 M	.43 H	87
SUPPORT FUNCTIONS			
48. Building/grounds maintenance	.25 M	.96 H	284
49. Building security	.09 L	.77 H	755
50. Fleet/vehicle maintenance			
a. Heavy equipment	.33 H	.94 H	184
b. Emergency vehicles	.33 H	.89 H	169
c. All other vehicles	.29 H	.94 H	224
51. Payroll	.12 M	.96 H	700
52. Tax billing and processing	.18 M	.79 H	338
53. Tax assessing	.12 M	.72 H	500
54. Data processing	.24 M	.94 H	291
55. Delinquent tax collection	.16 M	.79 H	393
56. Legal services	.54 H	.91 H	68
57. Secretarial services	.06 L	.94 H	1,466
58. Personnel services	.08 L	.95 H	1,087
59. Public relations	.12 M	.91 H	685

Note: N = 596 cities. Privatization diversity scores are mean scores for each service. The term *rating* is used in the table to describe the amount of privatization within services. Ratings are defined as: Low (L) = 0 –.10; Medium (M) = .11–.25; High (H) = .26 or greater. Increases and decreases represent changes in the indices between 1982 and 1992. Although most services include all 596 cities, there are cases in which cities did not provide some of the services (i.e., snowplowing for cities located in warm climates such as Florida).

Source: Jeffrey D. Greene, "How Much Privatization? A Research Note Examining the Use of Privatization by Cities in 1982 and 1992," *Policy Studies Journal* 24 (winter 1996), pp. 632–640.

Privatization Resources
on the Internet

There are many privatization resources available on the Internet. This partial listing provides some of the major sites, which link to numerous other sites. Many of the sites included here were used to locate case studies and other information used in this book. There are Web sites that favor the use of privatization and sites that adamantly oppose privatization.

The Reason Foundation

A site dedicated to promoting privatization at all levels of government. The site includes numerous studies and commentary about privatization.
http://www.reason.org

The Reason Foundation's Public Policy Institute

A site dedicated to increasing the use of the private sector in a wide variety of policy matters. The site includes many resources about privatization.
http://www.rppi.org

Privatization.com

A Web site that includes an extensive database about privatization that includes trends, cost savings, and a variety of case studies. The Reason Foundation also maintains this site.
http://www.privatization.com

AMERICAN FEDERATION OF STATE, COUNTY, AND MUNICIPAL EMPLOYEES

This is the Web page for one of the largest public employee unions in the nation. It includes extensive material and case studies about privatization failures. The site also includes the latest on-line version of *Government for Sale,* which includes many cases of disappointing results that have occurred with privatization.
http://www.afscme.org

THE CANADIAN UNION OF PUBLIC EMPLOYEES

This public-employee union site opposes the use of privatization and includes an anti-privatization database with examples of privatization failures.
http://www.cupe.ca/private.html

THE PUBLIC POLICY CONNECTION PRIVATIZATION PAGE

A listing of numerous privatization resources available on the Internet, both in favor of and against the use of privatization.
http://members.aol.com/Adriantm/privitin.htm

NATIONAL CENTER FOR POLICY ANALYSIS

A Web site that includes extensive information about public policy, including privatization at all levels of government. The site includes numerous studies and other resources.
http://www.ncpa.org

CATO INSTITUTE

A libertarian institute that includes numerous articles and resources about privatization. Because the CATO Institute includes most policy areas, simply type in "privatization" on the site's search feature to access numerous articles and studies.
http://www.cato.org

THE PACIFIC RESEARCH INSTITUTE

A public policy institute that focuses on many policies, including privatization.
http://www.pacificresearch.org

THE REASON FOUNDATION PRIVATIZATION LINK PAGE

This page includes links to numerous public-policy institutes.
http://www.reason.org/links.html

THE NATIONAL COUNCIL FOR PUBLIC-PRIVATE PARTNERSHIPS

A site that represents both the public and private sectors and promotes cooperative public-private ventures.
http://www.ncppp.org

Privatization.org Web Links Page

This is the link to the Reason Foundation's privatization links to organizations. This is not the same page or links provided on their main Web site of the Reason Foundation's Home Page. When one reaches the site, click *Privatization on the WWW*. The list of links is extensive.
http://www.privatization.org

The Alliance for Redesigning Government

This Web site, which is part of the National Academy of Public Administration, has many resources and studies about privatization. One must use their search engine to locate their privatization page. Simply type "privatization" into their search feature.
http://www.alliance.napawash.org

Cornell University's Cooperative Extension Service

This site maintained by Cornell University provides a rich database on privatization that includes articles, studies, and abstracts of most major studies. Use their search engine to locate privatization materials.
http://www.cce.cornell.edu

INDEX